Reviews of
Peasant Consciousness and Guerrilla War in Zimbabwe

'Ranger's present book has all the many-sidedness of a 25-year historiographical and political engagement... Oral historians are at home when listening to a voice directly or indirectly from the 1890s or 1940s. They are less used to treating as already historical a voice from the 1970s. But Ranger's book should be seen as a major event in contemporary oral history...' Logie Barrow, Professor of History, Hamburg in *Oral History*

'... undoubtedly much the most important book to be written on Zimbabwe and it transforms our understanding of the whole colonial experience.' Richard Brown of the University of Sussex in *British Book News*

'... ambitious and wide-ranging... comparisons with Kenya and Mozambique.' Hugh Macmillan of the University of Zambia in *Journal of African History*

'... a fascinating analysis of the imposition of colonial rule at the end of the nineteenth century, and the consequent alienation of much of their land, up to the conclusion of the bloody and successful struggle for independence during the 1970s, in which the role of the ordinary farmer played such a central role.' Michael Crowder in *The Times Literary Supplement*

James Currey
LONDON

University of California Press
BERKELEY AND LOS ANGELES

DAVID LAN

Guns & Rain

Guerrillas & Spirit Mediums
in Zimbabwe

For Nicholas Wright

DAVID LAN
Guns & Rain
Guerrillas & Spirit Mediums
in Zimbabwe

Preface by Maurice Bloch
Professor of Anthropology, London School of Economics

James Currey
LONDON

University of California Press
BERKELEY AND LOS ANGELES

James Currey Ltd
54b Thornhill Square, Islington, London N1 1BE

University of California Press
Berkeley and Los Angeles

First published 1985 in Great Britain by James Currey Ltd
and in the United States of America by the University of California Press
Reprinted 1987, 1989

British Library Cataloguing in Publication Data

Lan, David
Guns and rain : guerrillas and spirit mediums
in Zimbabwe.
1. Guerrilla warfare——History——20th century
2. Zimbabwe——History——1965–1980
I. Title
303.6'4'096891   DT962.75

ISBN 0-85255-200-9
ISBN 0-85255-201-7 Pbk

Library of Congress Cataloging-in-Publication Data

Lan, David, 1952–
Guns and rain.
Guerrillas and spirit mediums in Zimbabwe
(Perspectives on Southern Africa ; 38)
1. Spiritualism——Zimbabwe. 2. Guerrillas——Zimbabwe. 3. National
liberation movements——Zimbabwe. 4. Zimbabwe——Politics and
government——1965–1979. I. Title. II. Series.
BF1242.Z55L36 1984   303.3'72   85-40287
ISBN 0-520-05557-8 (alk. paper)
ISBN 0-520-05589-6 (pbk. : alk. paper)

Typeset in 10/11pt Times in Great Britain
Printed and bound in Great Britain

vi

Contents

vii

List of Figures, Maps and Plates

Figures

Maps

Plates

Between pp. 118–19

Acknowledgements

In Dande: Senator F. Moyo, District Chairman E. M. Chafesuka and Branch Chairman D. Mudzonga welcomed me and gave me their support, assistance and advice, without which my work would have been impossible. My greatest debt is to Village Chairman Penias Katsvete who accepted me into his family and looked after me with great concern and affection. Without him, his wives and his children, I would have learned far less than I did about what it means to be a member of Dande society. Of the many others who gave of their time and knowledge, I am especially grateful to Mutswairo Fumhe, William Madzivah, Nigel Mukokoti, Kaitano Goredema, Daveson Kwainona, Isaac Maudzenga and my research assistant Lazarus Basiyao who helped me to learn ChiKorekore and accompanied me on many gruelling journeys through the Valley.

In Harare: Professor G. Chavunduka and Dr M. F. C. Bourdillon of the University of Zimbabwe granted me affiliate status in the Department of Sociology. I am grateful for their interest and encouragement. Dr D. N. Beach and A. Hodza, also of the University of Zimbabwe, both allowed me access to their unpublished materials and the benefit of their contrasting views on mediums, tradition and history. I am grateful also to Dr S. I. Mudenge of the Ministry of Foreign Affairs, for sharing with me a little of his knowledge of the Portuguese documentation of Dande in the eighteenth and nineteenth centuries.

Mayor Urimbo MP and Air Vice-Marshall Josiah Tungamirai discussed many aspects of the organisation of the resistance with me. Mayor Urimbo supplied me with letters of accreditation from ZANU/PF which greatly facilitated the first months of my research. J. White, C. J. K.

Latham and R. Faulkner all spared time to give me insights into the organisation of the Security Forces during the years of the war.

To A. S. Kamba and P. Mazikana of the National Archives, Harare I owe a special debt for incorporating parts of my research into their Oral History programme and supplying me with excellent transcripts of the many recordings I have deposited in their collection.

Phyllis Johnson and David Martin of the Zimbabwe Publishing House provided me with a room in which to live and work while in Harare, as well as arranging a number of meetings and interviews. Thanks also to Margarita Vismara, Laurence and Sue Bartlett and Andrew Meldrum.

In London: This book is a revised and in part expanded version of *Making History: Spirit Mediums and Guerrillas in the Dande Region of Zimbabwe*, a PhD thesis submitted to the London School of Economics in 1983. Fieldwork and research for this were funded by the Economic and Social Research Council and the Central Research Fund of the University of London.

The thesis was supervised by Professors Jean La Fontaine and Maurice Bloch. Without their ceaseless advice and encouragement both in Dande and in London, book and thesis would have taken far longer to complete, would have been much less enjoyable to do and would lack a number of what I think are their more unusual features. My debt to Maurice Bloch is increased by the very generous preface he has provided for this book. Dr J. P. Parry suggested the original project of which this book is a total but perhaps not final transformation.

Dr D. N. Beach, Dr G. K. Garbett, Dr. R. P. Werbner, Andrew Ladley and Janet Carsten all provided extremely useful and detailed criticisms of *Making History*. They will find a number of their suggestions incorporated in this version.

Michael Stewart, Dr Byron Foster and Judith Cornell listened to this book being thought out either in London, in Harare or in Dande. Nicholas Wright has lived with it from beginning to end in all three places. For their advice, criticism, support and tolerance I am grateful to them all.

David Lan

Acknowledgements for illustrations
Plates 6, 7, 8, 9, 11 and 14, David Lan; Plates 2, 3 and 4, Nicholas Wright; Plates 1, 5 and 10 are reproduced with the permission of the Director of National Archives of Zimbabwe; Plate 13 is reproduced with the permission of Prof. D. P. Abraham from 'The Monomotapa Dynasty', *NADA* 1959, p. 58. Maps are drawn by George Hartfield; line drawings by Ingrid Crewdson.

Preface

It is the successful intertwining of three distinct levels of analysis that makes this book of such great importance.

Firstly, it makes us understand an historical event of world importance, the liberation of Zimbabwe, from the point of view of ordinary people. Secondly, it analyses the general problem of politics in the real world: that political action is a matter of joining, not of creating, a political and cultural stream; that therefore one may be swept up by the stream to a place quite different from where one thought one was heading. Thirdly, it makes us understand the internal logic of a particular social theory and social practice: that of the Shona people. These three levels are, in reality, inseparable but rare indeed are those who, like David Lan, can keep them all in sight as the argument unfolds.

When the ZANLA guerrillas entered Zimbabwe, they realised that if they were to be successful they would have to be seen to be liberators by the people whom they had come to free. It was not in terms of the political analyses of socialist theoreticians that their actions would appear legitimate but in terms of the political ideas and interpretations of history of the peasants of Zimbabwe themselves. These folk ideas had been forged by history, both remote and recent, and by the peoples' continual struggle to make sense of their history and their environment.

If the guerrillas were to be helped by others, they had to recognise others and so, to a degree, lose their autonomy of thought and action. The Shona have always seen the relation between their past and their present as mediated by their ancestors. The young fighters therefore had to enter into a dialogue with these ancestors, to justify and explain their actions and to seek ancestral help.

The inevitability of a dialogue between past and present is universal. This dramatic representation – spirit mediums speaking the words of the ancestors while the guerrillas spoke the words of the living – is a particularly moving and forceful formulation of this view of history. David Lan explains this dialogue with wonderful vividness, never forgetting the political reality in which spirit mediumship takes place.

The successful combination of levels of analysis presented in this book offers a guide to the direction in which the academic tradition of social anthropology will develop successfully.

The strength of anthropology has lain in demonstrating the internal consistency of the practices and ideas by which ordinary people from very different cultures live their lives. In the process it has often given the false impression that these people live in impenetrable 'other realities', undisturbed by history and world events. This is a travesty of the modern situation and it makes the work of anthropologists a complete irrelevance. A common reaction against this dangerous distortion has been to characterise ordinary people as the passive subjects of their political and economic circumstances which they neither seek to change nor to understand. Their beliefs and practices then appear as quaint folklore, out of touch with the 'real' world which has irretrievably changed. This reaction is equally false and, indeed, it is insolent.

The truth lies in a subtle balance between these two extremes. This balance, extraordinarily difficult to evoke and analyse, is the great achievement of this book, which, as a result, is not only a specific study of great brilliance but also a model which shows how anthropology can contribute to politics and history.

Maurice Bloch
Professor of Anthropology
The London School of Economics
and Political Science

Introduction

Chindunduma is a school in north-eastern Zimbabwe built after Independence to enable many of the young women and men who had left their homes to join the armies of liberation and fight for the freedom of their country to complete their interrupted education. In July 1981 a group of these young ex-guerrillas were describing and reliving some of their experiences of the war. They spoke of their life in the guerrilla camps in Mozambique and of the campaigns in which they took part inside Zimbabwe, of the lessons in politics and development they had received, of their fears and their triumphs, their setbacks and their rewards. And time and again they spoke of the help they had received during the war from their ancestors. As one young man recounted:

> I didn't believe all the things my father used to tell me until I was in the bush myself. Then – well, you just had to believe. One time we had no tobacco, nothing to smoke. One of the boys went into a trance. He said that his father's brother had sent us some. His father's brother had died a long time before so we asked him how this would happen. He said that the tobacco would be brought to us by a snake. Then the boy came out of trance, went looking in the bush and found the snake. The body of the snake was all curled up but there in the middle was a lump of tobacco. The boy clapped to the snake very politely and the snake uncoiled itself. Then he took the tobacco and we all had a smoke.[1]

Many ex-combatants tell similar stories of how long-dead members of their families had assisted them and led them to sources of food or other supplies. But these ancestral spirits and their mediums performed more crucial tasks as well:

> At one time there were many deaths in our camp. We used to bury up to eight in a single day. So we went to see this spirit medium who lived nearby. He told us that we should not bathe in the rivers. We should build a bathing hut

far from the river and carry water to this place in tins. The medium told us that when we got back to our camp a certain child would have died but that this would be the last one who would ever die from this cause. And he was right. This is just what happened.[2]

Many of the so-called *Chimurenga* songs – the songs of the war of liberation – that were sung by guerrillas and peasants celebrate the role of the ancestors. For example:

Isu nemidzimu yedu	*We and our ancestors*
takabatana	*worked together*
muno muhondo	*here in the war*

The especially important part played by the *mhondoro* (royal ancestor) spirits as protectors of the land and bringers of the rains is also recognised in popular song. In this one a number of senior *mhondoro* are celebrated together:

Takapinda nekuGaza	*We entered [Zimbabwe] at Gaza*
kusunungura Zimbabwe	*in order to free Zimbabwe*
Ambuya Nehanda	*Grandmother Nehanda*
Sekuru Chaminuka	*Grandfather Chaminuka*
Mwene Mutapa	*Mwene Mutapa*
Mulambo	*Mulambo*
midzimu yehondo	*the ancestral spirits of war*

What are we to make of a guerrilla war fought to liberate a colonised country from its oppressors, whose leaders professed a socialist ideology and a commitment to leading Zimbabwe into the modern world, when the fighters themselves describe their experiences of the war in these terms? The students of Chindunduma come from all over Zimbabwe and they are not exceptional. Reports from many of the Shona-speaking areas describe the peasants' and guerrillas' experience in strikingly similar terms. According to Frantz Fanon, one of the major theoreticians of African liberation, beliefs of this kind are quite simply not supposed to persist:

After centuries of unreality, after having wallowed in the most outlandish phantoms, at long last the native, gun in hand, stands face to face with the only forces which contend for his life – the forces of colonialism. And the youth of a colonized country, growing up in an atmosphere of shot and fire, may well make a mock of, and does not hesitate to pour scorn upon the zombies of his ancestors, the horses with two heads, the dead who rise again, and the djinns who rush into your body while you yawn. The native discovers reality and transforms it into the pattern of his customs, into the practice of violence and into his plan for freedom.[3]

The youth of Zimbabwe have certainly grown up in 'an atmosphere of shot and fire' and many have spent a good number of years with 'gun in hand . . . face to face with . . . the forces of colonialism'. And yet far from pouring scorn on these 'outlandish phantoms', their ancestors, they seem to believe in them as strongly as their fathers and their fathers before them. In fact all categories of participants in the war – guerrillas, those who joined them in the bush, those who stayed in the villages, those who fled to safer places – maintain that their ancestors protected and advised them either in dreams or by means of signs that gave them warnings and instructions. Even the future prime minister of Zimbabwe, Robert Mugabe, was himself assisted in his escape from Zimbabwe by an ancestor of the family which had given him shelter. The introduction to a volume of his collected speeches relates that the 'next two days were fraught with potential peril. Mugabe and Tekere were staying with Chief Tangwena. Mrs Tangwena had a spirit medium who advised them to leave the following day by the mountain route.'[4] Mugabe did so and after a long and arduous journey arrived at a village on the Mozambican side of the border.

It was not, however, only members of the resistance who believed that the ancestors had taken an active part in their struggle. Many Shona members of the government forces – soldiers, policemen, local government officers – also relate accounts of timely warnings and miraculous escapes which their ancestors engineered. However, it was only within the guerrilla army that this belief in the participation of the ancestors was elaborated into a system of ritual practices believed to place the combatants under their protection. While on active service within the borders of Zimbabwe, the guerrillas were not allowed to have sexual intercourse, they were not allowed to kill wild animals in the forest and they were not allowed to eat certain foods. These ritual prohibitions were imposed on them by the spirit mediums. It was believed that by observing them the guerrillas could protect themselves from the dangers of war and increase their chances of victory.

As we shall see, the fact that the majority of the guerrillas observed most if not all of these ritual prohibitions did not prevent them from taking part in the programme of peasant mobilisation or of political education that their political party put into action. We shall also see that these beliefs and practices were not invented by the guerrillas nor by the spirit mediums but were part of a wider pattern of beliefs and rituals that had existed for some hundreds of years. And, finally, we shall see how these ancestors who had protected their descendants during the war were celebrated and applauded at the ceremonies that marked the achievement of Independence. Their faces beamed out from banners hung all over the cities, their names were praised in speeches made by political leaders. In the first months of the new era, the most important of the Shona ancestors were installed, in effect, as the protectors and advisers of the new state of Zimbabwe.

Although this book deals with political and religious processes that are working themselves out at the heart of political life in the capital city today, it is based on research in one of the more remote corners of the country, an area in the extreme north known as Dande. This book is a study of the interaction of the ideology of the peasants of Dande with that of the guerrillas who lived among them between 1971 and 1979. I describe in some detail how these peasants viewed their world and how their society was organised, what the guerrillas intended to achieve within it and how far they were successful. Throughout, all events, symbols and processes – the whole of Zimbabwe in fact – are described from the point of view of Dande. I make no attempt at a complete analysis or description of the guerrilla war. No more detail of individual battles appears than is necessary to provide background from time to time. I deal only with the Zimbabwe African National Union (ZANU) and ZANLA, its guerrilla army, and not at all with their counterparts, the Zimbabwe African People's Union (ZAPU), and its army, ZIPRA. There is no reference but the most glancing to the major contribution made to the struggle by the Ndebele people or to that of any of the other minority ethnic groups of Zimbabwe. The reason is simply that they were not represented in Dande, where I lived for almost two years collecting the materials I present in this book.[5]

One final point. The purpose of this book is not primarily to describe *why* the peasants of Zimbabwe offered resistance to the Rhodesian state, though I deal with this at some length. Rather my intention is to describe *one of the forms that this resistance took*: the remarkable act of 'co-operation' between ancestors and their descendants, the dead and the living, the present and the past. In this account, it is neither the guerrillas nor the politicians who occupy the centre of the stage. It is the relationship between the guerrillas – the bearers of guns – and the religious leaders of the peasants – the mediums of the *mhondoro* spirits – the bringers of the rain.

The book is divided into four parts. Part I introduces the main events and the territory in which they took place. Chapter 1 contains an account of the first meetings between guerrillas and spirit mediums in the Zambezi Valley. Chapter 2 is an outline of the political, economic and kinship organisation of Dande, the background against which the rest of the book plays itself out.

The first two chapters of Part II deal with the range of religious experience that exists in Dande. The spirit mediums get most attention. I describe how people become mediums and how they live their lives after that. Chapter 5 is a detailed analysis of the mythological histories of the senior ancestors and of the ritual practice of their mediums. Here I dismantle and explore the basic concepts out of which political and religious ideology are constructed. I begin to show how these can be put together to form small-scale chieftaincies, large-scale political parties or the ideological apparatus of a state. Chapter 6 completes Part II, describing the integration of 'strangers' by their participation in the rituals of the *mhondoro* spirit mediums.

In Part III we move from Dande society itself to the war that took place within it. Chapter 7 contains an outline of the causes of the war together with a range of accounts by residents of Dande of their individual experiences of guerrillas, mediums, mobilisation, political education and so on. Chapter 8 takes a fresh look at the incidents described in Chapter 1. It shows how, as a reaction to colonialism, the authority of the spirit mediums rose while that of the chiefs fell, thus leading to the co-operation between these mediums and the guerrillas. Chapter 9 is a discussion of the protective behaviour that the guerrillas practised on the mediums' instruction, drawing on the materials laid out in Chapter 5 to explain them. In Chapter 10 all of these themes are drawn together in a detailed account of some of the actual battles – military, political and ideological – that were fought between mediums, chiefs, guerrillas and the local representatives of the state.

Part IV carries the analysis begun in Chapters 5 and 9 into the present day with, first, a discussion of the relationship between the newly elected village committees and the ancestors and, secondly, a brief assessment of the place of the ancestors in the ideology and the symbolism of the new nation state.

NOTES

1 From an interview conducted by Nicholas Wright at Chindunduma in July 1981.
2 ibid.
3 Fanon (1967, p.45).
4 Mugabe (1983, p. xiii).
5 A description of how these materials were collected can be found in the Appendix on p. 230.

PART I

The Operational Zone

We then proceeded to Kadzi River. When we arrived there we met up with the local people who were to carry the weapons and also the spirit medium who we were supposed to move with . . . We then left this place being 13 terrorists, one spirit medium and 8 locals who carried our weapons . . . We then proceeded to Mauhwe. Before we reached the mountain the porters went back . . . The spirit medium said that he was only going as far as this place as he was not going to climb the mountain.

Extract from the transcript of an appeal against the death sentence passed on three ZANLA guerrillas, heard in the High Court of Rhodesia on 6 June 1973.

1
Guerrillas and Mediums

By the mid-1960s all of Britain's former African colonies had achieved independence. The one exception was Rhodesia. The obstacle that prevented Rhodesia from joining the modern post-colonial world was the refusal of its government to extend to the majority of its citizens the right to vote in national elections. As long as the Shona, the Ndebele and the other smaller ethnic groups were unable to vote their own leaders into power, a negotiated independence was impossible. In 1965, as an act of defiance of the government of Britain, the Rhodesian parliament issued an Unilateral Declaration of Independence (UDI) together with a clutch of promises and guarantees that power would remain in the hands of the tiny white minority for all time to come.

Over the next few years international economic sanctions were imposed against Rhodesia but Britain, whose colonial authority had been flouted, took no direct action at all. The nationalist opposition within Rhodesia however did not wait long to respond. Within one year the first armed attack on the Rhodesian state since the 1896 rebellion took place. It was carried out near the town of Sinoia by a small group of guerrillas belonging to the Zimbabwe African National Union (ZANU). The guerrilla war had begun. In 1979, fourteen years after UDI, Independence with majority rule was finally achieved.[1]

The first meeting in the Valley

Early in 1971 a small band of ZANU guerrillas crossed from Mozambique into the north-eastern corner of Zimbabwe. After a few days in the densely wooded scrubland of the Zambezi Valley, they were led into the village of an ancient female spirit medium. Her name was Kunzaruwa. The name of her spirit was Nehanda.

3

Cde Mayor Urimbo was the leader of this group. He has described this medium as:

> a small woman, very thin and very old, with white hair and skin that was exceedingly black. She was dressed in a piece of black cloth that was wrapped around her body and she wore bangles, some of them gold, on her wrists, and other ornaments around her neck. Her skin was dry and cracked with age, and dung was regularly rubbed on to protect it from the sun.[2]

When I talked to Urimbo in 1980 I asked him how he and his guerrillas had met this medium and how she had helped them. 'When we arrived in the area,' he told me:

> we had to start by talking to the masses. We spoke to the old people who said we must consult the mediums. We were taken to Nehanda. She was very old. She never bathed and ate only once or twice a week. Her food had to be ground with a mortar and pestle. She hated all European things. We told her: 'We are the children of Zimbabwe, we want to liberate Zimbabwe'. She was very much interested. She knew very much about war and the regulation of war. She said: 'This forest is very, very difficult for you to penetrate', but she gave us directions. She told us what kind of food to eat, which routes to take, what part of the forest we were not allowed to stay in or sleep in, where we were not allowed to fight. She said we were forbidden to go with girls and she taught us how to interpret many signs in the forest which would allow us to live safely and to know when our enemy was near.[3]

Right at the first moment of meeting between guerrillas and mediums the major themes of this book spark into life. The mediums are experts on ritual who 'hate all European things'. If the guerrillas obey the ritual prohibitions that the mediums impose, they will be safe and the war they are fighting will meet with success.

In the years that followed, the guerrillas in the Zambezi Valley met and lived with a number of other mediums. Many of these, such as Chiwawa, Musuma, Mutota and Madzomba, will play a large part in the pages that follow. But the first that they met with was known as Chipfene. This medium was a short man, powerfully built and bearded like most male mediums. About 40 years old, he was usually dressed in a sky-blue toga-like cloth. I spent a day with him in November 1981 at his present home on the Msengezi River near the border with Mozambique. We sat in the shade on the rich soils on the bank of the river and he told me how time after time he had gone into battle with the guerrillas, always in the front line. Unarmed but protected by his spirit he had survived the entire war without injury. One of the district commissioners who had had responsibility for this part of the country in the early days of the war described Chipfene to me as 'a sort of phantom'. He had received countless reports of his exploits but never caught as much as a glimpse of him. A reward had been offered for his capture or death but it was never paid out.

Chipfene led the first party of guerrillas to two other mediums, Chiodzamamera and Chidyamauyu. Chidyamauyu, the youngest of the three, was charged with the care of the old medium of Nehanda. Chiodzamamera, his senior by ten or twelve years, had been a schoolteacher at the Evangelical Alliance Mission in the town of Banket when the illness that announced his possession by a *mhondoro* spirit first struck. Today he is perhaps the most widely respected medium in Dande. Much of the detail of the life of a *mhondoro* medium contained in this book I learnt from him. (See Plates 10 and 11 between pp. 204–5.)

The guerrillas intended that these four mediums who had given them their support should live and travel with them. None of the first group of guerrillas came from the north-east. The mediums would explain to the villagers that the guerrillas were from Zimbabwe and not foreigners from Mozambique or Zambia. They would tell them why the guerrillas had come and assure them that they had their interests at heart. They agreed to advise the guerrillas on the safest routes to carry weapons through the Zambezi Valley and up on to the Plateau, and to provide medicines to protect them in battle and to cure the wounded. But in 1972 the build-up of guerrillas in the Zambezi Valley was discovered. Government helicopters and ground troops began to patrol, searching them out. The three male mediums could easily vanish behind the camouflage of the shoulder-high grass and the mile upon mile of identical spindly grey trees. But the medium of Nehanda was feeble and weak. Fearing that she would be captured and punished for the support she had given them, the guerrillas decided to take her out of the country.

At first the aged medium refused to go, preferring to remain in the thick of the fighting. But eventually she agreed and was carried on a stretcher to the Zambezi River. Together with her three companions and aides she crossed into Mozambique, spent two weeks resting at Papai in Tete Province and then moved to a camp at Chifombo on the Mozambique–Zambia border where they remained for eight months. During this period, according to Urimbo, the medium 'was doing her command work, directing us in Zimbabwe'. Chidyamauyu put it this way – '*Vaititungamira muhondo yerusununguko*' – she led us in the war of liberation.

In mid-1973 the medium of Nehanda died. Her spirit had directed that she should be buried in Zimbabwe but the war made this impossible. Instead her followers chose a site at the side of a road used by guerrillas on their journey into Zimbabwe. She was carried to the grave covered in a white cloth and buried, like a chief, on a wooden platform sunk in the earth surrounded by a hut built and thatched in a single day.

Throughout the war the surviving mediums were joined by others and continued to work hand in hand with the guerrillas, either in the camps in Mozambique or guiding insurgents into Zimbabwe and leading new recruits out. After the war Urimbo, now National Political Commissar of ZANU/PF and a member of parliament, completed the story of Nehanda. 'Her house,' he told me, 'is still there. Fire comes and goes but it will never burn. When we crossed into Zimbabwe, we put our weapons there and praised the ancestors and said: We are going to liberate Zimbabwe.'[4]

Nehanda and the tradition of resistance

Unlike all other *mhondoro* mediums, Nehanda is believed to have two separate, equally legitimate traditions of mediums, one in the Mazoe region near the capital, Harare, the other in Dande. A medium of the Mazoe Nehanda, a woman named Charwe, was a major leader of the 1896 rebellion against the new colonial state. When the rebellion failed she was amongst the last of the leaders to be captured. Together with another leader of the rebellion, the medium of Kagubi, she was sentenced to death and hanged. (See Plate 1, between pp. 118–19.) A powerful and prolific oral tradition grew up around her name, her part in the rebellion and especially the last moments of her life after she was condemned: her refusal to accept conversion to Christianity, her defiance on the scaffold and her prophecy that 'my bones will rise' to win back freedom from the Europeans.[5]

In time the career of the medium and the healing and protective powers associated with the spirit became inextricably fused. In songs, in verse and in myth, Nehanda came to represent the inevitable but so-long awaited victory of the Shona over their oppressors. As a hero of the nationalist resistance she was rivalled only by Chaminuka, a *mhondoro* or royal ancestor of the Zezuru peoples of central Zimbabwe, who came to be regarded as her brother. In many of the new versions of old myths that grew out of the years of the struggle, this brother and sister pair are characterised as the original founders of the Shona nation. In recognition and perpetuation of this tradition two of the early ZANU operational zones in the north-east were named Nehanda and Chaminuka.[6]

But it was not only in myth that Nehanda's authority was recognised. She also appears as an inspirational figure in many important works of Shona literature published since the 1950s. In the novel *Feso* by Solomon Mutswairo (first published in 1957 and later banned by the Rhodesian Front government) the 'Vanyai' who represent the enslaved Shona people regard Nehanda as their protector and liberator.

Where is our freedom, Nehanda?
Won't you come down to help us?

6

Our old men are treated like children
In the land you gave them, merciful creator.[7]

In the poem *Soko Risina Musoro* published in 1958 by Herbert Chitepo, president of ZANU until his assassination in 1975, an old warrior bemoans the destruction of the Shona nation:

The sun of the kingship is setting,
the rising wind is screaming
a tale of death. The rivers have dried up;
leaving only pools filled with corpses of the dead.
Where are our heroes of old?
Where is Chaminuka and Nehanda?
Where are our tribal spirits?
Our complaining and our prayers,
have they failed to come where you are?[8]

In view of Nehanda's national reputation it is no surprise that when the ZANLA guerrillas discovered their good fortune in having a medium of this spirit, the most recent representative of this long tradition, active in their operational zone, they should have urged her to join the struggle. But the white administration was also conscious of its traditions. The attempt by 'native commissioners' to capture the mediums who had led the 1896 rebellion had been described by a number of local historians and was no more forgotten by government administrators than by their old adversaries.

In the late 1960s an administrative assistant in the Urungwe district to the east of Dande reported his belief that a spirit medium in his area had knowledge of guerrilla activity. Charges against this medium were eventually dropped but memories had been stirred. A nationwide survey of mediums of all kinds was begun. As the first spate of attacks intensified into a war, so attempts were made to use the mediums to counteract the influence of the guerrillas. Tape recordings of mediums denouncing the guerrillas while, supposedly, in trance were broadcast from aeroplanes. Leaflets bearing similar messages were scattered over the operational areas:

TO ALL THE PEOPLE OF THE LAND

Some of you have been helping terrorists who came to cause disturbances to you and your families. Your spirits have told your spiritual medium that they are disappointed because of your action. *Mhondoro*, your tribal spirit, has sent a message to say that your ancestral spirits are very dissatisfied with you. As a result of this there has been no rain. It is only the government which can help you, but you have to realise your obligation to help the government also.[9]

Though opposed to each other in every other way, the guerrillas and the government forces were united in the seriousness with which they regarded the ancestors and their mediums. In the course of this account of the mediums of one small section of the country, I shall pause many times to consider just how justified this attitude to the ancestors and their mediums proved to be. And with that question hanging in the air we begin the journey that will enable us to answer it, a journey into Dande society. The journey I describe here recreates my own.

I start with what first becomes visible to the dim-sighted traveller: the geography, the climate, the demography and the history of the various peoples who live in this part of the Zambezi Valley.

NOTES

1 Many of the towns of Zimbabwe acquired new names after Independence. I use the names that were current at the times of the events that I describe. The only changes that concern us are these: Salisbury became Harare, Sinoia became Chinoyi, Sipolilo became first Chipuriro and then Guruve.
2 Martin and Johnson (1981, p. 75).
3 Interview with Comrade Mayor Urimbo in Harare, 7 January 1981.
4 ibid.
5 Although it sometimes happens that more than one medium claims to be possessed by the same spirit, typically each of these mediums will deny that the others are legitimate and may challenge them to prove their authenticity. In the case of Nehanda, however, two separate traditions exist and the mediums of each will acknowledge the legitimacy of the other. However competition may arise between mediums within each tradition.
6 For the named operational zones see Martin and Johnson (1981, p. xx). For a description of the ascendancy of Chaminuka to the status of nationalist hero, see Ranger (1982a). For a full-blown history of Zimbabwe in nationalist-mythological terms, see Chigwedere (1980).
7 Mutswairo (1974, p. 66).
8 Quoted in ibid., p. 249.
9 Quoted in Frederikse (1984, p. 130).

2
The People
and the Land

The Valley and the Plateau

The road to Dande leads due north out of the capital, Harare. For over 300 km it runs between vast white-owned farms, their huge white houses set far back out of sight behind acre upon acre of cotton, tobacco, maize. Three times the road winds its way between Communal Lands dotted with clay-walled huts and tiny fenced-off fields. Then it straightens out and flows through white-owned farms again.

Twenty-five kilometres before the edge of the Plateau, the tar surface gives out and gravel begins. The journey slows down. At the side of the road men hover by whitewashed shops and beer halls in their faded formal clothes. Women saunter through the grass verge, children at their heels. Jam-packed buses, tractors, trucks and donkey carts dash along or crawl between the villages, the farms, the local town. Just as the road starts its descent, it makes a wide curve round the edge of the Escarpment. The Zambezi Valley spreads out, flat and wide, north, further north, east, west. On a clear day the Zambezi River sparkles 130 km away in Mozambique. And then the road falls 6000 m into Dande in fewer than 15 km.

For most citizens of Zimbabwe, Dande is unknown territory. It is 'the bush', a place of wild animals and backward people, drunkards and witches, left behind by modern times centuries ago. The people who live there and those on the edge of the Plateau speak the same language and live in some respects quite similar lives. But the break is felt as sharp and critical. On the Plateau the climate is mild, the soils are fertile though badly overworked, like all the Communal Lands. Here are the jobs, the markets, the centres of political power. In the Valley the heat is fierce, a remorseless 90° or 100°F in summer before the rains come, if they come, for rain is even less reliable here than in the rest of this often drought-

9

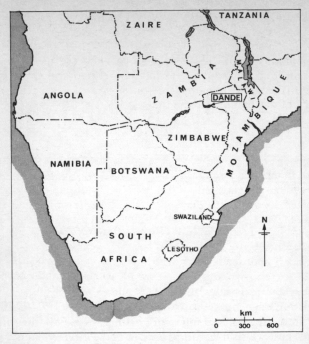

Map 2.1   Dande in relation to South Central Africa

struck land. The soils are poor. Tsetse fly make it impossible to keep
cattle to pull ploughs. There are few shops, few schools, no beer halls,
no jobs, no markets. The centres of power seem very far away.

From the bird's-eye of a geographer, Zimbabwe is divided into four
regions: high mountains on the eastern border; highveld and middleveld
forming a vast central Plateau; valleys to the south and north. But from
Dande the world appears as made up of two spheres: *panapa* and
mugomo, this place and on the mountain. In fact from the foot of the
Escarpment only the first row of hills can be seen. But as the road runs
north, the great, stout haunches of the mountain rise up blunt and grey
behind. And if the rains do come, the huge dark clouds seem to well up
from the height of the Plateau and to be forced off the edge by the wind,
soaring across and down the Valley sky, touching down almost to the
fields as they empty themselves of their rain.

The people of Dande live out most of their lives on the Valley floor
but the Plateau and the people who live up there are never long out of
their minds.

Four large rivers drain off the Plateau through the Valley and into the
Zambezi. In the Valley the villages cling to their banks and the banks of

their tributaries. Away from these rivers and villages, Dande is wild with pale, sharp grass, dense with thin contorted trees, scattered with towering baobabs. All this is home to the buck, baboons, monkeys, wild pigs, elephants, buffaloes, birds of a hundred species and, it is rumoured, lions. A few villages have boreholes and so survive away from the rivers and streams but for most a plot on the banks of a tributary of the Zambezi is the first essential of life.

Work

A village may be no more than a man, his wife or wives and their children living in a few mud-and-pole huts, a square bedroom and a round kitchen for each wife. Or it may be a group of such households, fathers and sons and brothers-in-law, gathered around a central men's house (*dare*) where the men eat, relax, entertain, hold court. Each household has its own fields where the men work in the early morning while their wives care for the children and prepare the morning meal. Women and men return to work till midday, eat and rest until mid-afternoon then return to the fields until the sun goes down.

There are very few families in Dande which rely entirely on the land for their subsistence. Most have a father or a son, a brother or a male cousin in work, or seeking work, somewhere 'on the mountain'. Without these wages it would be hard to make it even through the better years, almost impossible to survive the worst. But all these wage earners return to work their own fields when they can. Work in the towns, on the farms, in the mines has of course a powerful influence on shaping their view of their world. Nonetheless work in the fields is somehow a more basic form of work, 'real' work, providing a crucial framework of identity – as member of a household, a lineage, a chieftancy and ultimately of a clan as well. On the other hand, for those who farm away from where they were born, work in the fields may provide a sense of difference, of alienation from the land in spite of the effort spent. But over time, through work, differences may fade and strangers find that, almost without knowing it, they have come to feel at home.

In the chapters that follow we will advance deep into the undergrowth of mythology and ritual, of symbolism and belief. As we pick our way between these constructs and imaginings, it will be useful to keep in mind this central image: the villages, their fields near the banks of the rivers, the women and men of Dande working them, following the same paths over the fields, first to hoe out furrows, then back to the start and across again dribbling fertilizer (*mushonga*, or medicine) into the earth's new wounds, then back and across to sow the seeds, then back and across to weed and again to weed, day after day, with one eye on the sky, the birds, the soil, insects, winds, the mountain top seeking the signs of rain, and then back and across one final time to harvesi the heads of sorghum, the tufts of cotton, the pale green cobs of maize. The final time, that is, until next year.

The dry season lasts from April to December. The heat begins to build up in August and is intense until the rains fall. Then the grasses grow two metres or more and the rivers rise, isolating settlements one from another. When the rains end the grasses burn and all but the deepest of the rivers run dry.

The one advantage Dande has over most other parts of Zimbabwe is the large area of unclaimed land. In much of this the soil cannot hold water well enough to support the growing of grains but there are some fertile tracts away from the rivers. These the more ambitious and risk-taking of the farmers use. Poor soil and unreliable rains are the main inhibitions to economic growth. Tsetse fly carried by game is a third. Cattle brought into the Valley die within months and so most cultivation is done not with a plough but by hand with a hoe. A fourth is that few families can muster sufficient labour power to cultivate by hand the 3.25 ha of maize that they need to provide a subsistence and cash for basic needs. A fifth is that the cultivated areas are at constant risk of destruction by the elephants, buffalo, pigs and baboons that emerge from the bush when the crops grow ripe and often destroy in a single night a great part of the work of the year. Despite these disadvantages, many people have settled in Dande over the past twenty years, some because government legislation deprived them of their lands, others because by constant redivision and overworking, their lands can no longer support them. Few have been able to make full use of the available land. The hardship of putting and keeping together the cash to buy the tractors and ploughs necessary to overcome the difficulties has defeated all but the very few who brought into Dande large earnings made by wage labour on the Plateau. Until the war, there were no more than ten working tractors in the whole of Dande, four of these in a single village. Even today all tractors belong either to chiefs, schoolmasters or members of the Independent Churches to which less than 8 per cent of the population belong. For these people, and those who can afford to hire a tractor to plough a small area each year, it is possible to make reasonable returns on the cash-cropping of cotton or maize. But only a handful of those who try succeed. For most, the market provides only a tiny proportion of the money they need each year to buy soap, oil, bread, milk, matches, tea from the local stores and clothes and furniture from the towns.

The household head is officially in charge of agricultural production though his wife may deputise if he is working away. Men cut down the trees and clear the bush for new fields. All other agricultural tasks may be carried out by women or by men separately or together, though

12

usually when working together they form two single-sex groups carrying out the same tasks in the same field, talking and joking only between themselves though hurling the odd criticism or instruction from one group to the other. All household activities (fetching firewood and water, cooking, caring for children, cleaning and sweeping) are women's work. Women also maintain gardens on the river banks to provide vegetables to eat as a relish with *sadza*, the staple food, a thick porridge made by boiling ground grain. Gathered foods are not much desired but are eaten when, as is often the case, neither meat, fish nor garden vegetables are in the house and no money can be spared to buy dried or tinned goods from the shop. Some men hunt using dogs, traps and spears. Pigs, rabbits, birds and small buck are the main game. Fishing fills many gaps in the diet and is done in the wet season after the sowing of crops while the rivers are still high.

All but the youngest members of the household participate in agricultural work of one sort or another. Until the 1950s, work parties of neighbouring households assisted each other with large productive or development tasks. These no longer operate except for those organised by the Women's Clubs who use the money they earn to finance visits to other centres, knitting and baking competitions and other similar projects. The few tractor-owning large-scale farmers hire some wage labour for sowing, weeding and harvesting but this is not yet a significant feature of the economy of Dande as it is of the Plateau.[1]

One further contrast. For most Shona peoples cattle are a major source and store of value. Wealth, prestige and morality can be expressed by the accumulation of herds and their controlled dispersal. But as cattle cannot survive in the Valley, the people who live there do not have this means for the expression of value available to them. This is one of the sharpest distinctions between the Plateau Korekore and those who live in the Valley below.

The past

In this preliminary account I describe the history of Dande as a series of waves – waves of people bearing with them original political ideas, economic innovations, cultural idiosyncrasies. Some of these waves were absorbed, as it were, into the terrain. Others in time rolled back leaving only traces behind. The terrain itself was not deserted. The people who lived there perceived, accepted, rejected these waves in a highly complex and discriminating manner. The question of what changes over time and what remains, of what is washed away, what alters and what holds firm, is a central preoccupation of this book. What fundamental changes were worked in Dande society by the recent war? What is there in it that can survive not only this most recent victorious war but also the unsuccessful wars, the upheavals, the defeats of the past? These questions imply two others: what is victory if the key concepts of a society are altered by it; what is defeat if little that is cruicial is lost? Here I only describe the upheavals, the storms, the waves and what they left behind. What they flowed over and washed around I describe in the chapters to come.

There are four groups of people within Dande: the Tande, the Korekore, the Dema, the Chikunda. The people we can think of as the autochthons are those who gave it its name, the Tande. I use the clumsy word autochthon for want of a plainer term that conveys the partly mythical, partly historic, partly attitudinal references that it contains. To call a people autochthons, literally 'those who came out of the ground', implies that they are thought by themselves and others to have a special ritual intimacy with the territory they occupy because they are thought of as the earliest ever to have lived there. The Tande consider themselves to be the true owners of the land. According to their mythology, they are the people whom the Korekore conquered when they came to the Valley. It has been argued that the Tande are a subgroup of the Tavara, the autochthons to the north and east of Dande and across the border in Mozambique. They themselves deny this. The genealogy of their ancestors shows no linkage to the major Tavara ancestors. However, if one uses the word Tavara to indicate a loose collection of dynasties resident in the Valley before the Korekore, this would accommodate the Tande. Although their dialect is distinctive, the identity of individual Tande remains ambiguous. Because of the higher prestige of the Korekore as 'conquerors' and as members of a group with marginally higher economic status and mobility, many Tande claim to be Korekore. The name Tande is considered by some, though not the royal lineage, to be derogatory, indicating poverty, backwardness, wildness etc. They have only one chief, Matsiwo. His territory lies between the three Korekore chieftancies of Dande but members of both groups are scattered throughout both notionally distinct areas. The royal clan is Elephant (*Nzou Samanyanga*, literally Elephant, Keeper of the Tusks).[2]

The Korekore, the first of the waves that washed into Dande, are members of a major Shona language group which occupies a huge swathe of the northern Plateau as well as the southern section of the Valley. In all accounts published so far the Korekore are considered to be the descendants of a number of Karanga lineages which travelled to the north of the Plateau and the Zambezi Valley from the south of present-day Zimbabwe in the fifteenth century. Although the name 'Korekore' does not appear in records until the nineteenth century, it is said to have been given to the 'invaders' by the people whose land they took and is interpreted as a corruption of *kure-kure* (the people from afar) or of a word meaning 'locust' in reference to the effects of the pillaging that ensued. Political alliances between these 'conquering' lineages are thought to have formed the basis of the Mutapa state.

Northern Zimbabwe has known three major concentrations of political power in the recorded past. The Mutapa state, the first of these, was the focus of the highest levels of political authority over a large part of the Plateau and Valley from the fifteenth century to the eighteenth century. Over this period it achieved a fluctuating degree of control over its many subject chieftancies including those in Dande. In the eighteenth century Dande increased its independence, ruled by a house which had ancestral claims to the Mutapa state as a whole but which was unable to enforce them except for one brief period. At this time Dande seems to have extended much further west and south than it does today including an area of the northern Plateau. In this book I use the term 'Dande' as it is used by the people who live in it today who regard its boundaries as the Angwa River in the west, the Msengezi in the east, the Zambezi in the north and the Escarpment in the south.[3]

The wealth of the Mutapa state derived from three main sources: cattle-herding on the Plateau, agriculture, and trade in ivory and gold. From the fifteenth century, highly profitable trade routes from the Plateau to the sea ports via the Zambezi River passed through Dande. In some areas tolls were paid to chiefs. Thus Dande was linked to the international network of trade between Europe and the Far East – ivory and gold exchanged with Portuguese traders for cloth and beads from India. One reason these items were desired was as a means of storing wealth which could be transformed into food when the rains failed. The saltpans in the north-west of Dande provided another item for trade, this time with the people of the Plateau who had otherwise to extract salt from cattle dung or the leaves of certain plants.[4]

As the Mutapa state lost ground to that of the Rozvi its centre moved to the Valley where, according to some accounts, it persisted until the early twentieth century. Its legacy is complex. Some of the institutions and political rituals of the state continue to shape political and economic experience. The relationship of the present-day chiefs to 'their' land and the people who live there seems to derive from this period as does the hierarchical ordering of the chiefs themselves. Remnants of the calender of the state continue to order the rest days of the week and month. The genealogies of the rulers of the state as it existed during its last days in the Valley are the key institutions defining and delimiting the royal status of the present chiefly lineages. Although they give the impression of endurance over time, they are in fact frequently re-ordered and reconstructed and are crucial tools for the expression and manipulation of authority.[5]

I am concerned with only four of the many Korekore chieftancies.

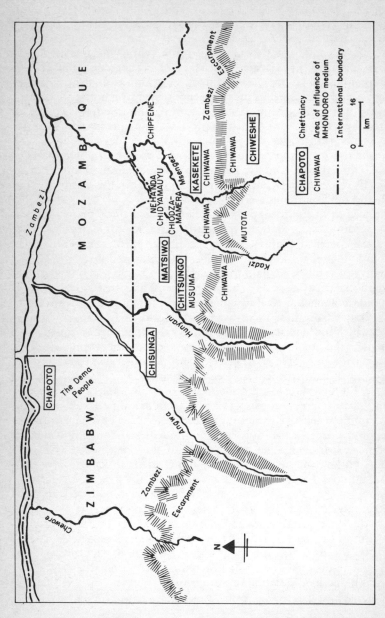

Map 2.2   The chiefs and the major mhondoro, c. 1980

Three of these (Kasekete, Chitsungo and Chiweshe) claim descent from the ancestor Chiwawa who will appear frequently in the pages that follow. The fourth (Chisunga) claims descent from the ancestor Nyamapfeka. All four chiefs claim ultimate descent from the original 'conqueror', Mutota. The royal clan is the same as that of the Tande: Elephant, Keeper of the Tusks (*Nzou Samanyanga*).

It was during the later Mutapa period that the Dema people were brought to live within Dande. Their name means 'the conquerors' but their mythology describes their incorporation within the state as unwilling, as the result of military defeat. It was only ever partially accomplished. They have achieved some notoriety throughout Zimbabwe because of the widespread belief that they suffer from a congenital deformation of the foot giving them the appearance of having only two toes. In fact, only one Dema family, and no more than two members of it, has ever had this characteristic but as the tale appealed to white racism it has had a long, not yet completed currency. This is only one of the many calumnies they have had to bear. In the mid-nineteenth century A. M. Pacheco reported that they were cannibals; a hundred years later the historian D. P. Abraham described their initiation practices as 'disgusting', and so on. Their reputation, as well as their present condition as semi-foragers in the Doma Hills with little access to fertile land, possibly derives from their prolonged resistance to incorporation within the Mutapa state. They speak a dialect distinct from the Korekore and Tande but in the main comprehensible to both. Their clan is *Mvura Tembo*. *Mvura* means water. *Tembo* may be translated either as zebra (Korekore) or, north of the Zambezi, as elephant. They are a small population and in keeping with their elusive and recalcitrant style they appear only occasionally in this book.[6]

The Rozvi state was the second major concentration of political power in northern Zimbabwe. Its influence was not significant in Dande and it need not detain us here. The third political force was the Portuguese. Traders had maintained a presence in the Zambezi Valley since the fifteenth century. As their political fortunes rose and fell they either extended their trade south onto the Plateau establishing market centres, or withdrew to the river. Their participation in succession disputes eventually split the Mutapa leadership and contributed to its decline. Their *prazos* or farms lining the banks of the Zambezi remained in Portuguese hands until the start of this century. Many of the riverine peoples were assimilated into their slave armies. The descendants of these people are known today as the Chikunda. The majority of Chikunda are found in Mozambique and Zambia. Only one Chikunda chieftancy is within Dande. This is Chapoto, a descendant of the nineteenth-century Portuguese land-holder José Rosario Andrade. Their dialect is closer to Tande than Korekore. Their clan is Pigeon

(*Hangaiwa Marunga*). The intermarriage between coloniser and colonised that produced the Chikunda contrasts markedly with the colonial experiences of the Korekore and the Tande. It is for the sake of this contrast that I include them in this book.[7]

The pioneer column that founded the state of Rhodesia arrived at Fort Salisbury in 1890. The effects were barely felt in the Valley for almost twenty years. Even the nationwide rebellion of 1896–7 involved the peoples of the Valley only marginally. Tavara and Korekore were much more heavily involved in resistance to the Portuguese in the insurrections of 1905 and 1917. The boundary between Rhodesia and Mozambique, slicing through the northern section of Dande, was drawn in 1891 and the focus of trade and labour recruitment switched from its northerly orientation towards the Zambezi River to a southerly orientation towards the farms and mines of the Plateau.[8]

By 1920 the Rhodesian state at last made its presence felt in the Valley. The Korekore chieftancies were reorganised. The power of the friendly was increased, that of the hostile reduced or removed altogether. Taxation was imposed. Headmen and chiefs were charged with collecting it. Having over centuries fought for and achieved a degree of political and economic independence from the Mutapas, the Valley peoples now began their incorporation into the Rhodesian state.

The early diversification of the Shona economy into various forms of trade had been encouraged by the need to find sources of income not reliant on the rains. This had been sufficiently successful in the Valley to give travellers an impression of plenty and ease. The collapse of the Portuguese trade routes coinciding with the inception of taxation forced the most significant contributors of labour to the local economy, the young men, out of the Valley onto the capitalist market. The inherently unstable agricultural economy thus lost two of its main props one after the other. The fate of the families in the Valley now depended on the success of their menfolk in the uncontrolled, fiercely discriminatory labour markets on the Plateau. The profound long-term consequences will be described in Chapter 7. In brief, none of the old forms of trade is carried on today. Apart from the small quantities of cotton and maize sold to the government marketing boards at a guaranteed price, the only trade is in baskets and mats woven by the men from bamboo and river reeds and, less significantly, in clay pots moulded by the women. The trade in pots is mostly local. Mats and baskets are bought by local entrepreneurs and sold door-to-door in the towns.

Over the succeeding years the churches came to Dande: the Catholics built missions in the south-west and north-west, the Evangelical Alliance Mission in the west and north-east, the Anglicans near the centre. Two of these missions opened schools (the first in 1941), and later clinics. Little other development took place until the mid-1960s.

The need to patrol this sensitive border region against the incursion of guerrilla forces led to the construction of gravel roads east–west along the base of the Escarpment and north towards the border. Police and District Administration camps were built; at the final count there were eight.

In 1971, as we have seen, ZANLA guerrillas entered Dande for the first time.

Modes of incorporation

Within a short period of their arrival in Dande, the ZANLA guerrillas were incorporated into local social categories. The category into which they were placed was 'descendants of the *mhondoro*', which is to say that they were regarded as members of the royal lineages. This was not the only way in which they were perceived nor was their incorporation into this category absolute and complete. It was nonetheless remarkable, for few of the guerrillas active in Dande were born in the region or had any historical connection with the ancestors believed to take care of it. Despite this, notions of descent, by definition a closed category, were opened out to receive them.

To show how the assimilation of these strangers, the guerrillas, occurred requires an analysis of all the techniques that can be used to achieve incorporation into Dande society. In this section I give an outline of these techniques. How they were made use of by the guerrillas and their supporters during the war is described in Part III.

Descent – lineage and chieftancy

In Dande, as in many African societies, ideas about political authority are expressed in terms of 'ownership of the land'. The principal holder of political authority, the chief, is the leading member of a patrilineal lineage that claims descent from an 'owner' of the land. These 'owners' may be thought of either as autochthons, the first people ever to have lived there (as in the case of the Tande and Tavara) or as the conquerors of earlier owners (as in the case of the Korekore). In Chapter 5, I will show that ownership by autochthonous right and by conquest do not achieve equally profound 'depths' of ownership. Nonetheless both autochthonous and conquering ancestors are referred to by their descendants as *varidzi vepasi*, the owners of the land. For the moment I will treat both styles as equally capable of conferring the authority to rule.

The notion that a territory within Dande is 'owned' by a particular lineage has a number of consequences for the way it is conceptualised.

19

For a start, the claim made by a lineage to an area of land causes it to be conceptualised as a 'territory' in the first place. These claims always refer to specific, usually natural, boundaries providing a chieftaincy or other territory with a precise delimitation. Secondly, the history of the ancestors of the lineage permeates and, to some extent, organises the sensory experience of the territory by its inhabitants, the members of the ruling lineage and others. The ruling lineage lends the territory its traditional name. Chief Chitsungo's territory is known as 'Chitsungo' and so on. A link between the chief's lineage and the territory is formed by the notion that the chiefs of the past (the ancestors) were buried in its soil. Another equally common way of expressing the bond is that the territory belongs to the chief's lineage because its ancestors *lived* in it. The most important sites in the territory (hills, pools, certain trees) are named after the ancestors, are near where their villages were sited or are associated with significant events in their lives.

The consequence is that a strong emotional bond exists between individuals and the territory of their ancestors. The desire to live there is equalled only by the desire to be buried there. An important notion in the organising of political and moral experience is the idea of living 'at home'. Home for the living is essentially the home of the dead. Life is good if you live where your ancestors lived before you. However, within a chief's territory live many people who are not descended from the royal ancestors, who are not 'at home' in the territory where they live. In fact it has been calculated by Dr Kingsley Garbett that only between one-quarter and one-third of those living in a chieftaincy are members of the royal lineage. Nonetheless, despite its small size, the royal lineage is able to stamp its personality on the territory it shares with other lineages and thereby make unthinkable the possibility that the land might not belong to it.[9]

The people who live within a chieftaincy may be divided into two categories: (1) members of the lineages descended from the royal ancestors. These are known as *machinda* (sing. *jinda*). I refer to them as royals. Only a few of these lineages are by tradition entitled to provide candidates for the position of chief; (2) people who are descended from royal ancestors who have authority in other parts of the country. These are called *vatorwa*. I call them strangers.[10]

Royal lineages possess long genealogies of their ancestors, up to fifteen generations deep, which link them to the original 'owners of the land'. Strangers may have long genealogies linking them to their own royal ancestors, or they may have forgotten these ties and remember only shallow genealogies that extend no further back than the father's father of the oldest living member. In Dande, as in Europe, family trees which make a claim to land or political authority because they link the present bearers of an aristocratic name to a conqueror, king or landholder of the past are valued and remembered. The landless and the powerless have no need to remember who their ancestors have been. This distinction between royals and strangers, that the first can trace their ancestry back to the 'owners' of the territory where they live whereas the second cannot is of great importance. But apart from this, and the exclusive right of certain of the royal lineages to succeed to the chieftaincy, there are no other distinctions of status between these two categories of people.

How did the strangers come to be living away from their own home territories? In some cases they may be members of lineages that migrated from an area of land shortage and received permission from the chief to live where they do. They may have been resident in their present home for generations. Or they may have another reason for being where they are.

Amongst all Shona groups, as throughout Central and Southern Africa, bride price is paid by a husband and his lineage to the lineage of the wife. In return for this he receives rights in the woman as a wife and as a mother and the incorporation of her children into his lineage. Usually bride price is paid in cattle and the woman goes to live in the village of her husband. But amongst the Korekore and the Tande, payment for a wife is usually made by the husband going to live in the village of his wife's father and working for a period of years in his fields. Occasionally a small sum of money may be paid as well but generally no more than a ritual payment and other prescribed gifts change hands.

The first reason for the high incidence of bride-service (or *kugarira*) marriage in Dande is the absence of cattle due to tsetse fly. The system can therefore be seen as operating within the 'wives for cattle' framework but, by force of circumstance, without the cattle. The second reason is the relative poverty of the people of the Zambezi Valley compared with those on the Plateau. Even those who earn money by migrant labour find it difficult to put together sufficient cash to pay for their wives once and for all. The period of bride service may be as long as fifteen years. When it has been completed husband, wife and children may return to the husband's father's home but frequently they remain in the father-in-law's territory on land allocated by him. If this occurs, the allocation of land to a son-in-law must be approved by the senior local representative of the royal lineage, the chief or ward head. In addition, it must be ascertained that the local *mhondoro* (royal ancestor) agrees to allow this 'stranger' to live in the territory he controls. A gift must be given to the *mhondoro* (typically a black or white cloth) and a payment (known as a *badza* or hoe) made to the chief.[11]

The consequence is that a chieftaincy is not merely a patrilineal lineage writ large although the terminology of descent used to describe the relationship would make it appear as though it were. The chief is said to be 'father' to his people; his ancestors are their *sekuru* or grandfathers. The first technique of incorporation into Dande society is that of descent, 'a genealogical connection recognised between a person and his ancestors'. But the relationship between chiefs and strangers is in fact quite different from that which exists between fathers and their descendants. Descent in itself cannot explain the basis on which this relationship rests.[12]

Substance – the clan

Another way in which the relationship between lineages is conceptualised is as members of clans.[13]

In the most complete discussion of Shona kinship to date, Professor Holleman deals only cursorily with the clan. He considers the two main features of clans to be that they are patrilineal and exogamous (ie clan members may not marry each other). In his researches he found no example of a clan functioning 'as a corporate group: either as a recognised political unit, or as an occasional, all-inclusive gathering for particular purposes'. He adds that clans are divided into sub-clans, also patrilineally inherited, that they are dispersed and that they are named, usually referring to an animal, and finally that 'people are expected to refrain from eating their totem animal or a specific part of it.'[14]

In his detailed study, *The Shona Peoples*, Dr Michael Bourdillon makes the important observation that 'sub-clans are often related to geographical areas suggesting that the sub-clans originated as local pockets of a particular clan'. The more substantial point that clans as a whole are associated with geographic areas was made by W. H. Stead who mapped a section of Charter District in central Zimbabwe in terms of clan affiliation. Another aspect of clan mentioned by Bourdillon is that 'when two people with no traceable kinship ties meet, they may adopt rules of behaviour towards each other based on any relationship which they know exists between other members of their respective clans'. Lastly he notes that 'clan names are most commonly used in a respectful greeting or when one wishes to show gratitude'. They are also used as endearments in lovemaking and are celebrated at length in praise poems.[15]

To summarise: the most important features of clans are that they are exogamic (in some cases it is permissible for different sub-clans of the same clan to marry); they are patrilineally inherited; they are named after an animal or other object which must be avoided or not eaten; they are associated with geographic regions; they are dispersed with no corporate or ritual functions.

For all the writers I have quoted, the clan is a means of incorporation based on the notion of descent. It is a collection of lineages, loosely and non-specifically related to each other, deriving its coherence from an undemonstrable claim to common descent from an unspecified ancestor. In other words, clan members are said to experience a sense of relatedness to each other in more or less the same way as members of the same lineage. The difficulty with this conclusion is that all the features of clans that distinguish them from lineages – association with a named animal or object, the territorial aspect, the mystical punishment for eating the tabooed animal and so on – remain unexplained. There is no doubt that descent is one aspect of clan membership but having said that, there still remains a good deal more to say.[16]

First, how do people actually describe their sensory experience of their clan affiliation? They say that they know they belong to a particular clan because if they eat the animal associated with it they will become sick. They may add that their teeth will fall out. This is clearly seen in this extract from a conversation recorded in Mauhwe village:

> *Question*: How do you know which clan you belong to?
> *Answer*: If a man eats a chicken and it makes him sick, then he knows he is a member of the chicken clan.

A subtle but crucial distinction is being drawn here. It is possible to say that you are a member of clan X because you avoid eating food X – an argument of 'doing' derived from a notion of law. But it is also possible to say, as my informants did, that because you are a member of clan X, if you eat food X you will become sick – an argument of 'being' derived from a notion of substance. What you are 'being' is that same sort of thing as other members of your clan and this is demonstrated by the typical reaction to the introduction of a particular substance (the clan animal) into a clan member's body. It is not a question of common descent but of common substance with other members of your clan.

This is not to say that clan membership has no descent component. One acquires one's clan from one's father and the word *rudzi* which is used for clan (it also means type, nature or colour of a thing or person) can also be used to mean lineage, though *dzinza* is more commonly heard in Dande. But there is no suggestion that clan members are in some way descended from the clan animal and it is rare in my experience that descent from a common ancestor is given as an explanation of clan membership. The way to discover a person's clan is to ask not from whom they are descended but what animal they taboo (*unoerei*?) This type of incorporation must therefore be distinguished from incorporation by descent. I will refer to it as incorporation by common substance.[17]

Secondly, Stead and Bourdillon's suggestion that clans (and subclans) are associated with specific geographic regions should be put much more forcefully. There is, in Dande at least, a very clear association of clan with place. By pointing in various directions, people can indicate precisely where each clan of significance to them has its origins. Dande is the home of the Elephant clan, to the south on the Plateau is the home of the Monkey clan, to the north-east is the Pig clan, to the north-west the Pigeon clan and so on.[18]

This leads to an interesting paradox. Throughout Dande people are adamant that clan membership can never be changed. When this subject is discussed, it is common for people to strike themselves over their hearts insisting that their clan identity stands at the very centre of their personalities and can never be altered. Although women adopt the clan name of their husbands at marriage, they return to that of their father if they divorce. Their father's clan is their 'real' clan and this remains true all their lives. But in fact both royal lineages and individuals change clan affiliation fairly frequently.

I deal with royal lineages first. If the association of clan with area operated as it is said to do, one would expect that the autochthonous people of a territory would be members of the clan associated with that territory while the 'conquerors' would have the clan of the area from which they came. In fact in Dande both members of the Tande royal lineage, who stand as autochthons in relation to the conquering Korekore *and* the conquerors themselves are members of the same Elephant clan. That this is an anomaly is recognised and attempts have been made recently by a senior spirit medium to alter Korekore clan affiliation on a large scale so that the autochthon/conqueror opposition may be clearly reasserted. But the Tande royal lineage insists that they are the real Elephants, while the Korekore royal lineages maintain that they are Elephants as well.[19]

Two principles are said to regulate large-scale changes of clan affiliation. A number of versions of the first of these were given me in Dande:

> If an individual or a group is defeated in battle, they will flee to the territory of another clan. They will hide in the bush for a few days until they hear how the people who live there address each other, that is, until they learn what the local clan is. Then they emerge from the bush and claim to be members of the same clan. Once they have adopted the new clan it is impossible for their enemies to find them.

This account expresses very powerfully the close association of clan with territory and asserts so complete a merging of individual with clan that clan membership can obscure all distinctive features of the individual.

The second principle comes into play when the conquered cannot flee from their territory and they adopt the clan of the conquerors. In this case the new ruling lineage would occupy a territory associated with a clan different from its own. There are many accounts of this occurring throughout Zimbabwe.

These two principles imply that changes in clan membership are a last resort and involuntary. However, some individual changes of clan take place without any sort of compulsion. Despite the claim to a profound identification of an individual with her or his clan, numbers of people are known to have changed their clans when they moved from an earlier place of residence to where they live at present. When I discussed with people their own particular experience of shifting clan allegiance, it was described to me as a gradual process of, as it were, assimilating a new clan identity. In all cases this occurred because they were living in a territory not associated with their clan and because they had been there, or their lineage had been there, for a very long period of time. If you live for a long time in a 'foreign' territory, gradually you may come to be adopted into the clan of that territory and to be treated as such by other clan members.

But it is not enough simply to live in a territory to acquire an identity as a member of the local clan. Above all you must work the land in that territory and take part in the communal rituals of the agricultural cycle. The members of a stranger lineage that has worked the land and acknowledged the local royal ancestors for a generation or two may come to be so closely identified with their new home that very few of their neighbours will suspect that they were ever members of any clan other than the one to which they now belong.

The ideology of descent, our first mode of incorporation, suggests that the social identity of an individual is acquired at birth and fixed for all time. It is an ideology most frequently expressed by members of the royal lineages. The ideology of clan membership, incorporation by substance, is more ambiguous. The association of clan with territory gives it a flexibility which is denied as often as it is exercised. Territoriality is therefore a third mode of incorporation. It is brought into operation by the fourth, duration. By working the land in a certain territory for a long period of time an individual or a lineage can alter their clan affiliation.

Women and men

In Chapter 5, I describe the symbolism and ritual practice of male supremacy and in Chapter 11, I discuss the extent to which these persisted through the years of the war. I give here a brief, preliminary account of the status of women in Dande.

Women share with men the basic agricultural tasks of sowing, weeding and harvesting but the central feature of the relationship between them is the moral, legal and intellectual supremacy of men. Only men can inherit or attain positions of authority within the lineage or chieftaincy. Every adult man of sound mind is considered capable of settling disputes. Before the new practices introduced during the war, no woman of any age was believed to be capable of this, just as women are believed to have no knowledge of the past. In fact, many women possess knowledge of the past as detailed as their husbands who frequently refer to their wives for forgotten details of the histories of their lineages. Despite this, the belief persists that the past and the authority and morality that derive from it are domains into which women can never enter.

The women's domain is the household and the garden. They venture into the bush only to collect wild vegetables when there is no other food in the house. While their presence *en masse* is required at the major ceremonies, there are no individual ritual roles open to women except as mediums of lineage ancestors. Very few women become mediums of the royal ancestors.

At marriage, which is usually to the man of her choice, a woman adopts the clan name of her husband and this may be used as a term of address for her. But her ties with her own lineage and her lineage ancestors remain strong. If divorce should occur, she will return to the territory of her father and take up his clan name again. Should she become sick in her husband's home it is likely that she will return to her father's home to be cured. Her husband has need to remain on good terms with her father's ancestors for they will make his children ill if he does not.

Men may have more than one wife and can expect their extramarital affairs to be tolerated and enjoyably gossiped about by all but the kinsmen of the woman concerned. Women are expected to be virgin at marriage and to remain faithful to their husbands throughout life. Adultery by a wife is sufficient grounds for divorce.

Succession to all positions, statuses and properties held by men on behalf of a social unit (the position of chief, of village head, the control of chief's names or non-royal lineage names and so on) are inherited adelphically (see p. 57). A man's own name and the property he has acquired during his lifetime are inherited by his sons. The eldest of his sons who lives at his home will inherit the term by which he was addressed. This son's brothers and even his mother will call him 'father' in his father's stead.

At the death of a woman her property is inherited by members of her lineage unless she specifies that it is to go to a daughter. It is distributed without the ceremony appropriate for men. Although women may be said to 'own' the fields they work on, they do so in the name of their husbands and lose rights over them when their husbands die. A widow may be inherited by a brother of her dead husband but a woman is free

26

to refuse subsequent marriages if she wishes and to return to her father's home. The only time at which men and women act towards each other as though they were equals is when drinking beer. However even here the equality is only partial and weighted on the side of the men. Women who drink are thought to lose an aspect of their feminine nature, to become foolish, mad or sexually irresponsible.

Unlike many neighbouring peoples (for example the Ndebele, Zulu, Hlengwe, Tsonga) the Shona today have neither an age-grade system nor specialised military institutions. Neither males nor females undergo a ceremony of initiation into adult status. Adulthood is achieved at the birth of the first child. The practice of teknonomy, by which parents are addressed as mother or father of their child, marks this transition.

NOTES

1 For work parties and more on Valley economics see Garbett (1963a, p. 105).
2 Bourdillon (1970, p. 103) contains a map indicating the location of the Tavara. See also Beach (1980, p. 66). In his recent study of the Middle Zambezi Valley, Lancaster (1981) applies to all the peoples of Dande the same name as he uses for the subjects of his study, the Goba. This name has the inference: 'people who live in a low-lying area'. See his map on p. 134. From the point of view of Dande, this name is not acceptable. For one thing the people who live in Dande maintain that the Goba live in a north-easterly direction. They point, in fact, towards the Middle Zambezi Valley. For another, Lancaster's Goba are matrilineal whereas the Tande and the Korekore are not. Nor can they be characterised as 'matriarchal' which, according to Lancaster, 'his' Goba can. Note that in the past Dande extended into what is now Mozambique. I was unable to make visits across the border.
3 For the Mutapa state see Beach (1980, Ch. 4). Pacheco (1883) gives the borders of Dande as 'The Mussengùse river to the east, the Zambèze to the north, the Changuè to the south, and the Sanhata to the west'.
4 Beach (1977) contains the best brief description of the Shona economy. Bhila (1982) contains a map showing Portuguese trade routes.
5 D. P. Abraham and other writers following him have described these genealogies as though they related to the highest levels of the Mutapa state as it existed from the fifteenth century onwards. I discuss this claim in detail in Lan (1983, Ch.5). For the role of spirit mediums in previous centuries see Mudenge (1976). For the political institutions of the Mutapa state see Randles (1981), Beach (1980), Mudenge (forthcoming). For the 'last days' of the Mutapa state see Ranger (1963a).
6 See Roberts (1974, p. 89) for the history of the 'two-toed' legend, and Beach (1980, p. 66) for hints on the relationship between the Dema and the Mutapa state.

7 On the Rozvi influence on Dande see Mudenge (1972, p. 90). The Chikunda
   have been exhaustively documented and analysed by Isaacman (e.g. 1972,
   1976). Newitt (1973) has written a detailed history of Portuguese settlement
   on the Zambezi.
8 See Ranger (1963b) on resistance to the Portuguese. See Axelson (1967) on
   the drawing of the national boundary.
9 A full-scale discussion of how this is achieved is the subject of Chapter 6
   below.
10 This analysis is based on Holleman (1952) and Garbett (1967).
11 See Garbett (1967, p. 308) for *kugarira* marriage. He has calculated that 83
   per cent of Korekore marriages are uxorilocal, that is bride-service
   marriages. My impression is that the figure may be higher for the relatively
   less well-off Tande. See Kuper (1982) for a summary of the 'wives for cattle'
   system. Lancaster (1981, p. 151) contains a discussion of bride-wealth
   versus bride-service marriages among the Shona and their neighbours in the
   Zambezi Valley.
12 The quotation is from Fortes (1959, p. 206).
13 I include this extended treatment of clanship here not only because of the use
   made of the principles of clan acquisition by the guerrillas but also because
   it has been suggested to me that this analysis may be of use in interpreting
   clanship amongst other Southern and Central African peoples. The
   distinction which the Korekore draw between lineage as descent and clan as
   substance is, I believe, recorded here for the first time. It allows some of the
   advances made in other areas (e.g. Strathern, 1973) to be applied to an
   African context.
14 Holleman (1952, pp. 23, 24).
15 Bourdillon (1982, p. 21); Stead (1946). For Shona praise poems see the
   excellent collection by Hodza and Fortune (1979).
16 For the purpose of my argument it is not necessary to consider why clans
   exist in the first place and as to the particular 'totemic' characteristics that
   they display, Levi-Strauss's (1969) conclusion that these are elements of a
   structured symbolic classificatory system fits this case as successfully as it
   does his many other examples. I am concerned here only with clan
   membership as a mode of incorporation into Dande society.
17 Among the Chikunda, it is said that if one eats one's clan animal, the teeth of
   one's brother's son will fall out. This neatly demonstrates the possibility of a
   descent group stress alongside and secondary to the 'consubstantial' aspect
   of clan membership. One illustration of the significance of substance as a
   mode of incorporation is the belief that it is possible to protect oneself from
   sickness by eating a small quantity of the soil of one's home territory.
18 From the local point of view, the clans that Europeans are thought to have
   are 'French', 'Scottish' and so on, each indicating a different type (*rudzi*) of
   people and a different place of origin.
19 The various versions of why and when the Korekore and the Tande acquired
   their present clan and subclan are difficult to reconcile. I interpret them not
   as historical accounts but as claims to the ownership of land along the lines
   explored in Chapter 5 below. See Matthews (1966), Abraham (1962),
   Kaschula (1965a), Beach (1980, p. 118).

PART II

The Lions of Rain

They helped us. The ancestors really helped us. If not for the ancestors this war would never have ended. If the war had gone on we would have had such troubles here. But these ancestors said: no, help is needed. We must help.

The medium of the *mhondoro* Kavhinga on the role of the ancestors during the war.

3
The Land and the Dead

In Chapter 2, I suggested that the history of Dande might be seen as a series of waves that washed across the Valley floor. First came the Korekore conquerors, then the Mutapa state, then the Portuguese and then the century of settler rule. All were partly absorbed and partly resisted. All left greater or lesser traces of themselves behind.

One set of traces of the past has yet to be described. These are the spirits of people who lived and died in Dande long ago but who despite their death still have influence over those who live there now.

The mediums with whom the ZANLA guerrillas came into contact were possessed by the *mhondoro*, the spirits of the chiefs of the past. But there are many other kinds of spirit as well. Some are thought of as the remnants of ancient populations which died out and whose descendants are unknown. Others are animal spirits. A third category are the spirits of ordinary people who share some of the characteristics and skills of the *mhondoro*. All are capable of possessing human mediums from time to time.

Midzimu *and* mhondoro

All women and men are expected to provide for and protect their families as best they can. Even when they die and leave their bodies in the grave they do not cease to care for their descendants. The richness of their personalities and the depth of their experience do not come to an abrupt halt and dissipate for all time. Death is like a weir in a river. For a while the flow of life is held up. The current eddies round and round and streams back on itself as the processes of dying and burial get underway. But then the weir gates are winched open and the flow of life continues, though now on a different level. Women and men with their limited powers, their ignorance and weaknesses have been transformed into

31

ancestors or *midzimu* who know the future before it happens and can cure every ill. Ancestors make the perfect parents. Human life is greatly enhanced by the ending of it.

The form an ancestor takes is *mweya* (breath or air). Ancestors have no material form and so can be in all places at the same time. But they continue to have sensory experience. They can see and hear, they have emotions and desires. But they are never frivolous or mean. The welfare of their descendants is their sole concern. There is only one reason why they might make a descendant ill. This is to give a sign that they wish to possess her or him, to speak through her or his mouth to all their descendants to warn that some disaster is about to strike or to complain that they have been forgotten and to ask that beer be brewed or a child named in their memory.

As with ordinary women and men so also with chiefs. In life a chief should look after all his followers. He should provide them with grain from a common store in time of drought and maintain the peace by enforcing the law through his court. When a chief dies he is transformed into a *mhondoro* and becomes the source of the fertility of the land itself. He provides rain for the fields and protects the crops as they grow. Rain will only be withheld if the *mhondoro*'s laws are disobeyed. If incest, murder or witchcraft take place drought follows and the crops will fail. But if the descendants of the *mhondoro* obey his laws and perform his ceremonies in due time, they will live in peace and plenty.[1]

The royal ancestors, the *mhondoro*, may be referred to as *midzimu*, or ancestors, for they too are the 'remnants' of dead people transformed and enhanced by their death. But their powers are as superior to those of ordinary *midzimu* as the authority of chief is to that of their followers. As the *midzimu* takes care of the lineage that has lost its human protector so the *mhondoro* cares for the *nyika*, the country, that he ruled over when alive.

Although the *midzimu* are unceasingly generous and concerned only with the welfare of the living, their protection is not automatic. It must be won by performing certain rituals, the most important of which is *kutamba guva* (to dance the grave). This should be performed within a year of the death of chief and commoner alike. In the course of the ritual the ancestor is led out of the bush where it has been living since its death back into the household which was its home in life. Only after this ritual has been performed will an ancestor extend its protection to the living. And from time to time beer must be brewed and distributed in its name, for the ancestors cannot bear to be forgotten and will withdraw their protection from their descendants if they are.[2]

The word *mhondoro* means lion. When a chief dies his spirit makes its way into the bush where it enters the body of a lion. Some people say that a few days after a chief is buried, a tiny lion without a mane crawls

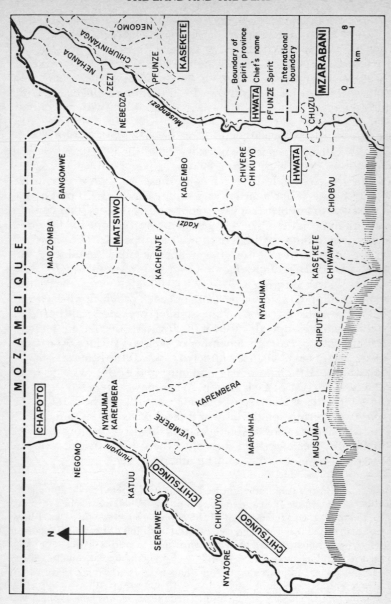

Map 3.1   The mhondoro of southern Dande, c. 1960 (adapted from Garbett, 1977)

33

up through a hole left for it at the side of the grave and scampers off into the forest. When I asked why this happens to chiefs and not to other men I was given one of two answers. Either I was told that it is simply because chiefs are chiefs. They own and rule the land when alive and it is just the same when they are dead. Or I was told that chiefs eat certain medicines which at their deaths transform them into *mhondoro*. Only chiefs know these medicines. They have the monopoly on power now and for all time.[3]

One of the most unusual features of the *mhondoro* is that each is thought to rule over a specific territory which he is believed to have conquered or been given when he was alive. Following Kingsley Garbett's pioneering lead, I refer to these as 'spirit provinces'. No part of Dande is unclaimed. Every square centimetre is part of one spirit province or another. They vary enormously in size. Some contain no more than a scattering of villages, some spread out for fifty-odd kilometres containing hundreds or thousands of people. Their borders, which are usually rivers, cross the boundaries of chieftaincies and administrative districts and some spill over into Mozambique.

These provinces are grouped to form 'spirit realms' under the control of the most senior of the local *mhondoro* but each province is itself a unit of communal ritual activity. In the smaller provinces, all heads of households must co-operate in the annual rituals that bring the rain. The larger provinces contain a number of separate shrines. At each of these, rituals are held but all are directed towards the same *mhondoro*. All men who work the *mhondoro*'s land must make offerings of grain to it at the first harvest of each season. When newcomers (strangers or sons-in-law) settle within a spirit province, a gift must be made to the *mhondoro* and permission to cultivate a piece of its land obtained.

Here is an account by a young man of his first meeting with the medium of the *mhondoro* who controlled the spirit province where he had recently arrived to live with his mother's father:

In the morning my grandfather showed me the field where I could plough. We walked all round the field and then went home. When we reached there we saw a man who was the medium of the *mhondoro* called Chiwawa. I have never seen this man before. I greeted him but he didn't answer me. I sat down near to him. Then he started to sing and his spirit came out saying: 'Eee. Aaa. Who are you? Get away. I don't want to see you here.' I got up and was about to go but my grandfather said to him 'This is your *muzukuru* [grandchild] and my grandchild. He wants to live with his grandfather in this area. Welcome him and look after him well.' Then the *mhondoro* said 'Well, he can stay here but the field you gave him, he mustn't plough it. I will be there checking. Tomorrow I want to give a chicken to this boy'. Then he stood up and went away. I was very surprised. I asked my grandfather 'What made him do all this?' Grandfather said 'This is the one who looks after us.' I said

'Why does he say I mustn't plough my field?' Grandfather said 'He means you mustn't go to the field early in the morning or you will be eaten by the lions. That is the time that he is working in his land.' I asked 'Does this mean he has his own lands?' He answered 'The land of this *mhondoro* is from Fumhe to Nyarutombo. He is the one who makes the rain fall. If someone breaks his law he can strike him with lightning or make him ill.' I said 'He wants to give me a chicken. How will he give it to me?' He answered 'The chicken is not a real chicken. It might be a buck or another wild animal. He means that he will let you catch the buck easily in the forest and that means that you are welcome here.'

The ngozi *and the witch*

Two categories of people cannot become *midzimu*. These are *ngozi*, people who have led an unsatisfactory life, and the *muroyi* or witch.

People who die childless cannot become *midzimu* because, so it is argued, they have no descendants to look after or to act as mediums for them. When such a person dies she or he becomes a *ngozi* who wanders through the villages angry and malicious, bringing harm and destruction for no other reason than its unquenchable fury and spite. To prevent this, childless (or in some cases unmarried) people are buried with a rat, a plank or a seedless maize cob tied to their backs. This object takes the place of the child (or the spouse) and will keep the *ngozi* still.

The word *ngozi* is commonly used to mean disaster or accident. This is especially appropriate to another kind of unquiet spirit. This type of *ngozi* rises from the grave of a person who has been murdered and seeks revenge on members of the murderer's lineage until the crime is acknowledged and reparation has been made. A third type is a person who has not received adequate burial. Either they have not been buried at all, as may happen when a person is murdered and abandoned, or they were not buried in their home territory in which case the 'bringing home of the spirit' will not have been performed.

A *ngozi* is a stranger, either an unknown body dumped in the bush or an ancestor with no descendants to remember her or him. It is what is left of a person who has failed in one of the crucial experiences of human existence. A *ngozi* is unmarried or childless, unburied or done to death. For such a person death is not an enhancement but a degradation. She or he is not welcomed but feared. As a *mudzimu* expresses order, fertility and concern, the *ngozi* presents the violent consequences of lack of fulfilment: distress and despair.

The second category of people who cannot become ancestors is the witch or *muroyi*.

The typical act of witchcraft is cannibalism or, more accurately, necrophagy. Witches kill people, including their own children, or rob graves to find human flesh to eat. They commit incest and adultery. They run about to do their evil deeds naked and at night. They ride on the backs of hyenas. They can transform themselves into hyenas, crocodiles or snakes at will. A typical ploy of a witch is to disguise himself as a snake, sneak into a hut, hide in a clay pot until the husband of the house has gone outside and then pounce on his wife and seduce her. Or, disguised as a crocodile, a witch might lurk on the banks of a river ready to seduce any woman who comes down to the water to bathe or wash her clothes. The three animals I have named may also act as familiars for witches, as may *zvidoma*, very small people the size of children who carry out the witches' commands.

People become witches in one of two ways. They may be involuntarily possessed by the *shave*, or non-human spirit, of the hyena, an animal that hunts by night and eats dead animals found in the bush. Once the hyena *shave* has control of a woman or a man, the *shave* of witchcraft is handed down from generation to generation, from mother to daughter and from father to son. Alternatively, people may become witches out of free choice by apprenticing themselves to a practising witch and eating certain medicines. Once they have achieved witch status, they carry out their murders either by magical acts, that is in ways non-witches know nothing about, or by the use of poisons.

Why do witches do these appalling things? Envy is the motive most commonly ascribed, either envy of the rich by the poor or of the fertile by the barren. But witches are also thought to be driven by unprovoked malice or simply by a relish for human flesh. It is universally agreed that the punishment for witchcraft should be death. It is common for the most inoffensive, not to say puny, individuals to declare themselves willing to kill any witch they might discover, however close a kinsman it might be. It is firmly believed that there are hundreds, maybe thousands of active witches about, but who they are cannot be known unless a *n'anga* (traditional healer) or a spirit medium is requested to explain a particular misfortune and names an individual as the cause.

However, despite the violence of the conventional response to witchcraft, villagers often live side by side with people believed to be practising witches and make no protest at all. To explain this I need to consider the specific directions from which people feel they are under attack. Unlike the characteristic witch of Europe, the witches of Dande are rarely strangers. In general they fall into two categories. First, and most commonly, they are members of one's own *dzinza* or lineage; secondly they may be close affines.

The term *dzinza* (like *rudzi*) can be used in a limited sense to mean lineage or to refer to a broad category of people of a similar 'kind' to oneself. The use of this term implies that only the same 'kind' of person as you can bewitch you. For example, it is said that only a member of the

Elephant clan can bewitch another Elephant. If an Elephant wants to bewitch a member of the Monkey clan, he must find a member of that clan willing to help him. As this was vividly put to me: 'An Elephant will say of an Elephant: he is our brother, let us kill him. An Elephant must help a Monkey to kill an Elephant.' This idea may be elaborated to include more or less closely defined groups of people but if you suspected that witchcraft had been used against you, you would look in the first instance among the closest members of your lineage. These need not be living in your own household. I can illustrate this belief from my own experience of living in Dande. When I first arrived there I was told that as I was the only white person living in Dande I was safe from witchcraft. No local witch could harm me without a white witch to give them a hand. But after a year had gone by, the quasi-kin ties I established removed this protection and I became open to attack.

The second, less frequently encountered, category of potential witch is a close affine. Men say that they will always consult an older member of their kindred (their mother's brother, father's sister or a grandparent) before they choose a wife. They fear that they will marry into a family of witches and not find out until it is too late. Although witchcraft accusation between co-wives is common, the source of the aggression is often believed to be the mother of one of the wives. But an accusation may be made by the lineage of the wife as well. If a woman who lives in the village of her husband becomes ill she often returns to her original home and puts herself under the protection of her own ancestors. Husbands of such women never stand in their way for they fear that if their wives should die in their married homes they will be accused of having bewitched them.

'He is our brother, let us kill him.' Nothing expresses more powerfully the fear that witchcraft will strike from *within*, that evil lies, sharp-toothed, poised to pounce, just where you most expect and need affection, ease, support and care. Fear of witchcraft tears whole families apart. On the other hand, it is this belief that enables people to live at peace with known witches provided always that the witch is not a member of their own lineage nor one of their affinal kin.[4]

On the whole you can rely on your ancestors to protect you against a witch's attack but if you do not maintain good relations with them they may punish you by 'opening the door' to the witches and allowing them in. The enormous concern with the ancestors that characterises every member of Dande society can in part be accounted for in this way: If your ancestors do not protect you, you are left at the mercy of your closest living kin.

The *mashave* (sing. *shave*) are the last category of non-material beings we need be concerned with. I have already mentioned the hyena *shave* that gives to its medium the characteristics of the witch. All *mashave* are the spirits of animals or of foreigners. They are spirits that emanate from outside known human society. Their common feature is that when they possess a medium, they confer a particular quality or ability. This may be the skill of hunting or of curing with great facility or it may be the trick of dancing in an unusual style associated with the home of the spirit. Once possessed the medium is required to wear beads on his wrist or at his neck which indicate the nature of her or his *shave*. Occasionally the medium should brew beer for the *shave* and dance in company with other *shave* mediums and allow the spirit to enter its human vessel. This is done either to alleviate illness caused by a *shave* aggrieved at having been ignored or forgotten, or to prevent an illness occurring.

The key distinction between *mashave* and the ancestral spirits is that the *mashave* dances of possession never climax in speech as do the dances of the others. The *mashave* shoulder no moral responsibility and have no message to communicate. Mediums of *mashave* never dance with mediums of *midzimu* or *mhondoro*. Each type of medium dances only with others of its own kind.[5]

Figures 3.1 and 3.2 summarise the material presented so far. Figure 3.1 contrasts the four most important types of spirit in terms of two characteristics: whether it is hostile or benign and whether the spirit derives from inside or outside the lineage.[6]

	Inside	Outside
Hostile	MUROYI (witch)	NGOZI (spirit of the childless or murdered)
Benign	MUDZIMU and MHONDORO (ancestral spirits)	MASHAVE (animal or foreign spirits)

Figure 3.1   Major categories of spirit types and their characteristics

Figure 3.2 summarises the animal, spatial and moral symbolism by which the ancestors are characterised. It requires a brief explanation. Of all wild animals, lions are acknowledged to be the most dangerous to people. They dominate the bush and keep people out of it more effectively than any other animal. Lions divide the country (*nyika*) into two sectors: the bush which is their home and the villages which are the home of people.

But *mhondoro* are also the spirits of chiefs. Chiefs are people but they are people of a very distinctive kind. Unlike lineage elders who control only a village and its cultivated land, a chief owns and controls the whole 'country': villages, fields and the uncultivated bush. There would appear to be a contradiction between the 'lion' aspect of the *mhondoro* spirits as 'owners' of the bush and their 'chief's ancestor' aspect as owners of the bush and of the villages as well.

But there is more in the bush than lions. Hyenas and crocodiles are found there too. It is true that lions kill people, but they kill publicly and they never feed on corpses found in the bush. They represent the positive, creative side of the wild. Hyenas and crocodiles kill in private, either under cover of night or by dragging their victims under water. They are the familiars, spirits and transformations of the witch who by its evil deeds (incest, murder, sorcery) causes drought. These animals represent the negative, destructive aspect of the wild.

The chiefly lineage claims that its ancestors control the rain. This control of nature by the spirits of a particular lineage is symbolised by the most human-like controller of the bush, the lion. It is from these chiefly lion spirits, rulers of the wild and of the civilised, of the bush and of the villages, that rain and fertility derive.

Country		
royal ancestors		chiefs
Bush		**Village**
hyenas	lions	people
witches	royal ancestors	lineage ancestors
night	day	
drought	rain	
barren	fertile	

Figure 3.2   Symbolic characteristics of ancestral spirits

The Churches

There are three main Churches active in Dande. Two are established, the Catholics and the Evangelical Alliance Mission. One is independent and known as the Apostolic Church of John Marange. Its members are referred to locally as *vapostori*.

The Evangelical Alliance Mission is the smallest of the three with between fifty and sixty members all told. A large number of these are people who have set up home in one of the towns on the Plateau for an extensive period of time, unlike the majority of the peasants whose experience of the towns is as migrant labourers living as single men in farm compounds or the dormitories of the mines. As this Church lays great emphasis on the Scriptures and their interpretation, the majority of its members are literate.

The Evangelicals are aggressively opposed to what they see as the backwardness that results from traditional religion and kinship. Members may have only one wife, they may not drink beer and – as the ancestral spirits are characterised as 'Satan's chief method in seeking to deceive and bind the believers to his old heathen fears' – members may not participate in any of the ancestral rituals and ceremonies.

The Catholics make a rather broader appeal and perhaps one-third of the peasants have some association, if only of the most casual kind, with this Church. The priests and catechists who serve the Dande congregation are divided about how much of ancestral ritual should be condoned by the Church. In practice, apart from a handful of the most fervent, most members continue to participate in possession ceremonies and to make offerings to the local *mhondoro*. It is not unusual for people who have danced at a possession ritual that began on Saturday evening and continued throughout the night to go straight to the service at the Catholic church on Sunday morning wearing a silver crucifix alongside a string of black ancestral beads around their neck.

The Apostolic Church is as passionately opposed to the practice of ancestral religion as are the Evangelicals but its relationship with the ancestors is rather different. The Evangelicals express contempt for them. The Apostolics never underestimate their power. Unlike the established Churches, the Apostolics practise possession but in their case this is by the 'Holy Spirit'. They believe that ancestral possession is a cause of sickness and they spend a great part of their services exorcising those of their members who have succumbed. In their terms all ancestral spirits are placed within a single category: witches.

The Apostolic Church was founded by the prophet John Marange in the 1930s. It ties its members (about 8 per cent of Dande) tightly together by a set of ritual prohibitions. Only those who observe these will be saved when the world comes to an end and is engulfed by fire. These prohibitions have been described in detail elsewhere. All I wish to point out is that many of them are explicit contraventions of ancestral ritual and belief. The Apostolics may not drink beer, which is a key feature of possession rituals, nor may they make use of musical instruments such as drums or finger pianos as spirit mediums do. The men shave their heads whereas mediums let their hair grow long. On their holy days they wear elaborate costumes which are either white or red. Mediums wear black; red is a colour forbidden and dangerous to them. They have their own rest days, their own meeting places, their own ways of curing diseases. The *mhondoro* bring the rain: the Apostolics, as it were, bring the fire which will herald the end of the world. In addition to their avoidance of 'traditional' medicines and rituals, the Apostolics are also forbidden to use Western-style medicines and they do not recognise state courts. All matters of law are settled by their own leaders in their own religious courts.[7]

Despite the Evangelical and the Apostolic characterisation of the ancestors as aspects of the devil, many of their members participate as openly and almost as often in ancestral ritual as the Catholics. Serious sickness will cause members of any one of these Churches to visit a spirit medium or a traditional healer. Apostolics may even go as far as to leave the Church altogether for the period that they or their children are receiving forbidden treatment either at the clinic or the medium's village.

For some people the existence of alternative belief systems is problematic and occupies a great deal of intellectual energy, not so much in an attempt to reconcile the two as to decide which is appropriate in which circumstances. For others the two systems are easily reconciled. After all, Jesus died and rose again after three days. The only difference this illustrates between Jesus and the Shona ancestors is that the ancestors wait a year after their deaths before they rise up and become active again. Furthermore, it is argued, the Bible instructs us to love, honour and obey our parents. It does not say that we have to stop this after they are dead.

To conclude this chapter here is an extract from an account by a member of the Apostolic Church of his encounter with a witch. It illustrates as clearly as any other account I have heard the intensity of this aspect of Shona religious experience.

It is true that in this country there are witches. You can't see them when they are moving during the night. They can come when you are having your supper and you can eat with them but you can't see them. But we Apostolics can see them because of the Holy Spirit. A witch can kill a person any time he wants. We don't agree with them at all. If it is a witch who uses magic we take the magic and burn it. If the witch is a medium (*svikiro*) we exorcise the spirit by the power of the Holy Ghost.

One day I was asleep. There came a witch. The witch stood at my door. I was filled with the Holy Spirit and I saw him. I got up quietly and opened the door so we were standing face to face. I asked him 'Who are you?' He didn't answer. So I asked him again 'What do you want here?' I pushed him with my staff but I didn't hit him. Then I saw that his face was changing and becoming like a hyena. His ears were growing and his mouth was getting long. His eyes were getting bigger also. White fur was appearing on his face. He did this so I would be afraid of him and so that I would not know who he was. When I saw

41

him change his face I wanted to hit him with an axe but the Holy Spirit didn't
want me to do that. I started saying 'Amen! Amen!' He ran away. I chased
him and I know who it was because I had a good look at his face. That was
the first time I ever saw a witch.

NOTES

1 In Chapter 6 below, I describe how all those who live within the spirit
province of a *mhondoro* may come to be regarded as his descendants whether
they can trace a direct line of descent from the *mhondoro* or not.

2 For descriptions and analyses of the *kutamba guva* ceremony see Holleman
(1953) and Bourdillon (1982, p. 200).

3 A lion which is not inhabited by a *mhondoro* spirit may be referred to as
shumba. Alternatively a distinction may be drawn between *mhondoro
dzemwari*, the lions of god, in other words ordinary lions and *mhondoro
dzemidzimu* which are lions in whose bodies the spirits of dead chiefs make
their homes.

4 One example. In the village in which I lived, a barren woman was accused by
the son of her co-wife, a man named Enias, of having killed five of his
children. One by one they had inexplicably sickened and died. His belief in her
guilt was unshakeable and his accusation was vigorous and repeated. As the
law of the land forbids action to be taken against witches, the solution Enias
found was to move his entire family out of the village. Even then he attributed
the death of one further child to this woman's vicious influence. Other
villagers with no kin ties to this woman of course knew of the accusation but
were totally unafraid of her. There can be no clearer demonstration of the
inconsistency in the attitudes taken to this woman than that when elections to
the local village committee were held she was appointed Welfare Officer, thus
attaining a unique combination of roles each justified by her relationship with
different parts of the village.

The fear of witches within the lineage is very strongly marked at the burial
ceremony. After death, the body is carried to a site outside the village where
other members of the dead person's lineage have been buried. When the grave
has been dug, a shelf is hollowed out at the base. The body is placed on this
shelf and sealed off with a mat and wooden poles. The grave is then filled with
stones and a mound of stones is built on top of it. These precautions are taken
to make it difficult for witches to get at the body. Funeral orations always
contain exhortations to witches to leave the body alone. What is very striking
is that no member of the lineage of the dead person may participate in the
process of burial. It is unthinkable for a fellow lineage member to carry the
dead body or to climb into the grave in order to place the body on the shelf or
to help to seal the grave. The final part of the ceremony is the sweeping of the
grave and the surrounding area so that if witches visit, their footprints will be
seen. This is performed by the *muroora* of the dead person, that is the wives of

his or her sons or classificatory sons (i.e. affines). At all other rituals the main officiant is the *muzukuru* (sister's son, son's son or daughter's son). The main officiant at a burial is the *sawhira* who is a friend, a non-kinsman. The *sawhira* relationship is inherited patrilineally forming reciprocating lineages of 'ritual friends' who may be trusted to organise burials. It is forbidden to visit a grave without a *sawhira* of the dead person present.

    I have described here only the case of Dande. People in other parts of Zimbabwe have other methods of acquiring witchcraft powers. See Bourdillon (1982, p. 163).

5 In the two villages in which I collected this information, approximately half of the households had at least one member who from time to time became possessed by one sort of spirit or another. Of course it was impossible to collect this sort of information about witches.

    A class of ghosts or *zvipoko* are also found in Dande. (The name probably derives from the Afrikaans *spoek*.) Fire burning high above the ground, tiny people met with by the side of the road and towering figures with excessively ugly faces may all be termed *zvipoko* and are believed to be the dead returned to haunt the living. They are only met with at night which is 'their time' and their hostility to people is explained by their anger at seeing living people moving about during their period of the day. They do not take mediums and have no influence on the living except to frighten them. To account for them requires a different order of theory to that appropriate for spirits which achieve material form only by the possession of mediums, and I do not deal with them here.

6 This table is based on the model developed by MacGaffey (1970).

7 The main source is Daneel (1971, 1974). See also Dillon-Malone (1978) and Bourdillon (1982). For a discussion of the social and economic grounds for the rejection of ancestral beliefs by Apostolic churches see Long (1968).

4

The Great Spectacle
of the Past

Every year in the month of September, when the new moon appears, Quiteve ascends a very high mountain situated near the city called Zimbaoe, in which he dwells, on the summit of which he performs grand obsequies for the kings, his predecessors, who are all buried there . . . When the king has feasted for eight days, he begins his lamentation for the dead . . . until the devil enters into one of the Kaffirs of the assembly, saying that he is the soul of the dead king, father of him who is engaged in these ceremonies, come to converse with his son . . . he begins to cough and speak like the dead king who he represents, in such a manner that it means the Kaffirs recognise that the soul of the dead king has come as they expected . . . Then all withdraw, leaving the king alone with the demoniac, with whom he converses amicably as if with his dead father, asking him if there will be war, and if he will triumph over his enemies, and if there will be famine or misfortunes in his kingdom, and everything else which he wishes to know.[1]

From this extract from a journal published by João dos Santos in Portugal in 1609 it is clear that possession by royal ancestors or *mhondoro* has taken place in northern Zimbabwe for at least four-hundred years. Dos Santos' account suggests that it was not known in advance who the *mhondoro* would possess; that mediumship had not yet become the institutionalised role, almost the profession that it is today. At this period it was to the 'king' rather than to the medium that the peasants turned for 'rain when it is required and other favourable weather for their harvest . . . firmly believing that he can give them all that they desire or have need of, and can obtain anything from his dead predecessors, with whom they believe that he holds converse'[2] However from the evidence of two journals written in the 1860s, we can see that

44

by this date at least the *mhondoro* mediums had acquired all the features that identify them today. David Livingstone included brief accounts of a number of meetings with what he calls Pandora (from the Chikunda *póndoro*). On 26 May 1860 at the village of Defue on the Zambezi he wrote:

> At the last village a man who pretends to be changed into a lion occasionally came and sat down near us to salute . . . At the present village there is a house under the tree we lodge under for the Pandora. He presides over the superstitions of the village and gives medicines to enable the villagers to kill game, and occasionally lies in his hut and roars a whole night.[3]

A month later he attempted a little research into the subject:

> A man came to see us who stated that he was the Pandora of the place. Asked him to change himself into a lion then, that we might see and believe. Said that it was only the heart that changed, that he pointed out witches to be killed, that he told when rain would come.[4]

The Portuguese soldier and administrator Albino Pacheco, has left an account of a meeting with a *mhondoro* on 10 June 1862:

> Being at the village of a medium I wanted to see for myself what stratagem he makes use of in order to be accepted as the incarnation of the deceased ruler. I must say that in view of the repugnant faces that he made, the howling to imitate the roaring of a lion, the barely intelligible answers to the questions put to him by a big crowd of stupid people . . . I had an urge to tell one of the detachment of soldiers to give him a good shaking. The tragedy is that there is no human influence capable of making those unfortunate people see and those mediums live off their blindness magnificently and that accounts for the great number of them that there are.[5]

Pacheco's response, equal parts of contempt and fascination, was to be echoed by many administrators and commentators from that time to the present. So too was his desire to make 'those unfortunate people see'. See what? That the mediums they trusted were charlatans, holders of illegitimate power by means of cheap and callous deception. But if the authority of the mediums is based on a fraud, how is it that so many thousands of people have believed in them for so many hundreds of years? Pacheco is happy to write off the people of Dande as 'a big crowd of stupid people'. It goes without saying that for us this will not do.

This chapter is an attempt to dismantle the structure of belief in which the *mhondoro*, their mediums and their followers are entwined. I start with two accounts of rituals in which *mhondoro* mediums play a leading part. Then follows an analysis of how individuals come to think of themselves as mediums in the first place. In the major part of the chapter I show how the authority of the mediums is tightly bound up with the authority of chiefs and headmen. And I conclude with a fresh look at the question of belief. If the peasants 'believe' in the mediums, what precisely is it that they believe?

POSSESSION I: SEED AND RAIN
13 November 1981 at Tsokoto

Late afternoon. The sun burns out of a massive cloudless sky. The thin contorted trees are bare of leaves. In the beds of the rivers lie stagnant pools. From time to time a whirlwind rushes out of the undergrowth across the path and back into the bush casting up sand and brittle leaves. Unless the rain falls soon there is not a chance that crops will grow this year.

But still the seed must be prepared. To do this the local household heads and their wives make their way towards the village of the medium.

As they arrive the women and men go off in separate directions. The women put down their bags, unload children from their backs, greet their relatives and friends, set out to look for firewood to cook the evening meal. The men make for the open space at the centre of the village. The medium is lying on a reed mat on the ground, surrounded by a group of elders drinking beer. He is young and bearded, strongly built and dressed in a long black cloth draped across his right shoulder and reaching to his feet. At his side lie his ritual axe and staff, insignia of a *mhondoro*, the spirit of a chief.

The medium's wife brings out a large clay pot, kneels, sets it at the medium's feet. He ladles out a mug of beer, tastes it, hands it round. This beer was brewed from grain collected from local households. To refuse to contribute is to put at risk your fields, which will stay dry when all your neighbours get their share of rain, or your house which will be struck by lightning when the first rains fall. Young boys drag up the huge trunk of a tree, set fire to twigs and grass beneath one end and watch it burn.

After sunset. The meal is over, plates tidied away, mats and blankets laid out on the ground. The youngest children sleep. The young boys who have tried their hand at drumming all day long make way for their fathers. The cross-rhythms of the four hide drums become more complex, overlaid and sure. In the darkness an old woman sings out the first line of a song to the ancestors. Other voices follow. Some women dance – advancing, sway, retreat, advance again – turning a circle in the sand. The medium has retired inside his hut. With a few close friends he is discussing local and national affairs.

The men round the fires drink on. The singing dies down. The women stretch themselves on the earth to sleep. The moon is full and rising in the sky.

Two hours before dawn. The medium's assistants go among the people, waking them. More than two hundred men gather in a semicircle at the door of the *mhondoro*'s hut. The women, sitting close together to one side, sing and then fall silent. Loud bursts of clapping rise from the men. It dies away, picks up and dies again. Singing. Clapping. Silence. Clapping. Silence. Silence.

The medium bursts from the door of his hut. A long white cloth is wrapped around his body covering his head. The singing pours out. He leads it, his long staff bobbing and dipping above the sea of heads. The medium's body stands before the crowd, but it is the *mhondoro* who waves his arms and sings.

He sits. The singing stops. The men clap, women ululate. Silence. The *mhondoro* speaks. His voice is low and rough but his speech is clear. He explains why he has called the people to his village. A discussion starts. Problems are raised by the elders and by younger men as well. Herds of elephant have gathered in the bush outside the villages. The crops will be destroyed as soon as they grow ripe. What is to be done? Some men object to the siting of a new village. They fear the fields will encroach on their own. In three villages children have sickened and died for no good reason. They address the *mhondoro* face to face and soon the awe his appearance had called up wears off. The discussion is respectful but vigorous and free.

The medium listens but says nothing until everyone has had his say. Then he gives his advice and his instructions. When everybody's problems have been raised he asks who is to take the offering to the senior *mhondoro* who controls the rain. Forty dollars have been collected, black and white cloths and a mound of tobacco prepared. A headman is selected and told which medium to take the offering to. It will be passed from medium to medium until it reaches the most senior of them all.

The light is rising. Dawn is near. Two weeks before, the medium's assistants had collected seed from every local lineage head. Two large winnowing baskets have been filled mostly with sorghum and maize. Seeds such as cotton grown only for cash may not be added to the rest. The baskets are taken inside the hut. The medium sprinkles onto them ground roots which protect the seeds from locusts and other pests. The baskets are taken out and the seeds divided between the household heads to take home and distribute among their sons and sons-in-law to mix in with their own.

A few people elbow their way into the hut to consult the *mhondoro* about their health or other urgent matters. He listens and prescribes a cure. Some ask only for a pinch of *bute*, the *mhondoro*'s snuff which brings good health and luck. When the last of these is satisfied the sun is high, the women have packed their baskets, bound their babies to their backs, set out for home. Young boys have taken back the drums while their fathers drink a final mug of beer.

After a while the medium emerges from his hut dressed in his long black cloth. He stretches, yawns, sits in the shade. The *mhondoro* has gone.

Two days later. Early morning. In a small clearing in the middle of the bush half a mile from the medium's village stands a single hut, the *dendemaro* or house of the spirit, with its two doors, one for the medium and *mhondoro*, the other for those who consult him. Beer has been brewed near the *mhondoro*'s shrine, a large tree on the bank of a stream. Here men and women sit together passing a mug of beer from hand to hand. The medium's assistant empties one mugful onto the ground before the shrine. Men clap, the women ululate. The assistant crouches, claps and says:

> Ancestor, you cared for us in the past. Do so again. Bring us rain. How can we grow our crops without rain? Do not fail your children. Send us rain.

A full pot of beer for the *mhondoro* is placed beside his tree.

The medium arrives late, sits to one side, drinks and talks but is not possessed and has no special part to play. From time to time the old women dance in a tight circle and cry out the words of the ancestor's songs. When the beer has run out the ceremony is over. The people leave the shrine and walk to a nearby village where beer has been brewed for sale.

POSSESSION II: CURING
17 January 1981 at Utete

Except for a few children playing in the shade, the village of the medium is deserted when the man and his sick wife arrive. The oldest of the children runs off into the fields where the adults and the older children are working and returns with the medium's assistant, the *mutapi*. He offers them food and, while they eat, questions the woman and her husband about the sickness. He receives a small consultation fee and agrees that she may consult the *mhondoro* at dawn the next day.

That night the sick woman sleeps in the hut of one of the *mutapi*'s wives. Shortly before dawn the *mutapi* wakes her and leads her to the spirit's hut in the centre of the medium's village. When they arrive, the medium is already possessed. The *mutapi* leads the patient in. The hut is dark but she can just make out the medium lying on a low platform, propped up on one elbow, covered by a black cloth and wearing a large flat hat made of porcupine quills. The *mutapi* sits at the medium's feet. The woman has brought a length of black cloth as a gift to the *mhondoro*. The *mutapi* places it on a wooden plate, hands it to the medium, claps in respect and explains why the woman has come.

At first the medium's manner is gruff and offhand. He growls and roars and when he speaks he uses archaic words and obscure phrases which the *mutapi* translates and explains. Frequently he breaks into a chant, a formalised, rhythmic verse in a style all his own.

The woman is afraid, but the friendliness between the *mhondoro* and his *mutapi* gradually reassures her. The *mhondoro* begins to joke and call out to people waiting outside the hut. The respectful clapping that had preceded each question and response is quickly forgotten as is the mediation of the *mutapi*. The patient talks directly to the *mhondoro* and he outlines the cause of her distress. If the case is simple, a cure is prescribed right away. Otherwise the patient may be told to remain in the care of the *mutapi* for a while and return to the *mhondoro* after resting for a few days.

Becoming a mhondoro *medium*

When an ancestor feels the need to communicate directly with its descendants it chooses a woman or a man and uses her or his mouth to speak. It is said *svikiro inobatwa nemidzimu*, the medium is grabbed by the ancestor. The medium does not wish to be possessed. Indeed posession is a hardship and a trial. It is the all-powerful ancestors who make their choice, 'grab' their mediums and take control of their lives.

When possessed, the medium is thought to lose all control of body and mind. He may be referred to as *homwe* which means pocket or little bag. The medium is simply the receptacle, the vessel of the spirit. He has no specialised knowledge or unusual qualities of his own. But this attitude to the mediums contains a paradox. Although the medium is thought of as an ordinary person, when a particular woman or man is selected from all others, they are marked out as extraordinary, as unique. The medium combines in one body two contradictory aspects: he has no special qualities and he is as close as anyone can come to divinity. He has no influence on the will of the ancestor, yet the ancestor cannot act without him. He is a person of no special powers and he is a source of the most significant powers on earth.

All mediums start out on their careers in the same way. The first stages are identical for mediums of *mashave* (foreign or animal spirits), *midzimu* (ancestral spirits) or *mhondoro* (royal ancestral spirits). Whether he becomes a part-time low-level *shave* medium or a full-time *mhondoro* medium depends on the working out of the complex relationship that exists between the aspirant medium, the senior medium who initiates him and the community to which he belongs.[6]

The careers of all mediums develop out of a state of crisis. A woman or a man becomes sick. All attempts to cure them fail. Western and local medicines and techniques are tried one after another but the patient gets steadily worse or, at best, does not recover. Inevitably the suspicion grows that the sickness is not caused by disease but by a spirit. In time this suspicion may be confirmed by a *n'anga* (traditional healer) though usually she or he is unable to say what kind of spirit is involved.

One factor that influences the diagnosis of the traditional healer is the age of the patient. It is rare for possession to strike for the first time late in life. For elderly people to suspect that their illness is due to an ancestral spirit is considered ridiculous. At that age, it is said, you are almost an ancestor yourself. The illnesses of the old therefore tend to be diagnosed as the work of witches or simply as disease. But if the

49

traditional healer does attempt to resolve the crisis by suggesting that a spirit is involved, he will recommend that the patient attempts to achieve possession so that the spirit can reveal its identity, its complaint and its demand.

Unlike possession in many other societies, amongst the Shona possession is never spontaneous. It only occurs at highly structured rituals which in Dande are known as *humbikumbi* for *midzimu*, and *mashave* for *shave*. These require weeks of preparation. Beer must be brewed, a team of drummers engaged, all members of the patient's lineage as well as his mother's kin must be invited and given time to arrive from their villages or from the towns. To accommodate town dwellers these rituals are usually held on Saturday nights, starting soon after dark and continuing until long after Sunday's dawn. At the height of the possession season, which starts after the harvest when grain for beer is plentiful, there may be two or even three possession rituals in most villages each week.

The father of the patient takes charge of the ritual, usually in co-operation with the traditional healer who first diagnosed possession. Drumming starts soon after darkness has fallen. The drums are said to call the spirits. Different drums and varied rhythms are used depending on the type of spirit being summoned. The patient sits on a mat in front of the drummers, his legs extended, his head bowed with a half-white, half-black cloth covering his head. He will not have eaten for a day or more but is encouraged to drink as much beer as he likes.

After a while female kin and neighbours dance in a semi-circle facing the drummers, approaching and retreating from the patient, singing the same one-or-two line songs over and over, the lead singer calling out the verse and the crowd repeating it over and over again. A few men may dart into the centre of the dancing, leap about for a few moments, then melt back into the crowd that presses on the sides. Mediums who have been possessed many times before and who now have the knack of slipping easily into possession are invited to dance with the women and become possessed so as to encourage the spirit troubling the patient to appear. As these mediums, dressed in their black and white cloths and bearing their ritual axes and spears, one by one fall into trance, so the dancing becomes more aggressive and warlike. They brandish their ritual weapons, cry out, chanting, weeping. Once they join in, the only reason they ever leave the dancing is if their spirit starts to speak. Then they break from the centre, crouch in the darkness and wail out the anger and resentment of their spirit while a relative or friend tries to comfort them by clapping to the spirit to assure it of the high esteem in which it is held. (See Plates 2, 3 and 4, between pp. 118–19.)

If the patient does become possessed he will stand and hesitantly join in the dancing, encouraged and supported by other mediums. If not he remains sitting in front of the drummers. In either case, just before dawn the patient is led into a hut followed by close members of his lineage and the mediums. His mother's kin, his affines and neighbours wait outside, sometimes for hours, many pressed up against the door of the hut trying to make out the secrets the spirits are revealing about their mysterious world.

The identity of a spirit is discovered by question and answer. The father of the patient asks the main questions but the traditional healer and anyone else who has been allowed inside the hut may interrupt to encourage the spirit or to ask questions of their own. The spirit is always reluctant to speak, unwilling to reveal its name or its complaint. It must be cajoled and bribed with small coins placed in a dish in front of the medium, pleaded with, reminded of its duty to care for its descendants. Sometimes the spirit refuses to break its silence and the ritual has failed. But if it does relent, after the first faltering exchange it begins to speak with increasing fluency and force and even to deliver long and bitter harangues broken up by weeping and groaning, grunting and agonised cries, to the distress of people inside the hut and the delight of those outside. The atmosphere is always tense. At any moment the flow may stop, perhaps to continue after encouragement, perhaps not, in which case the ritual has come to an end. If during the patient's first possession the spirit is obliging enough to reveal its clan, its name and some of its history, this is highly satisfactory and no more could be expected. Some relief of the sickness may occur and plans will be made for a further possession ritual so that more information can be obtained. As these are expensive and time consuming, it may take years before all the demands of the spirit have been heard.

The first question put to a medium and the one which the spirit is often most reluctant to answer is the name of its clan. The asking of this question is called *kukonya*. The answer given is crucial, for this declares what sort of spirit it is. There are three possibilities. If possession has occurred but the spirit refuses to speak this may be taken to mean either that the spirit has no clan, which implies that it is either not human or not Shona, which means it is a *shave*. The rest of the session will be given over to determining what sort of *shave* it is. If the spirit does name a clan, this may determine a great deal about the medium's subsequent career. A *mhondoro* will never possess one of its own descendants. Therefore if the clan named by the spirit is the same as that of the medium it will be concluded that the spirit must be the medium's own ancestor. In other words it is a *mudzimu*, not a *mhondoro*. If the clan named is different from that of the medium it is possible, though by no means inevitable, that a great event has occurred: that the spirit is a major one, a royal ancestor, a *mhondoro*.[8]

If this is suspected, the patient will be sent to the village of an established medium where he will become possessed again. The medium may decide that the spirit is a *shave* after all. But if he is convinced that a *mhondoro* has indeed chosen the patient, he may agree to prepare him for the formal testing procedure. From this point on the aspirant will adopt the conventional medium's dress and may go to live in the province of his *mhondoro*.

An established medium will refuse to give help to an aspirant unless he has already received some recognition, for example at a *humbikumbi*. Either the medium's father or a representative of the lineage of the *mhondoro* believed to be possessing him must accompany the aspirant when he firsts visits the established medium. Men who believe themselves to be mediums but who can persuade no one to take them seriously are occasionally found wandering round Dande dressed as mediums but rejected by the established mediums and regarded by other villagers as mad.

The first years in the career of a medium are the most sensitive. At any moment the *mhondoro* may decide he is in some respect inadequate and abandon him. To discourage this, the medium should abstain from sex until his mediumship is confirmed, a process which may take five or even ten years to complete. During this time the medium may stay with his mentor, or he may return home. The *mhondoro* may disappear for months on end, allowing the medium to live an ordinary life. In time it may turn out that it has gone for good. Or it may unexpectedly return and dominate the medium's life again. Gradually the medium will begin to establish a reputation for some special powers. He may foretell the future with surprising accuracy or reveal secrets or threaten to punish those who do not believe in him and then persuade them that he has done so. Eventually, when the medium is confident of his powers, the full-scale testing procedure can begin.

At this large public ritual, usually attended by a number of practising mediums and local chiefs, the aspirant must become possessed and recite the genealogy of the royal ancestors as well as details of their history – where they lived, who they married, the battles they fought and so on. As only the *mhondoro* known this information, if he recites it accurately he is able to convince those present that he has remained entirely passive, that a *mhondoro* has spoken through him.

The final part of the test requires the aspirant to select from a pile of carved staffs the one used by the previous medium of the *mhondoro* or by the *mhondoro* himself when alive. Even now after the history of the royal lineage has been successfully recited, if the medium does not select the correct stick he is judged to have failed altogether. Failure does not imply that the medium is a conscious fraud. Perhaps the medium has inadvertently broken some law of the ancestors. Perhaps the ancestor simply changed its mind. The failed medium will be accepted back into the community but with the need to find an alternative explanation for his illness. If the aspirant does make a second or a third attempt and is at last successful, there is no thought that he has been coached in the true version or that he would cynically recite an acceptable account of the past. It is known that a *mhondoro* will kill anyone who fakes possession. A recitation of a more 'accurate' version is thought to be a consequence of the increased passivity of the medium which allows the *mhondoro* himself to come through loud and clear.

As to the state of mind of the medium in trance, I have found no evidence that suggests pretence or conscious fraud. The process of initiation structures the aspirant medium's perception of his own experience. Choices are constantly put in front of him. Once he has chosen he has to accept the institutionalised consequences of the choice he has made. The first suggestion that a spirit may wish to possess him is made not by the patient but by the traditional healer whom he consults. No one can organise a possession ritual for himself. They never occur unless there is general agreement that there is good cause. During the first questioning, the possessed medium makes a straightforward choice when he states the clan of his spirit and thereby determines the direction his initiation will take. It is possible for him either to withdraw before this stage has been reached by not becoming possessed at all, or to reduce the significance of his possession by not naming his clan and thus allowing his spirit to be interpreted *by others* as a *shave*. If he does name a clan his subsequent answering of questions and the detail of the history of the spirit that he gives determines whether or not his kin will decide to take the process one stage further by organising a subsequent ritual at considerable expense to themselves. Each choice the medium makes elicits a response from the listeners which determines the subsequent choice the medium makes. It is in the interaction between the medium and his 'audience' that a credible personality for the spirit is evolved and a patient converted into a medium.[9]

The word 'choice' stands inadequately for a complex range of individual psychological responses to the support or disbelief the patient receives from his kin and neighbours. But that the patient can at any stage opt out causing no humiliation to himself suggests that a conviction is gradually arrived at that mediumship will resolve his unusual and puzzling dilemma and bring him the relief and the rewards he desires.[10]

If only the *mhondoro* know the true history of the past, how do those present at the testing ritual know whether the aspirant medium has recited it correctly or not? Part of the answer is that it is the other *mhondoro* mediums present who will declare the authenticity or failure of the possession. But during and after the ritual the elders will discuss the version recited and speculate amongst themselves about its accuracy.

On what basis do they do this?

As far as living people are concerned, technical or practical knowledge can be acquired by experience or by teaching. Lineage seniority, age and duration (that is, the length of time a person has lived in the same place) are all loosely associated with superior knowledge. An elderly person who has lived most of his life in the same village will be assumed to have arcane knowledge of the history of that place including the period before her or his birth or arrival. But the sort of knowledge that the ancestors have, knowledge that gives power over life and death and over the forces of nature, becomes available only after death. This is expressed by a formula which I heard recited all too often when my questions touched on areas people either could or would not discuss with me. They would say: 'We eat *sadza* [food], we know nothing'.

This attitude is adopted by even the most senior of elders and headmen, even by the closest associates of the mediums and indeed by the mediums themselves when not in a state of possession. It implies that the fact of having a body and being subject to biological needs prevents human beings from themselves achieving the most important forms of knowledge. This notion can be experienced just as powerfully the other way round in the belief that anything the living know must for that reason be different from the superior knowledge of the ancestors.

In fact, this sharp distinction is not borne out in practice. The areas of ancestral knowledge which are most frequently drawn upon are curing and 'the past'. Most adult men and women know a great deal about these subjects. Some have reputations stretching miles into other territories for their ability to cure disease. Many adults, especially the associates of the mediums and the chiefs, have a wide knowledge of the ancestors of the provinces in which they live, though they rarely know more than a few fragments about other parts of the country. The true relationship between human knowledge and ancestral knowledge is as points on a continuum and, in day-to-day speculation, the existence of a continuum is unthinkingly accepted. It is only when a person reaches the limits of her or his knowledge, or when they reach the limits of the knowledge they feel it legitimate to admit to, that the continuum is denied. Then the everyday practical knowledge of work and social relations is subsumed within a category of ignorance and impotence characteristic of human biological nature.

Therefore at the *mhondoro* testing ceremony, although the elders will admit that the knowledge of the ancestors is far more elaborate and perhaps even of a different kind to their own, they believe themselves capable of assessing the aspirant medium's claims. In effect, to gain acceptance, the aspirant medium must speak a version of the past that approximates to what has been recited before, to the version commonly known and believed. But if his version is accepted it is immediately categorised as ancestral knowledge, as 'true' knowledge accessible only to immaterial beings who exist beyond the desires of the flesh and the need for food.

That human knowledge and ancestral knowledge are in fact one and the same does not mean that an elder can claim to be a medium simply on account of the knowledge that he has acquired. Long before he embarks on this test, the medium has been marked out by his inexplicable illness, his willingness to accept the diagnosis of the *n'anga*, his persistent attempts to achieve possession, his avoidance of sex, his inexplicable powers and his wearing of the ritual dress. Successful completion of the testing does not transform an ordinary person into a medium. Rather it confirms the generally accepted explanation of his behaviour, that a *mhondoro* has chosen his as the mouth through which it will speak.

Once established in their provinces, mediums usually continue to practise for the rest of their lives, but occasionally a medium will lose credibility and his reputation will dwindle. The most important quality of ancestral spirits is that they have the welfare of the people who live within their provinces at heart. If a *mhondoro* medium is suspected of greed or selfishness or of using his powers for illegitimate ends it may come to be believed that, whatever may have been true in the past, he is not possessed by a *mhondoro* any more.

For example, the mediums receive payment for the performance of their duties, as recompense for curing or as offerings for rain. Much or all of this money is used to cover the expenses of their shrine, especially providing hospitality to the flow of visitors that arrive. Kingsley Garbett has written of the senior medium of Mutota:

> what [he] retained as personal income was just enough to enable him not to work extensively in his garden and to keep his family modestly clothed. Over the year . . . he more or less broke even. In this region, therefore, the principal officers do not acquire a great deal of personal wealth through the operation of the cult.[11]

But if a *mhondoro* medium is believed to be accumulating large amounts of cash (like the traditional healers or *n'anga* who, free of the moral injunctions of ancestral mediums, typically accumulate small fortunes) he is open to suspicion as a fraud or, even more damagingly, as a witch. If this happens his following will fall away and the way is open for another medium to claim to be genuinely possessed by the same *mhondoro* and challenge the first medium to prove his authenticity.

All this is to view the institution only from the point of view of an individual entering it. In the next section I give a description of the institution as a whole. This will lead down a number of different paths. In the end we will arrive at the question that leads directly out of the one

I have tried to answer here. Here the question was: how is the authenticity of a medium established? The next question is: how is the authenticity of the medium maintained?

Chiefs and mediums

In João dos Santos' account published in 1609 and quoted at the beginning of this chapter, the chief or 'king' of Quiteve plays an active part in the major religious rituals of his people, speaking directly to the ancestors and interceding with them to ensure the coming of the rain. As political and religious leader he displays the standard characteristics of the chiefs of Central and Southern Africa as summarised by Audrey Richards. 'The chief,' she writes, 'combines executive, ritual and judicial functions . . . Like the family head, he is a priest of an ancestral cult, believed in many cases to have a mystic power over the land.'[12] But for the last hundred years at least, the Shona have been an exception to this. Shona chiefs have no ritual functions, no 'mystic power over the land'. These functions and powers are entirely in the hands of the mediums of the chief's ancestors.

When I discussed this question with the chiefs and mediums of Dande, they were perfectly clear about how, traditionally, their responsibilities differed from and complemented each other. The duty of the chief was to rule. The duty of the spirit mediums was to advise the chiefs. But this requires a little more elaboration. Strictly speaking, it was not the medium who was thought to advise the chief but the *mhondoro* that possesses him. In the terms by which the people themselves express the 'separation of ritual and secular power', the living chiefs took responsibility for the spheres of politics and law while the chiefs of the past were in charge of fertility and morality. The unique power of the spirit medium is his ability to allow the long-dead chiefs to speak directly to their descendants with the lack of self-interest, duplicity or error characteristic of the thoroughly dead. The opinions and attitudes of the mediums themselves have, according to the Shona theory of mediumship, no significance or influence at all.[13]

In what follows I make no attempt to explain why this separation exists. But I will try to explain how the double act of chief and medium operates in practice.

Any area of land within Dande is conceptualised in two separate ways: it is part of a chieftaincy and it is part of a spirit realm comprised of all the spirit provinces under the control of the senior *mhondoro*, the earliest known ancestor of the local chief. But despite the fact that the *mhondoro* are the ancestors of the chiefs, a spirit realm is not simply a reflection of a chieftaincy on the religious plane. Chieftaincy and realm do not necessarily extend over the same geographic area. One realm may contain more than one chieftaincy. People whose home is within one realm and are subject to the authority of a chief who lives there may journey to consult a medium who has influence in another realm altogether. The institutions of the chieftaincy – wards, villages, headmen, courts – organise the perception of the land as a place where people live and work in the present. The institutions of the spirit realm – provinces, mediums, shrines and their officials – organise the perception of the land as a place where the chief's ancestors used to live in the past.[14]

If you ask the people of Dande: 'What do these chiefs of the past, these inhabitants of the spirit realm, do?', the typical answer is *vanotichengeta*, they look after us. If you ask for details it will be said that they protect the crops, protect wild animals and wild vegetables and send the thunder, the lightning and the rain. They can cure and, as they are the spirits of dead chiefs, they know all there is to know about war. Finally, it is these chiefs of the past who select and install the chiefs of the present. All of these powers will be explored in the chapters that follow. In this chapter I deal with one of the most important: the selection of the chiefs.

The influence of the past bears down especially heavily on the present when a chief dies. A member of the royal lineage must be chosen to succeed him. For the new chief to be legitimate he must be selected from all other candidates by one of his ancestors. This ancestor, of course, can only make his choice known by speaking through the mouth of its medium.

Like most other inherited statuses, the chieftaincy is passed on by what is sometimes referred to as adelphic succession. This is explained in the following way: at his death each chief should be succeeded by a younger brother. This continues until there are no more men of that generation left alive. Then the chieftaincy should pass to the senior son of the next generation. This does not mean that every male member of the royal lineage has a spell at being chief for the 'brothers' referred to in the explanation are in fact the separate 'houses' (*dzimba*) which together make up the chieftaincy. Each of these houses is believed to be descended from a son of the man who originally founded the chieftaincy. The intention of this system is that each of these houses should in turn nominate one of their members to be a chief.

The unfamiliarity of this system makes it seem complex and clumsy. In fact it would operate with neither more nor less difficulty than the more common system of succession from father to son but for a number of factors that come into play and thoroughly complicate matters.

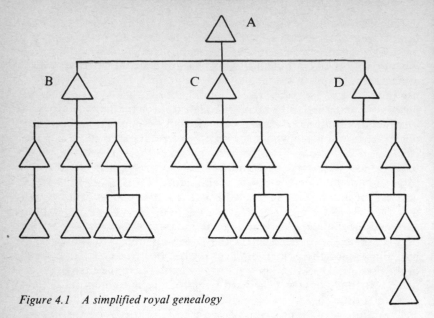

Figure 4.1   A simplified royal genealogy

Consider the simplified royal genealogy in Figure 4.1. A is the founding ancestor, now a *mhondoro*. The chieftaincy must pass between the houses B, C and D. If this were all there were to it the senior member of each house would become chief at the death of the senior member of the previous house and so on. But succession is not based on seniority alone. Political acumen, age, moral and intellectual suitability are all taken into consideration. The most senior member of a house may be rejected on any of these grounds. Secondly, each house is itself internally segmented and so the precise identity of the most senior member is not always easily agreed on. Thirdly, permanent records of each deviation from the strict order of succession were not kept in the past. Claims and counterclaims as to which line of succession is legitimate are frequently made by those who because of earlier 'deviations' have lost their turn. For all these reasons there are always a large number of contestants for the title within each house. In chieftaincies which contain many houses, disputes about sequence and precedence frequently arise between houses as well. As a result of all these factors chiefs tend to be elderly when selected and their reigns are often quite brief. All in all, it is not uncommon for disputes about succession to take place every ten or so years and sometimes more often than that.[15]

In the course of these disputes one of the candidates will acquire the support of the *mhondoro* medium. The way this support is expressed is highly significant. Speaking through his medium the *mhondoro* presents his choice not as the best candidate for the job but as the 'real' chief, the only legitimate heir. Once this has been revealed arguments about past manipulations of the succession rules should cease. Order has been re-established, justice has prevailed.

This is what the rules say should happen. Often it does but as often it does not and this reveals a good deal about the delicate nature of the medium's authority. If the choice the medium makes is supported by a sufficient number of people it will stand. If not, the medium may be accused of favouritism or corruption and the authenticity of his claim to possession may be thrown into doubt. I will deal with this in a moment. The point to hold onto as we go forward is that a chief is only legitimate if it is agreed that he has been chosen by his ancestor the *mhondoro*. The relationship between chief, medium and *mhondoro* is summarised in Figure 4.2. Line A represents possession of the medium by the *mhondoro*, line B the choice of chief which the medium makes and line C the descent of the chief from the *mhondoro* which is confirmed by the fact that he has been selected by the authentically possessed *mhondoro* medium.

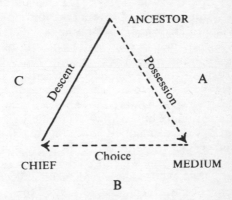

Figure 4.2   The sources of authority in the relationship between chief, medium and mhondoro

I turn now to the more complex question of the relationship between the medium and his assistant, the *mutapi*.[16]

The *mutapi* (pl. *vatapi*) is the manager of the shrine of the *mhondoro*. His main responsibility is to act as an intermediary between the *mhondoro* and those who wish to consult him. He receives visitors to the medium's village and looks after them during the consultation. During possession rituals he sits in front of the medium and claps to the *mhondoro*, summoning him to possess the medium and address his visitors. When the medium has become possessed and is therefore unconscious of the world around him, the *mutapi* takes care of him. He interprets or explains the statements the *mhondoro* makes. When the *mhondoro* has departed and the medium has come to himself once more, he repeats to him all that the *mhondoro* has said.

Some *vatapi* collect the medicinal herbs and roots prescribed by the *mhondoro* and administer them to his patients. If the rains are late, he collects money to be offered to the *mhondoro*, some of which he may be allowed to keep. He may also be sent on other errands taking messages to the chief, to other mediums or to the officers of the district administration. All in all, as the medium is by convention entirely passive, so the *mutapi* is his active counterpart.

Like the chieftaincy, the position of *mutapi* is inherited adelphically, that is from elder to younger brother, though in this case as there is only one lineage involved it is actual brothers rather than houses that inherit one from another. *Vatapi* make little financial profit from their skills. Indeed they complain of the amount of farming time they lose when the *mhondoro* has a large number of visitors. They are distinguishable from other villagers only by their knowledge of everything that concerns the *mhondoro* including the genealogies of the chiefs of the past.

The *vatapi* of the *mhondoro* Chivere are typical of the many similar lineages in Dande. Their name is Kwainona. They have lived within the spirit province of 'their' *mhondoro* for generations while mediums of Chivere have come and gone. They are royals of the Elephant clan and claim direct descent from the *mhondoro* himself.

At the height of the recent war the village of Kwainona was destroyed. All the residents were moved into the concentration camp within the spirit province of Chiwawa. There they remained until 1979. When the camps were dismantled Kwainona reasserted itself. Almost all of its member lineages returned to the burnt-out remains of their homes and built them again. And they did this even though Kwainona is sited on some of the least productive soil in the Valley. Dry, uneven, full of stones, however hard the fields are worked the level of production remains pitifully low. In fact, the Kwainonas have moved the site of their home six or seven times in the past twenty years but have always stayed within the limits of the section of Chivere's spirit province which the *mhondoro* declares it good to live inside. And there despite their poverty they feel they must stay.

What is typical and significant about this lineage of *vatapi* is their close attachment to the territory in which they live and their tendency to remain within their spirit province while mediums of the *mhondoro* arrive, either establish themselves or are rejected, eventually die or move away. The *mutapi* is a well-known figure, a respected family man.

By contrast one of the characteristics of a medium is that he is a stranger. By convention mediums never belong to or come from the territories that they make their professional home. They are unknown men, possibly dangerous, certainly unpredictable, who wander in from who-knows-where claiming to be possessed by a *mhondoro* who has been profoundly associated with that place for longer than the oldest inhabitant can remember.[17]

The first imperative for a new medium must be to gain the confidence of the established *vatapi*. If he does not his authenticity will be open to question and it will be impossible for him to carry out all the duties that I described in the first part of this chapter. The present Kwainona *vatapi* told me of two aspirant mediums of Chivere who had lived among them for a while and whom they had, as it were, seen off the premises. One had fled, one had died in mysterious circumstances. Neither had satisfied them that he was the true medium of Chivere.

The point I want to emphasise is that the *mhondoro* medium requires a *mutapi* for two separate but related reasons. First, he requires a *mutapi* because when he is possessed he is unable to carry out the activities that day-to-day consultation with his patients involves. The second reason takes us to the heart of the institution of the *mutapi*. A medium requires a *mutapi* because without one it would be impossible for him to establish himself within the province his *mhondoro* controls. I have mentioned the would-be mediums who wander about Dande unable to persuade anyone to believe in them, full of bitter stories of their rejection by the villagers who treat them as mad, dangerous or both. Their problem in essence is that they have failed to persuade anyone to act as *mutapi* for them, to organise the rituals that would enable them to become possessed and prove their claims. A medium cannot do this for himself. If a medium becomes possessed without a *mutapi* to intermediate, he will arouse a suspicion that he is the medium of a witch. And it is of no use if a man of no social standing, a man with no descent group following, offers to help. The essential characteristic of the *mutapi* is that he is a lineage head with intimate knowledge of the territory of 'his' *mhondoro*, acquired and handed down over generations. By accepting the mysterious stranger into the spirit province and agreeing to perform rituals on his behalf, the *mutapi* allows his own authority to underwrite the ambiguous authority of the medium, lending credibility to his claim to be possessed by the benign ancestral spirit of the place.

A moment ago we saw that the legitimacy of the chief rests on the fact that he was selected by the *mhondoro* from all other possible candidates and we have just seen that before a medium can establish his authenticity he requires a *mutapi* to lend him the authority of his position. Chief depends on *mhondoro* and *mhondoro* depends on *mutapi*. The circle is completed by the fact that the authority of the *mutapi*

61

ultimately derives from the chief. Almost invariably the *mutapi* is also the headman of the village in which he lives.

It might seem that the importance of the *mutapi* in the life of the community is enough to justify him holding this status as well as his others but this is only partly true. A brief account of a second lineage of *vatapi* will show that there is an important historical dimension to the combination of these roles.

It is said that when the most recent medium of Nyahuma arrived in the Valley there was no one living in his spirit province at all. With him came a man from his home village to act as his *mutapi*. That a new *mutapi* was appointed suggests that there had been no medium of Nyahuma for a long time, long enough for the previous lineage of *vatapi* (if there had been one) to die out or, more likely, move away.

The medium was moral leader of the new community. His *mutapi* became *samusha*, village head, and in time his son was appointed *sabhuku* or government tax collector. Gradually members of other lineages gathered around them, attracted by the space for gardens on the river banks, the game animals in this part of the Valley and the presence of the medium.

The medium of Nyahuma died in 1971. A few years later the residents of his village were moved into the concentration camp in Chiwawa's spirit province along with the people from Kwainona and many other villages. At the end of the war some residents of the camp stayed more or less where they were on land more fertile than that they had left, closer also to the facilities they would need if they were to enter the expanding cash economy. Others, including the lineage of Nyahuma's *vatapi*, made themselves a new home just within the borders of Nyahuma's spirit province. Here they can take advantage of the nearby facilities and still satisfy the moral injunction to live 'in the right place', within the province of their own *mhondoro*, though on the very edge of it. A son of the old *mutapi* has been accepted as village head. In their new/old home they await the arrival of the next medium of Nyahuma.

Taking this example and that of Kwainona together, we can extract two principles which are typical of many other lineages of *vatapi* throughout Dande. First, that so many communities destroyed during the war re-established themselves within the same spirit province demonstrates the sense of intimacy and belonging which people feel for the territory of their own *mhondoro*. This is perhaps felt most strongly by the members of the lineages of *vatapi*. Secondly, the belief that the lineages of *vatapi* have lived in the spirit province longer than anyone else is the reason that they so frequently function as village heads and are recognised as such by the chief.[18]

From the historical point of view, the information on the relationship between mediums and *mutapi* given so far can be summarised like this: if a medium is possessed by a *mhondoro* with an already existing territory containing a lineage of *vatapi*, he will attempt to persuade those *vatapi* to perform the necessary rituals for him. If a medium is possessed by a previously unknown *mhondoro*, as happens from time to time, the next most senior *mhondoro*, that has a medium will reveal the site of his spirit province. He and his *mutapi* will move into this province. The *mutapi* will become village head and a new community will assert itself. On the other hand, if a *mhondoro* has taken no mediums for a long period of time, the lineage of his *vatapi* may begin to disintegrate. People may shift their ritual allegiance to another nearby *mhondoro* or they may move away. If they leave, a few scattered households may remain, potentially the basis of a new cycle of village development, expansion and decline should a medium of the *mhondoro* eventually arrive. Of course not every village in Dande has its own *mhondoro* medium and not every headman is a *mutapi*. But within a spirit province all villages are dependent on the village of the medium for the performance of the annual rituals of agricultural production. The cycles of appearance, established possession and death of mediums affect most directly the villages of these mediums, and their headman the *vatapi*. But all villages are caught up in the swell and flow of change that the establishment and dissolution of these core villages creates.

From the point of view of the day-to-day functioning of the system, the three-way relationship between medium, *mutapi* and chief can be summarised like this: the authenticity of the mediums is constantly reaffirmed by the authority of their *vatapi* which derives from the chiefs whose own legitimacy was established by one of the *mhondoro* who possess the medium. One might say that it was his ignorance of this relationship (illustrated in Figure 4.3) that allowed Albino Pacheco, and some more recent observers as well, to dismiss the activities of the mediums as anarchic and fraudulent.

Neat though this view of the system is, it is only one view. It is the view of the people who operate it. It is the view from the inside. If we take a step backwards it is possible to see something more in this religio-political system than this efficient circle of transferred authorities. The way forward is to look once again at the crucial role of the *mutapi*.

Another term frequently used to refer to the medium's assistant is *munyai* (pl. *vanyai*). This term has an old and complex history. It means royal servant or messenger and can be used to indicate many different types of subservient relationship. The fullest description of a *munyai* is that given by Chet Lancaster in his monograph on the Goba people who live a short distance to the east of Dande:

> According to local reckoning, the confluence-zone Goba were collectively known as *vanyai* or followers of highland southern chiefs at least inter-mittently in the past ... The term *Nyai* referred to the local political

structure and to a hierarchy of status linking Shona-speaking groups occupying a fairly wide area. [This term can also refer to] a valuable periphery of dependent men . . . uxorilocal service husbands [whose labour] would be available for an indefinite number of years . . . They also acted as messengers, errand runners, bodyguards and henchmen for their leader, spying out local dissension, scouting for news of enemy attacks, and rushing to their defence or help if a raiding party were approaching. In addition, the younger men might form hunting, raiding or trading parties on behalf of their patrons.[19]

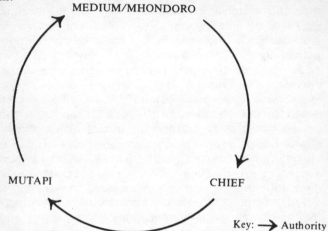

Figure 4.3 The sources of authority in the relationship between medium, mutapi *and chief*

In what sense is a *mutapi* a *munyai*? If he is a royal servant or messenger, who is the royal whom he serves? There are two answers to this question.

Within a chieftaincy are found many spirit provinces with many *mhondoro* mediums. A chief cannot be present at the shrine of the mediums of all his ancestors wherever and whenever they become possessed. The term *munyai* can be used for the *mutapi* to indicate his function as a 'messenger' of the chief. But he does not intermediate between the chief and the mediums. By convention the medium has nothing interesting to say. He intermediates between the chief and his ancestor the *mhondoro*. And this provides the second answer, for the *mutapi* is also the 'royal servant' of the *mhondoro*, the chief of days gone by. He may be sent by him to carry messages to the present chief but also to other mediums or other *mhondoro*, to officers of the state or to anyone else with whom he wishes to communicate.

The work of the medium's assistant in his role as *mutapi* is to manage the shrine and care for the medium. But in his role as *munyai* his function is to intermediate between the two parallel spheres: the spirit realm and the chieftaincy. He operates at the interface of the two conceptualisations of the territory. His authority comes both from his specialist knowledge of the ways of the *mhondoro* and also from his position within the political structure of the chieftaincy. He stands with one eye on the present and one on the past, one foot in a spirit province and the other in the territory of the chief.

Once the intermediary role of the *mutapi-munyai* has become clear, an extraordinary paradox is revealed. The chain of communication between the living and the dead excludes the medium altogether. Despite the flamboyant and idiosyncratic character of the medium, it is not he who is thought of as the intermediary between this world and the last, it is his assistant. This can be made quite clear by a survey of the full range of the *mutapi-munyai*'s responsibilities. As well as overseeing the rituals at which the medium becomes possessed, the *mutapi* also takes charge of those at which he does not, in which the medium plays no part at all. The supplication to the *mhondoro* for rain (*mbudzirume*) is organised by the *mutapi* as is the thank-offering made each year for the harvest (*musoso*) when the *mutapi* carries cobs of maize and ears of sorghum to the tree shrine of the *mhondoro*. It is also seen at the early stages of the possession rituals, especially those of a relatively inexperienced medium, when the *mutapi* sits and claps, sometimes for hours on end, beseeching the chief of the past world on behalf of the people of this to enter the medium and to speak.

From within the system, it is the chief, the *mutapi-munyai* and the *mhondoro* who are thought of as the three crucial participants in opening a channel of communication between the living and the dead. It was continually repeated to me (and I have continually repeated to you) that the medium is passive, that the medium makes no contribution of his own to the busy and varied life of the *mhondoro*'s shrine. In fact, the personality of the medium, his view of the world and his desire to act on it provides the independent input that gives dynamism and adaptability to the system. When the system is working well, the independence of the medium is invisible. If a possessed medium should make statements that contradict established history or convention, this is interpreted not as a new interpretation but simply as 'truth' never before revealed. What had been previously accepted becomes misconception and is swept aside. The medium may reveal previously unknown relationships between his descendants or reveal the existence of descendants never before heard of. He may announce his 'traditional' right to install chiefs in distant areas and his power to bring the rains to their fields. His potential is limited only by his ability to respond to the challenges of his environment.[20]

It is only when the system breaks down that the medium's true significance becomes apparent. This might happen if the innovations or changes proposed by the medium are too radical, too challenging of established rights and authorities. Then his originality and creativity force aside the veils and stand revealed. Or it might be that a medium is thought to be accruing too much personal benefit from his profession, making too much money or accumulating too many wives. Then his good faith may be questioned and belief in his ability or desire to deny himself for the good of the community may be suspended. If this should happen the consequences are disastrous. All at once, the channel between living and dead is at risk of being closed down. The system can only operate at all when the source of its energy, the creativity of the medium, is successfully (though unconsciously) concealed and denied.

The breakdown of the system is illustrated in Figure 4.4. Here the line C, 'descent', stands for the relationship between the *mhondoro* and the chief, *mutapi* or the people which may be stressed by them in order to justify their challenge (B) to the medium whose possession (A) by the *mhondoro* has become suspect.

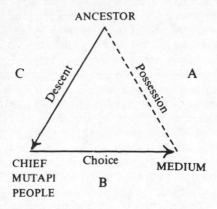

Figure 4.4   The sources of authority as they seem when the system breaks down

The following paragraphs summarise some conclusions which may be drawn from this chapter as a whole.

(1) The representative of the *mhondoro* on earth is the chief. His authority derives from the fact that he is descended from the *mhondoro* and that he has been selected by the *mhondoro* from all other candidates as the true heir to the chieftaincy. He is therefore a future *mhondoro* himself. The *mutapi*, the manager of the shrine of his ancestor, stands midway between this world and the last, the chieftaincy and the spirit realm. The medium is at once passive vessel and dynamo, originating and challenging but never in his own name or his own person.

66

(2) The *mhondoro* mediums and the chiefs are part of a single system first because the spirits that possess the mediums are the ancestors of the chiefs and, secondly, because the authenticity of the medium relies on the political structure of the chieftaincy for its expression. Unlike the Old Testament prophets, the *mhondoro* medium cannot wander off into the desert and live as a 'charismatic' on his own. If a would-be medium fails to find the backing of a village head or a senior member of his lineage there can be no communication between living and dead but only a dangerous stranger, a mad young man in the bush.

(3) The most important characteristic of the *mhondoro* is his altruism, his profound moral concern for all the people who live within his spirit province or, in the case of a senior *mhondoro*, within his realm. How is this altruism assessed? Ultimately by the extent to which it expresses the will and the desire of the people who live within his territory. Thus one aspect of the *mhondoro* medium's role is to express the consensus view of his followers. For example, if he selects a chief who has no popular support, he will be suspected of corruption and self-interest and the authenticity of his possession will be questioned. But another aspect of this system is that the means of communication between spirits and people are so constructed that the contribution made by the medium himself is invisible. Thus, the way in which one of the key distinguishing features of the Shona people, the twin roles of chief and medium, operates in practice allows the mediums a great deal of covert influence at the most significant levels of political activity while the chief has no authority to innovate within the sphere of ritual at all. But consensus and innovation must be delicately balanced if the medium is to survive. A successful medium must develop great skill in leading simultaneously from the front and from behind.

But it would be a mistake to interpret this to imply that the careers of mediums are shaped largely by opportunism. There may be mediums who make no statement unless they are certain that it will increase their prestige and support but there are others who are courageous and creative, who venture into uncharted regions of the political terrain. As we shall see some, like the medium of Chiwawa, succeed and their reputations are immeasurably enhanced. Others, such as the medium of Madzomba, are less sensitive and they lose almost every drop of authority they possess.

(4) As new areas of land are opened up for cultivation, so the spirit realm expands. New *mhondoro* and new spirit provinces appear. *Mutapi-munyai* are chosen. As soon as their rituals succeed and the *mhondoro* speaks through his medium for the first time, the ownership of the spirit province is established. What belongs to the chief's ancestor belongs to the chief. As long as the *mhondoro* continues to supply rain to

his followers, the chief's ownership of the land seems to be beyond question, beyond doubt.

The great spectacle of the past

There is one further aspect of the professional life of the *mhondoro* medium that contributes to the apparent inevitability of the ownership of the land by the royal lineage. Throughout the whole of their professional careers, the lives of the *mhondoro* mediums are constrained by a number of ritual prohibitions. By adhering to these prohibitions the mediums present the illusion that they are not simply the mediums of the chiefs of the past but that they actually are those very chiefs returned physically to earth.

In theory it is possible for every spirit province to contain a medium of its own *mhondoro* at the same time. This is rarely if ever achieved. Some *mhondoro* have long traditions of mediums stretching back over hundreds of years, others take a sequence of mediums over forty or fifty years and then return to the body of their lion and to silence for years on end. But the *mhondoro* mediums who are 'in residence' – and there may be fourteen or fifteen of these at any one time – present what amounts to a non-stop historical spectacle: the dead ancestors of the present chiefs returned to earth, the history of the land displayed and acted out, the heroes of the past available once more not to rule but to give the benefit of their wisdom, to tell the truth which only they, being dead, understand. It is as if the Duke of Wellington, Henry V, Winston Churchill and a dozen more heroes of the British state had all possessed mediums, moved into their old homes and invited the public to bring their problems and complaints to be resolved by them.

Four sets of ritual prohibitions create this illusion. The first affects the mediums' dress and controls the behaviour of their followers towards them. With the exception of a very few elderly women in the extreme north-west of Dande, everyone wears Western-style dress. Only the mediums are an exception. Their main garment is two lengths of black (or dark-blue) cloth. One is tied round the waist so that it falls to the ankles. The other is draped over both shoulders and tied under the right. These cloths as well as the staff which all mediums carry and the sandals which they wear on their feet make up the dress worn by Shona chiefs since the sixteenth century.[21]

Hats and shoes must be removed before entering the presence of a medium. This is not an unusual gesture of respect but it is precisely what is described as compulsory when addressing certain of the Mutapas, the leaders of the Mwene Mutapa state. Mediums may not see rifles. At certain periods it was forbidden to appear before a chief holding a rifle or any other weapon. In this case, as in the last, what may have been gestures of respect or measures to protect security when directed at a chief or a Mutapa have been transformed into a ritual when acted out towards a medium.[22]

This set of prohibitions and behaviours is shaped by a conception of what the chiefs of the past were like and how they were treated by their followers. Mediums are as quick as non-specialists to insist on the distinction between the medium and the *mhondoro* that possess them. But the rituals of their daily lives blur this distinction for they operate at all times, whether the mediums are possessed or not. The term *mambo*, meaning chief, is commonly used to refer to a medium. If you were near a medium's home and asked where the *mambo* was, you would be directed without hesitation to the home of the medium. The *gano* or ritual axe which all mediums carry is a symbol of the ownership of the chieftaincy as is the unique fur hat which some mediums wear. Even more strikingly, a medium is given precisely the same burial as a chief. His body is allowed to disintegrate, the flesh to separate from the bone, before it is finally placed inside the earth.

The blurring of the division between *mhondoro* and medium is so extreme that the name of the *mhondoro* is commonly used to refer to the medium. As often as I would stand corrected for using the name of the *mhondoro* to refer to his medium, so often would the person who had corrected my 'mistake' do precisely the same himself. Although it is constantly insisted that medium and *mhondoro* are totally separate entities, in practice the intangible essence of the one is lost within the material reality of the other.

As long as the forms of ritual behaviour which produce this merging are observed and the spectacle performed, so long will a challenge to the rights to own the land by the descendants of the ancestors be unthinkable. Rights to ownership in the present derive from rights to ownership in the past and with each royal ancestor returned to life and living in his spirit province, the past is available for inspection right now, right here, right in front of your eyes.

There are three more sets of prohibitions which the mediums observe that are yet to be described. All three of these reinforce the historical spectacle because they present the mediums as if they were the *mhondoro* made flesh. I deal with them separately for each has its own domain of meaning.

The second set controls the mediums' contact with the biological aspects of life: birth and death, reproduction and decay. Mediums may have nothing to do with death, with burial or with the destruction of life in any form. Blood, especially menstrual blood, is extremely dangerous to them. If the *mhondoro* sees it the medium will die.

The third set of prohibitions prevent the mediums from having anything to do with the artefacts of Western technology. They may not use Western medicines. They may not ride in cars or buses. Petrol fumes are dangerous to them as is the surface of asphalt roads. To have contact with any of these or similar objects can cause their death.

Finally, each medium has his own set of restrictions on his diet but all avoid consumption of onions and pepper and the use of strong-smelling soap.

I will deal with the last of these sets in Chapter 9. There I show how they stress the characterisation of the *mhondoro* (and therefore the medium) as a wild animal at home in the bush. The third set I deal with in Chapter 7 when I discuss the development of the mediums' attitude to the economic pressures of colonialism and to the colonial state. The second set, the mediums' avoidance of all aspects of biological life, is the main subject of the next chapter.

NOTES

1 Theal (1898–1903, Vol. VII, p. 197).

2 ibid., p. 199.

3 Livingstone (1956, Vol. I, p. 168).

4 ibid., Vol. II, p. 254.

5 Department of History, University of Zimbabwe translation of Pacheco (1883) p. 10. (I am grateful to Dr D. N. Beach for making this available to me.)

6 Very few *mhondoro* mediums are women. Those that there are, are possessed by spirits that stand at critical points on the genealogies of royal ancestors and will be discussed in Chapter 5 below. I use the male pronoun to refer to all *mhondoro* mediums and indicate specifically where the medium is a woman.

7 The critical point of difference between *n'anga* and spirit mediums in Dande is that the *n'anga* do not become possessed. This varies in different parts of the country. See Chavunduka (1978).

8 This process contains one of the reasons why women are so rarely considered to be the mediums of *mhondoro*. As far as possession by lineage ancestors, *midzimu*, is concerned, men are almost exclusively possessed by male ancestors of their father's lineage but women may be possessed by female or male ancestors of their mother's or their father's lineages. This has the effect that if a possessed woman names a clan other than her own (i.e. her father's lineage) this may be interpreted to be an ancestor of her mother's or her mother's mother's lineage and so on. For men, two paths are open: a spirit of one's own clan is a *mudzimu*, a spirit of another clan may be a *mhondoro*. For women, no matter what clan they name, it is possible to conclude that they are possessed by a low-level ancestor, a *mudzimu*.

9 I know of no moment in the initiatory stage of a medium's career, such as that described by Beattie for the Bunyoro, when the aspirant medium is encouraged to feign possession. See Beattie (1969, p. 166).

10 See Levi-Strauss's classic account of the initiation of a medium, 'The Sorceror and his Magic', on which I have leaned (Levi-Strauss, 1968, p. 167).

11 Garbett (1977, p. 75).

12 Richards (1940, p. 83).

13 The quotation is from Mitchell (1961, p. 34) who was the first to describe this peculiar feature of Shona social organisation.

14 Garbett (1977) has discussed the independence of the ritual sphere from the political sphere with great subtlety. I am especially grateful to Dr Garbett for criticism of earlier drafts of this section.

15 See Holleman (1952, p. 21) and Garbett (1966a) for a full discussion of chiefly succession among the Shona.

16 The *mutapi* may also be known as *nechombo* (Garbett, 1963a) or as *mutonje* (Bourdillon, 1971, p. 202).

17 Among the Tonga people of the Valley, the *basikatongo*, who corresponds to the Korekore *vatapi*, are said to inherit the shade of the first man to have lived in that area and their wives to inherit the shade of the first woman (Colson, 1971, p. 226).

18 Especially in cases where a lineage has provided the *vatapi* of the *mhondoro* for a long time, the *vatapi* may claim to be descended from the *mhondoro* for whom they care. If this is the case, it will be considered impossible for a member of the *mutapi* lineage to be possessed by 'their' *mhondoro*.

19 Lancaster (1974b, p. 77).

20 The conception of the medium as totally passive, as almost, though not quite, redundant in the communication between living and dead, goes some way to explain a peculiar anomaly noticed by myself and other researchers as well (e.g. Bourdillon, 1971, p. 59). Although the convention is that a *mhondoro* medium will be a stranger to the territory in which he practises, in fact it is very common for mediums to have been born at or near the place where they live out their professional careers. Nonetheless the dogma that mediums are strangers persists. The explanation I was given of why this must be is that if the medium came from the same area as his *mhondoro* he would know the history of the chieftaincy and his speaking of it during his testing would prove nothing at all. But this is not an explanation. Rather it is a commentary by insiders on an element of their social organisation the meaning of which their position within the system makes it difficult for them to see. The medium is thought of as an outsider because he is irrelevant to the system of communication which is operated between, as it were, people like us: our chief, our headman and the ancestor of our spirit province.

21 Beach (1980, p. 98).

22 Alpers (1968, p. 15).

5

The Valley of Affines

Through all the political and economic changes that have taken place in Dande over the last one-hundred-and-fifty years, the developments from within as well as the waves of history rushing in from without, two features have remained constant: the possession rituals of the *mhondoro* mediums and the belief in the power of the *mhondoro* to bring the rain.

If you ask which *mhondoro* bring the rain, the answer will be all of them. All *mhondoro* mediums may be addressed by the title *samvura*, literally 'owner of the rain'. But in fact the matter is a little more complex than this answer suggests.

For example, the famous *mhondoro* Nehanda is known to have *simba yehondo*, the power of war and also *simba yemvura*, the power of rain. In the nineteenth century her reputation as a rain-bringing spirit was widespread (in some accounts she is referred to as a 'rain witch') and this has endured. A medium of Nehanda in the Mazoe region in 1906 is referred to in government reports as a 'rain spirit'. In 1963 a District Assistant collecting information for the Ministry of Native Affairs recorded that 'Nehanda is the spiritual rainmaker' of the Korekore people in the Valley. Guerrillas who lived with the medium of Nehanda in the 1970s believed her to have this power and this is the generally accepted view in Dande today. However, when I visited the village where the most recent Nehanda medium lived before her journey to Mozambique and asked some of those who had lived with her: 'Can Nehanda bring the rain?', the answer was no. Not only that, I was told that Nehanda had never had any rain-making powers at all.[1]

The same contradiction arose with Nehanda's 'father', the *mhondoro* Mutota. (Figure 5.1 contains all the genealogies of the *mhondoro* of Dande linked together showing the ties of kinship believed to exist between them).[2] In the 1960s, Kingsley Garbett was told that Mutota was 'the big one', the senior *mhondoro* at the head of the genealogy of

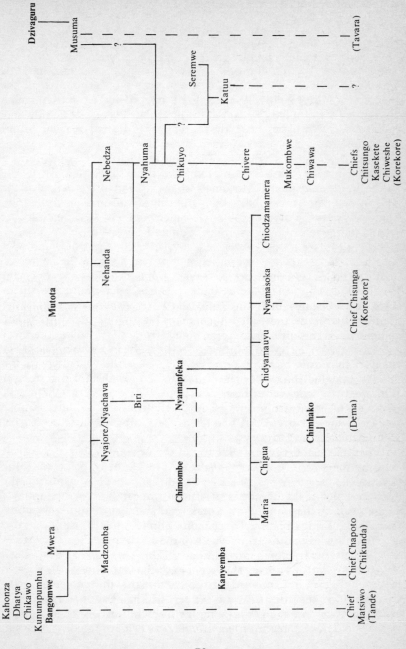

Figure 5.1   Ties of kinship between the main mhondoro of Dande (bold type indicates the senior mhondoro of each lineage)

73

all Dande Korekore royal ancestors and chief rainmaker. Twenty years later, in general discussion with people in Dande, I was told precisely the same. But at the village where his most recent medium was living at the time of his death in 1974, his followers say that the *mhondoro* Mutota cannot make rain. They say that only the *mhondoro* of the autochthonous Tavara people, Musuma, has this power. Moreover, I was told that every year during his lifetime the medium of Mutota had sent offerings of tobacco and cloth to Musuma to ensure that rain fell. When this is put to the villagers of Dande they agree and say: 'Musuma, *he* is the big one. He is the real one who brings the rain'.[3]

Only at Musuma's village is there no ambiguity. The medium of Musuma and his followers agree that everything said of him is true. As one follower described it, Musuma's village is 'head office', where all the minor *mhondoro* must make their offerings. Musuma produces rain simply by desiring that it should fall. The medium of Musuma told me: 'I control the tap of heaven. I turn it on and off as I will'.[4]

Two ideas seem to co-exist side by side. On the one hand, the Korekore ancestors are responsible for providing rain, the source of fertility and life. On the other the Tavara *mhondoro* is the only one who has this power. In ritual practice these two ideas are partially reconciled. Each year offerings for rain are made at each *mhondoro*'s shrine but the *mhondoro* is unable to produce the rain for his province by himself. The request must be sent up a chain of *mhondoro* until it reaches the most senior, the *mhondoro* who is in charge of the realm as a whole. The chain of *mhondoro* up which the requests are sent is the genealogy of the chieftaincy which links the present chief to his most distant ancestors. It is these very long genealogies which, as I described in Chapter 2, distinguish the royal lineages of the chiefs from all the others whose brief genealogies break off before they link up with an ancestor of significance to the territory as a whole.

When the request reaches the top of the genealogy, it may be dealt with by the senior Korekore *mhondoro* Mutota or transferred to the Tavara *mhondoro* Musuma. Whether the action of transferring the request takes place or not is of crucial importance for it implies a recognition by the 'conqueror' Korekore that only the 'autochthonous' Tavara can bring the rain. To make this admission is to admit that it is the Tavara who are the true owners of the land.

'Who are the true owners of the land?' This question has never been asked as urgently as during the recent guerrilla war. One of the ways in which the guerrillas expressed their conviction that the land belonged to them and to their followers was by performing certain rituals. These rituals demonstrated that they were the 'autochthons' in contrast to the whites who were categorised as 'conquerors' with no abiding rights in the territory they occupied. The ritual activities of the guerrillas will be described in Part III of this book. In this chapter I give an account of the symbolism out of which those rituals were constructed and adapted, the symbolism at the heart of the two features of the social life of Dande that have triumphed over political and economic change: the possession rituals of the *mhondoro* and the narratives spoken in Dande which describe – in terms of myths of origin – who has the power to bring the rain.

The myths

The first myth I analyse tells the story of Mutota's journey from Guruuswa. This is the most important myth belonging to the Korekore of Dande. Any Korekore asked about the history of his ancestors will probably begin by telling a version of this narrative. Or, to make the same point in a way that better illustrates the relationship between myth and ethnic identity, any person who answers questions about their past by telling this myth is making a claim to be a Korekore.[5]

Myth I

I collected many versions of this myth. The version given here is the one most frequently told in Dande. I mention variations only when they are pertinent to the analysis that follows the five myths presented here.

Nyakatonje lived in Dande which at that time was called Mbire. He travelled to the country of Guruuswa taking with him some salt. When he arrived he found Mutota living there. Mutota killed an ox to welcome him. When the meat was cooked, Nyakatonje added salt to his portion. Mutota saw him eating this and asked for some. When he tasted how good it was, he asked Nyakatonje where he came from and then set out with him as guide to find the land of the salt. With him went his son Nebedza and his daughter Nehanda as well as Zvimba and Chingoo. [In some versions Chingoo is described as Mutota's brother or his twin, in others as his friend. Other 'sons' of Mutota such as Samarengo, Nyajore, Madzomba and Chinengebere may also be said to have travelled from Guruuswa. They are all *mhondoro* of the Zambezi Valley or escarpment and are added to the narrative by those who claim to be their descendants].

They journeyed through many places, passing where Harare is today and on into the Mazoe Valley. When they reached a certain place, Zvimba said he had to stop as his legs were hurting him [the verb *kuzvimba* means to swell up painfully]. Zvimba remained there and that's how the place known today as Zvimba got its name.

Chingoo and Mutota continued. They found a tree with bees in it. They were unable to reach the honey, so Chingoo bent his spear into the shape of a curved stick [called *ngoo*] used to fetch down honey from trees and that's why he was called Chingoo. Some of the honey was wet and fell on Mutota and that's why he was called Mutota [the verb *kutota* means to become wet, especially with rain]. When they reached the country of Guruve, Chingoo stopped and made his home there while Mutota continued towards Dande.

As they travelled, Mutota told Nyakatonje to warn him before they reached the edge of the Escarpment and saw the Zambezi River in the Valley. Mutota needed time to prepare himself to perform certain magic [*mapipi*]. But Nyakatonje failed to warn him and Mutota saw into the Valley before he was prepared. Now he was unable to continue his journey. He returned back and made his home on the Escarpment. When he died the earth opened for him and he was placed inside a rock. Around his grave were planted eight small baobab trees [*tuuyu tusere*] brought from Dande by his followers. Before he died Mutota told his sons that if they wished to enter the Valley, one of them would have to have sex with their sister Nehanda. All the brothers refused to perform this forbidden act. Only Nebedza, the youngest, agreed. When this was accomplished, Nebedza inherited his father's position as head of the lineage and all the sons climbed down the Escarpment and made their homes in Mbire, now called Dande.[6]

The Mutota story contains not one but two accounts of the coming to Dande of the ancestors of the Korekore. First, there is the story of Mutota, heading for Dande but failing to arrive there. Secondly, there is

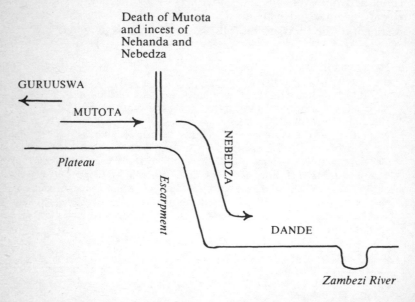

Figure 5.2   The journey from Guruuswa to Dande : 1

76

the story of the entry of Mutota's children into the Valley. I will treat the two sections of the story separately, dealing with each significant element in the sequence that it appears in the narrative. Figure 5.2 is a diagrammatic representation of these key elements.

Section 1: 'The failed journey of Mutota'

The first important element in the myth is:

Guruuswa – the home of Mutota before the journey

A large number of Shona groups in the northern parts of Zimbabwe name Guruuswa as their original home. But not all of these groups agree about where Guruuswa is. D. N. Beach writes that:

> the dynasties that claim to have come from such a place locate very different areas as their point of origin. In the lands between the lower Ruya and Mazoe Rivers, 'Guruuswa' is said to lie in the West; in the upper Ruya Valley, the upper Dande Valley, the Dande and western Chidima it is thought of as being in the south and the people of the Mafungabusi Plateau and the Umfuli-Umniati confluence area place it in the east.[7]

Guruuswa means literally 'long grass'. In order to explain the variety of directions in which Guruuswa is said to lie, Beach has suggested that the term is used by people living in highly forested or scrublands to refer to their 'original home' on open plains or grasslands. This interpretation is uncomplicated and therefore attractive but literal and therefore problematic. In this reading 'We come from Guruuswa' would mean simply: 'we came from a place where there were more grasslands than there are here'. But many other Central and Southern African peoples have origin myths strikingly similar to this one. The oral traditions of the Xhosa, for example, refer to their place of origin as *Eluhlangeni* or *umhlanga*. Today this is widely understood as being 'the place of reeds'.[8] For the Xhosa this place of reeds (or long grass) is the place of origin not only of a particular set of lineages but of all men and women and of all animals. And this is how Guruuswa was explained to me in Dande. Guruuswa, I was told, cannot be located geographically for it is not a place in the sense that a village or a country is a place. Guruuswa is where *everything* comes from, not only ancestors but all men, all animals, even all plants. It was also suggested to me on a number of occasions that the 'long grass' is not real grass but the hair that grows in the pubic region of the human female.

One simple observation brings all these interpretations together. On Map 5.1 are marked the homes of the Guruuswa traditions mentioned by Beach. All lie within the inverted bow-shape formed by the middle Zambezi River and all lie on tributaries of the Zambezi River from which in the past (and in some cases still today) they drew their daily supplies of water. In each case the source of these tributaries lies in the direction in which the communities say their place of origin is found. For example, many thousands of people in Dande live on the banks of the Msengezi River. The source of this river is in the south and south is where these people believe Guruuswa to be.

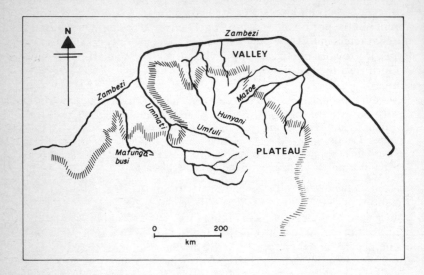

Map 5.1   Main tributaries of the Zambezi River in northern Zimbabwe (adapted from Beach, 1980)

My preliminary interpretation of these Guruuswa myths, including the Mutota version, is therefore as follows: 'our earliest ancestors and the waters of our river both travel towards our present home from the river's source, a place where water rises out of the earth in a patch of long grass.' This is a handy demonstration of how rival and apparently contradictory interpretations (Guruuswa as actual place, as mythical place, as source of water, as source of natural life, as vagina) can all find a home within one symbolic framework provided that it is sufficiently broad. And I emphasise that the clues to evolving this framework (that Guruuswa is where every living thing comes from, that the long grasses are a reference to pubic hairs) were suggested to me by people living in Dande. I do not mean to imply by this that my interpretations of these myths and rituals are their interpretations. Far from it. The meaning which I suggest they contain only has significance for the sort of sociological analysis that is contained in this book. But it seems to me that people's attitudes and responses to their own traditions should be

78

regarded as data and interpreted along with the traditions themselves.

One further piece of information about Guruuswa that the Mutota myth contains allows a tentative expansion of this interpretation. In no version of the myth is any reference made to a wife of Mutota or to any other affine. The people at Guruuswa and those who make the journey to Dande are all members of Mutota's own lineage – his sons, his daughter and his brother, twin or friend Chingoo. Not only is affinity absent but the notion of twinship or brotherhood re-emphasises that all the characters in this tale are members of the same lineage. In narrative terms, it provides companionship without introducing affinity.[9]

Guruuswa then is the source of social and biological life, possibly a source of fertility, which is found within the lineage of our hero Mutota. Fertility within the lineage implies a notion of motherhood. This is consistent with the interpretation of Guruuswa as a vagina out of which the ancestors of Dande emerge.

Nyakatonje – who brought the salt from Dande to Guruuswa and led Mutota back again

Nyakatonje appears in the myth as the name of an individual character but unlike all the other characters he is not regarded as the ancestor of anyone living today and is therefore not a *mhondoro*. It is unthinkable that Nyakatonje should ever possess a medium. In fact the word *nyakatonje* can be translated to mean 'acolyte, or interpreter, of a spirit medium'. This surprising information is underlined by the many references to Nyakatonje in various versions of the myth as a *muranda* (servant) or *munyai* (royal messenger), both terms that can be used in Dande to refer to the assistant of a spirit medium who is also an intermediary between the political realm and the spirit realm, the present and the past.

That Nyakatonje, the salt-bringer and guide, is also a *mutapi*, a religious functionary, has a long historical tradition. For example, in the version of the myth contained in Pacheco's mid-nineteenth-century description of the Zambezi Valley, the Nyakatonje figure is called Netondo. According to W. G. L. Randles in his book, *The Empire of Monomotapa*, the *netondo* was 'one of the three religious specialists at the court of Monomotapa'.

If Nyakatonje is a *mutapi*, it seems possible that in some way or other the Mutota myth may refer to the possession of mediums by *mhondoro* spirits. If we re-read the myth thinking of Nyakatonje in this way, the narrative seems to imply that the *mutapi* goes back (upstream) to bring Mutota, the senior *mhondoro*, to his descendants living in Dande. This is an interpretation of quite a different kind to the one suggested in the last paragraph but both of these, as well as a third contained in the next paragraph, are all compatible, interrelated and interdependent.[10]

The salt

In most versions of the Mutota myth, the salt is described as salt extracted from the earth (*munyu wepasi*) and is contrasted with the salt obtained by burning cow dung or certain leaves which had been in use in Guruuswa until the happy time of Nyakatonje's arrival. It is the attractiveness and convenience of Nyakatonje's mined salt that persuades Mutota to leave Guruuswa.

The trade in salt from the Valley to the Plateau was one of the main forms of commerce in Dande from the sixteenth century to the early twentieth century. The journey that the salt makes in the myth, from Dande to Guruuswa, precisely corresponds to this trade. Salt was exchanged for gold and ivory, and this third level of interpretation gains significance from the fact that the clan of the Korekore ancestors who travel towards the Valley (downstream) in the same direction as the gold and ivory is Elephant, Owners of the Tusks (*Nzou Samanyanga*). And there is still more to be said about this salt. It is characteristic of the societies of the Zambezi Valley that meat offered in rituals to the ancestors is unsalted. This is an extremely important point. Ancestors do not eat salt. Mutota, on the other hand has such a powerful craving for the salt with which Nyakatonje has flavoured his meat that he travels all the way to Dande to find more. Why should this be?

The answer to this question will become clear by the end of this chapter. Meantime here is a summary of the suggestions I have made so far. I have sketched out three levels of interpretation of Mutota's journey from Guruuswa. First, I suggested that it contains two references to the origin of all life. One is the source of the river on which the people depend for their water supply. The other is maternal fertility. Secondly, I picked out a number of allusions in the myth to the ritual of spirit possession. This may have some tie-up with Mutota's surprising desire for salt – surprising because it is in contradiction to the ritual offerings of unsalted meat which are made to the ancestors from time to time. And, thirdly, I suggested that the journeys made in the myth parallel the trade of salt for ivory carried on between the Valley and the Plateau.[11] One final point may be made before I move on to the next part of the myth.

Mbire – the pre-Mutota name for Dande

The only point I need to make here is that when the story begins Dande is already established as a defined and populated territory. Some versions stress that Mutota should not see the Zambezi River, others that he should not see the country of Mbire. Both amount to the same thing. On a clear day the Zambezi is just visible from the edge of the Escarpment. Indeed one section of the Escarpment is called *rukovakuona* which means 'river view'. The only point we need hold on to is that when

Mutota finds himself unable to enter Dande the boundary which he cannot cross is the Escarpment itself.

Section 2: 'The crime of Nehanda and Nebedza'

Nehanda and Nebedza are complex figures. A variety of traditions have accumulated around them and they have each acquired two traditional names. Nehanda means 'of Handa' or 'at Handa', Handa being a territory probably in the extreme north-east of Dande though the boundaries are unsure. The borders of Bedza, the home of Nebedza, have been loosely identified with the help of eighteenth- and nineteenth-century Portuguese documents as a territory near the foot of the Escarpment. Nehanda's full title is Nehanda Nyamita Nyakasikana. Her brother is Matope Nebedza Nyanehwe. Nehanda's names have been variously interpreted. To attempt to unravel their meaning would lead us deeper into pre-Korekore history than we have evidence to guide us or present cause to go. Nebedza's names however are relevant to our present journey and I will suggest an interpretation of them in a while. Throughout this chapter I deal with this brother-and-sister pair only as they appear in the Mutota mythology, though what I say may have relevance for the other traditions in which they appear as well.[12]

Nebedza as son

Nebedza is the youngest of the sons of Mutota. In Dande it is said that in the past at a man's death his estate (his property, his position, his wives and his titles) was inherited by his youngest son. The reason given is that as land was plentiful, older sons would move away from their father's home at marriage leaving the youngest to care for the father's lands. This information was given to me specifically to explain why it was Nebedza rather than any of his older brothers who became 'chief' after Mutota.

Nehanda as daughter

This brings us to the central problem of this chapter, the incest between Nehanda and Nebedza. The theme of incest is not uncommon in mythic narratives. Quite often it represents an action so powerfully condemned in ordinary life that when performed by the characters in the story, they are transformed and so is the society they are part of. I am going to suggest that the effect of this act of incest is that the descendants of the incestuous couple, namely the Korekore people of Dande, are forever afterwards able to acquire rain from their own ancestors.

You will notice that this is in contrast with the idea set out in Chapter 3 that if incest takes place drought will follow as inevitably as night follows day. Here I am suggesting that the meaning of the Nehanda-Nebedza incest is that incest *produces* rain. I will explain why I interpret this myth in the way that I do by comparing the Mutota/Nehanda/ Nebedza story with four other mythic accounts, two recorded in Dande and two recorded nearby on the Plateau.

Myth II

Chimombe travelled from the north bank of the Zambezi to the south and made his home in a place from which Nyamapfeka's people had been accustomed to take salt. Nyamapfeka set out to win back this land but a fog came up and Nyamapfeka's people were unable to find their enemies. They devised a new strategy. They sent Nyamapfeka's daughter, Semwa, to seduce Chimombe. She was successful and he married her. One night, after Chimombe had fallen asleep, Semwa cut his throat. Where the blood fell a river formed. Semwa returned to her father who became owner of the salt pans.

Today the ancestor Chimombe is considered to be an 'iron god', the only concrete manifestation of ancestral power that I know of in the region. The form the 'god' takes is a length of twisted metal which is said to have been found near the River Chiore. According to the myth, this river was formed out of the blood that flowed from Chimombe's wound. Chimombe cannot speak to his descendants and followers directly but has the medium of the *mhondoro* Mbaiwa, a descendant of Nyamapfeka, to interpret for him. (Chimombe is said to be the chief of the VaSoli people. Note that he travels from north to south, the direction of the rivers flowing into the north bank of the Zambezi from where the VaSoli are said to come. Despite the fact that Nyamapfeka is reported to have taken salt from Chimombe's home *before* Chimombe's arrival, Chimombe is in all respects treated as an autochthon. Nyamapfeka is the senior *mhondoro* of the Korekore Chisunga chieftaincy, members of the Elephant clan.)

Myth III

Musuma lived in Dande. His daughter was married to Nyahuma, a descendant of Mutota. One day while Musuma was thatching his hut, perched up on the roof beams, Nyahuma hid a red cloth beneath one of the bales of thatching grass. When Musuma lifted this bale he saw the red cloth which he is forbidden to do and he died. Before he died he said: as I am on the roof of the house, my home will be in the heavens, whereas you who are on the ground will own the land. That is why Musuma is the bringer of rain.

Musuma is the *mhondoro* of the Tavara people, a 'son' of the major Tavara *mhondoro* Dzivaguru. Nyahuma is a descendant of Mutota (see Figure 5.1, above).

Myth IV

When Chingoo parted from Mutota he entered the country of Guruve. He found Nyamazunzu living there, 'a great warrior and a man of miracles'. As he could not defeat him in battle, Chingoo offered him Peduru, the daughter of his descendant Dumbu. He said 'Take my daughter to be your wife. Let us be friends and stop fighting. You are my *mukuwasha* [son-in-law].' After beer had been drunk at Dumbu's village they travelled to Nyamazunzu's home where more beer was drunk. When Nyamazunzu was asleep, Peduru cut off his head and beat the ceremonial drum announcing victory. Chingoo entered the village and killed all of Nyamazunzu's people. That is how the country of Guruve was won.

The name Nyamazunzu is quite commonly applied to an autochthon. There appear to be no traceable links between him and any group of people living in Guruve today. Chingoo is the senior *mhondoro* of the Korekore Chipuriro chieftaincy on the Plateau who are members of the Monkey clan (*Soko Wafawanaka*).

Myth V

Chambavanhu came from Guruuswa and settled in Damba on the Plateau. Nyamakwere, a four-eyed man, was already there. Chambavanhu could not easily defeat him as Nyamakwere's arrows were guided by the wind. He was able to raise mists to hide his people and he could disguise himself by turning into an anthill. Chambavanhu tied a black cloth round the eyes of Nyamakwere during the night. He died and his body was thrown into a pool where he turned into a crocodile.

A different version, told by the people who claim descent from a *mhondoro* called Chigamauro who 'lived in Damba before Chambavanhu' relates that:

Chigamauro climbed a mountain of rocks where Nyamakwere the four-eyed man was living and said: 'We've come to fight', and Nyamakwere said: 'Why have you come to fight when I have married your daughter?' They both took up a bow and arrow and shot at each other. Nyamakwere's wife tied a piece of black cloth round his neck and strangled him. Chigamauro also died of his wound.

(Nyamakwere is another autochthon without descendants. Chambavanhu and Chigamauro are ancestors of different branches of the Korekore Bepura chieftaincy of the *Pwere* clan).[13]

An analysis of the myths

A comparison of myths II to V with the Mutota myth (myth I) will form the basis of my analysis of them all. The central point of my comparison is this. Myths II to V contain accounts of 'tricks' played by the conqueror to defeat the autochthons, the original owners of the land. In myths II, IV and V a female member of the conqueror's lineage seduces and defeats the autochthon. In myth III the conqueror kills the autochthon by tricking him into looking at the colour red. The Mutota myth appears to contain no trick comparable to any of these. True, there is mention of certain 'magic' that Mutota is prevented from doing by the absent-mindedness of his guide but this is a different matter. None of the tricks of the conquerors in the other myths can be described as 'magical'. Indeed it is the autochthons who perform 'magic', raising fogs and mists and so on. It may seem to you no surprise that Mutota does not perform a trick of underhand military strategy because, unlike the heroes of the other myths, Mutota's attempt to conquer a new territory is a failure. His quest for the country of the salt ends in his defeat. But, and this is the important point, although Mutota fails and turns back, his son Nebedza continues into the Valley. Perhaps it is to Nebedza rather than to Mutota that we should look to find the trick that wins the day.

Of all the narrative devices that myths II to V share, the most important is that in each a woman of one lineage marries into another. This is explicit in II, III and IV and implicit in V where the marriage of the conqueror's daughter to the autochthon has taken place before the myth begins. We need to look very carefully at who marries whom and what happens afterwards (see Figure 5.3).

Let us start by looking at III. Here the conqueror (Nyahuma) takes the autochthon's daughter, then kills her father and gains his territory. At the end of the story the conqueror has the woman. In II, IV and V it is the autochthons who get the women. But in fact this does not contradict III because all three of these marriages are deceitful tricks which end in the death of the husbands. In the first part of these myths, the conquerors give away their women. They seem to capitulate to the superior force or magic of the autochthons. But when the autochthons have been destroyed through the deceit of their wives, the conquerors take the women of their own lineage back again. This is explicity stated in II. When he has brought about the death of his temporary son-in-law, Chimombe, Nyamapfeka takes back his daughter.

When they pretended to capitulate, the Korekore chiefs established their status as conquered people by giving their daughters to their victors. It is logical, therefore, that when the Korekore eventually triumph, the defeated autochthons should yield their daughters to them. In other words, in the course of the myths the Korekore transform themselves from fathers-in-law into sons-in-laws, whereas the autochthons start off as sons-in-law and are fathers-in-law by the

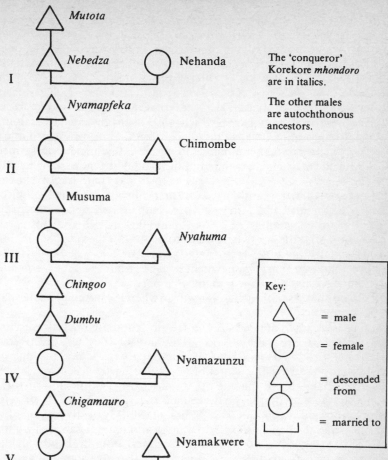

Figure 5.3   Kin relations in Myths I to V

end. What does this mean? Let us look briefly at the conventional attitudes taken towards each other by affinally related men, that is men who are related to each other by marriage.

This relationship bears perhaps the greatest weight of ritual stress of any in Shona society. During marriage negotiations a man is required to avoid coming into direct contact with senior members of his wife's lineage. Although after a period of married life avoidance ceases, the son-in-law must continue to display respect to all men who stand in relation to him or to other men of his lineage as father-in-law to son-in-law. He may be called on to give assistance to any of these men in any way they require. An example of the way in which respect is displayed is that on meeting a father-in-law, either his own or of a member of his lineage, a man will crouch on the ground, remove his hat and perform a special long, loud, hollow-handed clapping in greeting. In brief, the lineage that gives a wife has a higher status relative to the lineage that has received her and marriage with a woman who is mother-in-law to your lineage is regarded as incest.[14]

According to local etymologies, the term for father-in-law, *tezvara*, is derived from the verb *kuzva* which means 'to give life'. The local explanation given for this is that one's wife's father gives life to one's own lineage by supplying a female to perpetuate it. The term *tezvara* may be used for any male member of the affinal lineage and the female members may all be called *mezvara*. The customary pattern of exchange that occurs at marriage is that wife's father's lineage supplies biological fertility to the husband's lineage. It is compensated by a payment of money or the expenditure of labour on the father-in-law's fields.

To summarise the last two paragraphs: if one lineage supplies another with the fertility it needs to perpetuate itself, it will be partially reciprocated by a marriage payment or labour but the debt is so great that the wife-giving lineage remains in a position of superiority with a call on the services of the wife-takers even when the initial exchange has been completed.

Let us look again at myths II and III. Both contain references to the marriages that exist at the end of the stories they tell. In III the conqueror is married to the autochthon's daughter and in II the logic of the strategy used by the Korekore (pretending to accept defeat by yielding a daughter to the enemy) implies that the direction of wife-giving at the end of the myth will be the same as in III, that is: autochthons give to conquerors. Although this is logically sound, III is the only case in which it is explicitly stated and there is good reason for this. The reason is that what *is* explicitly stated, both in II and in III, is that apart from daughters the autochthons also give something quite different to their sons-in-law. They give water, either as rain or as river water. (Both sorts of water are expressed in Shona by the same word *mvura*).

As you can see from the text, the version of III that I have quoted was told specifically to explain why it is that the autochthons' *mhondoro* Musuma supplies the Korekore with rain. They supply them with rain because they were defeated by them, but the myth very carefully points out that it is as a father-in-law that Musuma gives this rain to Nyahuma, his son-in-law. In II the death of Chimombe, the temporary son-in-law, is the origin of the river on the banks of which the Korekore, the conquerors, and eventual permanent sons-in-law live. Although the myths present the relationship between their protagonists as affinal, it is not the exchange of biological fertility for labour or wealth that is stressed, it is the gift made by fathers-in-law to their conquering sons-in-law of natural fertility or rain.[15]

This relationship is explicit recognised by the mediums who operate the system. The terminology used by the medium of the autochthon Musuma to describe all the *mhondoro* he supplies with rain is affinal: 'I have many, many sons-in-law', he says, listing Nyahuma, Nyajore, Chikuyo and all the other Korekore ancestors. This terminology is reciprocated. The medium of the Korekore *mhondoro* Chivere describes Musuma as the father-in-law of himself and of Mutota, and so on.

Another example of how the relationships between the *mhondoro* of different lineages are expressed is that between the *mhondoro* Seremwe and Katuu on the one hand and Nyahuma on the other. Seremwe and Katuu who are father and son (see Figures 5.1 and 5.4) are members of the Eland clan (*Shava Mufokose*). There is no chiefly lineage in Dande that recognises them as ancestors. The only link they have to any other *mhondoro* is with Nyahuma, whose daughter Seremwe is said to have married. Although there are other *mhondoro* such as Chikuyo and Tombwe, who are geographically closer to them, Seremwe and Katuu refer requests made to them for rain to Nyahuma, just as Nyahuma refers requests to his father-in-law, Musuma. Once again it is wife's father who brings the rain (see Figure 5.4).

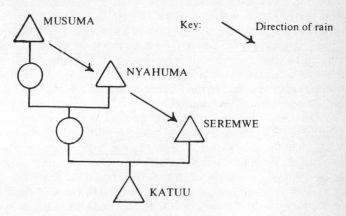

Figure 5.4   Affinal relations and the control of rain

Myths II to V therefore dramatise two separate but related acts of acquisition. The Korekore gained their new territories by defeating their original owners, the autochthons. They gained access to its fertility by marrying the autochthons' daughters. When the autochthon Nyamakwere (myth V) is attacked by his Korekore father-in-law, he says in astonishment: 'Why have you come to fight when I have married your daughter?' By the end of the myth, the autochthon is father-in-law and the new son-in-law has the land, daughter, biological fertility, natural fertility and all.

If we apply all this information to the myth of Mutota (myth I) the differences between myths II to V and the Mutota narrative become clear. Mutota neither gives nor takes a daughter. His son Nebedza neither kills an autochthon nor does he either give or take a wife to gain control of Dande. In myth I all the terms of myths II to V are reversed. Nebedza's own father dies and he has intercourse with his own sister.

Rain comes from wife's father say myths II to V, but if men marry their own sisters then own father *is* wife's father. Conqueror and autochthon are one and the same. The 'trick' Nebedza plays, more cunning than any dreamed up by the other conquering heroes, is to treat a member of his own lineage as if she were his wife. The result is that the Mutota lineage can supply itself with its own fertility, biological and natural. They need neither conquer strangers nor marry them to win the ownership of Dande. It belongs to them by right.

The meaning of the myth of Mutota, revealed when it is compared with myths II to V, is that the Mutota lineage has no need of affines. In some extraordinary sense they are both conquerors and autochthons. They can bring their own rain.

A little later I am going to turn to the rituals of possession and show how the symbolism they enact makes a very similar statement about the ability of the lineage to supply itself with everything it needs. But before I do that I want to press this analysis of the symbolism the myths contains a little further by describing an aspect of certain *mhondoro* that I have hardly touched on so far. This is that some *mhondoro* are regarded as women or as having a female aspect. These are Nehanda, Chigua, Chimombe and Musuma.[16]

These four *mhondoro* can be divided into two groups of two. In the first group are Nehanda and Chigua. These are the only two *mhondoro* who are unequivocally women. Nehanda is the daughter of Mutota, Chigua is the daughter of Nyamapfeka. The mediums who are possessed by them are always female. It is true that there are other female mediums in Dande as well but these are possessed by male *mhondoro*. Despite this I do not deal with Nehanda and Chigua in what follows because their 'femaleness' is purely functional. In order that the autochthonous lineages may be linked to the conquerors, women as marriage partners are called for. It is only these female ancestors who link lineages together that appear in the mythology or who possess mediums. All the other *mhondoro* are men. Chimombe and Musuma however, although they are men, have a female aspect. It is this female aspect of the male *mhondoro* that I want to explore.

Despite the fact that in myth II Chimombe is sufficiently characterised as a man to be seduced by the conqueror's daughter, the medium of the Korekore *mhondoro* Nyamapfeka regards him as his 'wife'. He refers to Chimombe both as *mukaranga* (ritual wife) and as *mukadzi* (wife/ woman). The feeling that there is a female aspect to Chimombe is shared by non-specialists as well, as this quotation from an interview I conducted in Nyamapfeka's spirit province shows:

> *Question*: Are Nyamapfeka and Chimombe related to each other?
> *Answer*: Yes. Chimombe is a *mukaranga*. If Nyamapfeka wants rain to fall nicely or if you plant a small field, if you can't get the food you need from that field, in the bush there is the fruit and the other things that you find, Nyamapfeka begs them from that woman because that woman has the power. That is the one who makes the rain fall very heavily.

According to the medium of Musuma, his *mhondoro* also has a female aspect. He refers to Musuma as a woman in some contexts as do other mediums and non-specialists as well.[17]

In order to emphasise this feature of the autochthons, I will compare the way the Korekore characterise their own *mhondoro* Chiwawa to their attitude to the autochthon Musuma. In some respects Chiwawa, one of the most important Korekore *mhondoro*, embodies the most extreme features of Korekore ancestors. I give his characteristics in order to make the contrast as clear as possible. I will have a good deal more to say about Chiwawa in Chapter 10.

Chiwawa is characterised by the Korekore as a recent *mhondoro*, as male, as a lineal descendant of Mutota and as a warrior. Musuma is characterised as the most distant *mhondoro*, as 'female', as an affine and as a rain-bringer.

Recent male lineal ancestors conquer. Distant female affinal ancestors bring rain. Now, let me remind you of the other place at which we found distant females producing fertility though in this case the females were not wives but mothers. These mothers were found at the source of the rivers in the Guruuswa myth. I presented you with an image of Guruuswa as the source of maternal fertility, the vagina, a wellspring surrounded by long grass from which the river and all life flows. Now let me reveal these wet and fertile mothers lurking in yet another place. This is at the very top, I might almost say at the 'source' of the Korekore royal genealogies.

Recitations of the genealogy of the Korekore royal ancestors always begin with Mutota. During the time that I lived in Dande I often tried to find out if anything about the time before Mutota were known. Eventually I was told as an item of the most arcane knowledge the name of Mutota's mother. She is called Nehate. Further back than that no one could go. Neither the name of Mutota's father nor of his mother's father was known. As the people of Dande put it, the *mhondoro* had never told

them. However, on one occasion at which I was present the medium of
Musuma, speaking in trance, described how at the time of the beginning
of the world Mutota's father had died. But he had not died as ordinary
people die. He had been drowned in a huge pool.

The history of the senior ancestor of the Chisunga chieftaincy
contains a strikingly similar sequence (see Figure 5.1, above).
Nyamapfeka did not come from Guruuswa. His birth was magical.
He remained in his mother's womb for three years. When he emerged he
could do magic (*mapipi*), he was dressed in skins, he carried a bow and
arrow and he immediately took his place as chief of his people. His
mother's name is Biri, a name that recurs in other genealogies as a
remote female ancestor. The name of Nyamapfeka's father is not
known and his magical birth suggests that he had none. However, in
certain contexts the Nyamapfeka lineage is linked to the Mutota lineage
as a junior branch. When this is done, it is said that the father of Biri is
Nyajore, a son of Mutota who is regarded by Nyamapfeka's descendants
as one of the three great rain-makers (the other two are Musuma and
Chimombe). The structure at the very top, almost unknowable edge of
both of these Korekore royal genealogies contains first a female element
and then the idea of water or of rain. This is illustrated in Figure 5.5.

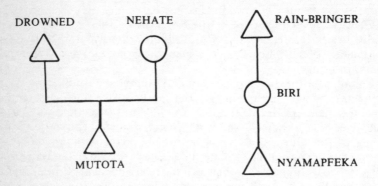

Figure 5.5   The source of royal lineages

Whether the imagery is natural/geographic and we look for the
source of life at the source of a river, or whether it is lineal/historical
and we look for the origin of life at the source of a genealogy, in both
cases we find a wet, water-related mother. And, as my analysis of the
myths has shown, this distant own-lineage source of fertility is
contrasted to the fertility that is needed in the place where people
actually live which is supplied to them by their affines. In the Guruuswa

myths especially, the contrast is very clearly drawn. The fertility that comes from affines comes in the form of rain.

Let me string all this imagery into one paragraph and then move on. Affinal lineages supply water in the form of rain and their representatives, such as Chimombe and Musuma, are regarded as wives by the Korekore. This sort of fertility comes unexpectedly, from some other place, is hard to control and will stop and start as it pleases unless certain measures (the annual rain-bringing rituals) are taken to control it. Mothers are also a source of fertility but this fertility always runs in the same river beds. It can be relied on to help you out when affinal fertility, rain, has let you down. Wives come and go but mother is always there. Ultimately, of course, rivers will run dry without the rain, but no one would deny that in the not-so-distant past our mothers were our father's wives.[18]

The rituals

The first thing to say about the rituals of possession by *mhondoro* is that whenever they take place, the colour red is absolutely forbidden. No one wearing any shade of red – scarlets, crimsons, even darker shades of pink– may attend. If the *mhondoro* sees this colour the medium will die.

The second thing to say about these rituals is that they only take place on nights when the moon is in the sky. On nights when the sky is dark, the *mhondoro* are unable to enter their mediums and speak to their descendants. The most important possession rituals take place only at full moon. Although experts deny that a full moon is absolutely necessary, during the time that I lived in Dande all the important possession rituals were held at full moon as were many low-level *mudzimu* possessions as well. None were held when there was no moon at all. Rituals at which possession does not occur may be held whether the moon is visible or not, at any convenient time.

The phases of the moon regulate another sphere of activity as well, day-to-day agricultural work in the fields. In the weekly and monthly cycles, certain rest days are observed. These are known as *zvisi* (sing. *chisi*). On these days no agricultural work or hunting may be done though the domestic work of cooking, fetching of water and fuel, tending of children and so on may continue. In the weekly cycle two *zvisi* are observed. Which days these are varies from area to area whereas the two rest days in the monthly cycle are the same everywhere. The first, *chiropa*, is the day after the non-appearance of the moon in the sky. *Rusere*, the second day following this, is indicated by the reappearance of the moon. The name means simply 'eighth' and it is probable that it derives from one of the rest days observed in the calendar of the Mwene Mutapa state. Not everyone observes *rusere*. Pressure of work in the fields may cause some to treat it as an ordinary work day. But *chiropa* is universally observed.

The typical activity of a rest day is to gather somewhere in the village and drink beer. This may be beer brewed for sale or, if a rest day has been chosen to offer beer to an ancestor, the beer will be free. Some people interpret the work prohibitions to refer only to work on their own fields. They claim that co-operative work parties may be held on these days and treat *zvisi* as an opportunity to earn money by working on the fields of those farmers who employ wage labour. Under ordinary weather conditions this argument is accepted and it is in these terms that people explain how their relatives employed in the towns escape punishment for working when they should be at rest. But unusually frequent thunderstorms or destructively heavy rains may be blamed on an unwillingness to treat the rest days seriously. In this strict inter-pretation, all agricultural work is forbidden and only domestic labour is allowed.

If male work is forbidden when there is no moon in the sky and *mhondoro* do not possess their mediums at the same time and for the same reasons, it seems possible that possession is in a sense thought of as male work. Let us follow this possibility and see if it leads us anywhere worth getting to.

The widest definition of a *chisi* is a day on which no work is done because someone has died. On this day villagers gather at the home of the dead person and assist with the burying of the body. The weekly *chisi* rest days are said to commemorate the death of particular *mhondoro*. It is believed that if people work on these days the *mhondoro* whose anniversary it is will strike them down with lightning. The monthly *chisi* is also associated with death. On *chiropa*, the day after the moon has vanished from the sky, the moon is said to be dead (*mwedzi wafa*). *Chiropa* is the rest day following the death of the moon.

The rest days therefore are days associated with death on which no male work, including possession, can take place. But on the anniversaries of these highly significant deaths (the deaths of the *mhondoro*, the chiefs of the past, the death of the moon) one kind of work, women's work may go ahead as usual. Does this mean that men's work is in some sense opposed to death, on a death-day it must cease, whereas women's work is somehow associated with death, so closely associated in fact that on a death-day this work alone may continue? We need to look a little more closely at what women's work, in the widest implications of this phrase, actually is. At the same time I will deal with the first set of ritual prohibitions observed by *mhondoro* mediums as promised at the end of Chapter 4.

Of all the ritual prohibitions the *mhondoro* mediums are subject to, the most powerful is the avoidance of blood (*ropa*). Mediums believe that if they see blood they will die. For example, it is said that during the war the medium of the *mhondoro* Chingoo died when he saw the blood of a man who had been shot. The medium himself suffered no violence at all but 'the one who was with him was the one who was shot. When Chingoo saw the blood, first he vomited blood and then he just died.'[19] Apart from the blood of a dead body, the other type of blood explicitly avoided by the mediums is the blood of menstruation and childbirth. A *mhondoro* medium may not eat food cooked by a woman during the period of her menstruation or for some time after she has given birth – to be exact until her child has cut its teeth. These teeth that announce that a woman and her child are no longer dangerous to a *mhondoro* medium are the second set to appear in this book. The first set were the ones that fall out of the mouth of people who eat their own clan animal. Unlikely as it may seem, a brief account of the gaining and losing of teeth will illustrate how the worlds of women's work and of men's work are symbolically differentiated.

When the punishment of losing your teeth for eating your own clan animal was first mentioned in Chapter 2, it may have seemed totally arbitrary. Why isn't it hair that falls out? Or why isn't the person who commits this indiscretion punished with blindness or deafness? You will begin to see the logic of the punishment of tooth loss when I tell you that the process of human ageing is imagined by the Shona as a process of drying out. At birth a child is thought of as thoroughly wet. The first stage of a child's development is marked by the closing of the fontanelle, the soft-skinned gap in the centre of a baby's skull. Until this happens the child is thought to be especially susceptible to the evil thoughts of witches. Medicines are rubbed on the scalp and protective charms strung round the waist until the fontanelle has closed and the head is hard. It is no coincidence that the word for fontanelle in Shona, *dziva*, is also the word used for a pool of water. When the skull is complete and hard, the child has become just a little more dry.

Burial practices make these conceptions especially clear. Young children who die before their teeth have emerged must be buried in the wet soil on the banks of a river. If they are buried in dry soil this will cause a drought. Adults, by contrast, must be buried in dry soil. Once, during the wet season of 1981, I helped a burial party to prepare a grave. Each time the hole reached below three or four feet water trickled in from the sides and the site was rejected. If an adult is buried in wet soil, the spirit will become a dangerous *ngozi* rather than a kindly *mudzimu* and this must be prevented at any cost.

The fullest demonstration of how age and the authority of the lineage are associated with dryness and bones occurs at the burial of a chief. At the death of this most senior member of a lineage and a future *mhondoro* the body is not buried immediately as happens with ordinary people. It is laid out on a platform either in a hut or an enclosed grave, with pots placed beneath to collect the bodily fluids as they emerge. Only when all the wetness of life has drained away and nothing but hard, dry bones remain may the head of the royal lineage be placed in the earth with his ancestors.

Young toothless children, remote from the ancestors and lacking all authority are wet, soft and bloody. The older people get, the closer to the ancestors and the more authoritative they become. They are dryer, harder and bonier. Both women and men gradually acquire dryness as they progress through life. But women periodically revert to utter wetness. It is only when they lose the ability to produce children, when they are least like women and most like men, that they have really begun to dry out. So it is that the only women who play an individual role in the rituals of possession by a *mhondoro*, the women who brew the beer, must be post-menopausal, thoroughly brittle and dry.

When a child gains its teeth, this is evidence that it has begun to move away from the world of its mother and of maternal blood. It has begun to be incorporated into the dry, male world of the lineage. At this point a *mhondoro* medium may come into contact with it or its mother without harm. How are we to relate these teeth to the teeth lost by eating one's clan animal? Although any part of the clan animal is dangerous, it is especially the heart and the liver that are avoided. The association of the heart with blood needs no comment. The Korekore use two words for liver. The first is *chitaka* which is of no consequence here, but the second is *chiropa* which may be translated as 'unpleasant thing of blood'. If you eat the heart or the liver of your own clan animal it is as if you are ingesting your own blood. If you should be so foolish or wicked as to do this, it is as if you have returned to a state similar to that in which you were at birth, polluted by the blood of your mother which is your own blood. You return to the state you were in before you acquired the male characteristics of dryness and hardness, the state before you had any teeth at all. As a consequence your teeth fall out.[20]

And that is what the losing of teeth has to do with women's work. Women's work is thought of as the reproduction of human life by biological means with all the wetness, softness and blood that that entails. Men's work, by contrast, is the reproduction of human life through the agency of the mediums, the recreation of the lives of the senior lineage ancestors by means of the rituals of possession.

This broad generalisation can be justified by a wealth of detail of which I give a small selection here. In discussing the constituent elements of the human body, men argue (and as far as I could determine women agree) that the woman is no more than a container within which the substance 'planted' by men is grown. The only contribution women make to the human body is blood. The burial of a young toothless child is attended only by women whereas the burials of adults are organised by men with women playing a very insignificant part indeed as they do in everything to do with the ancestors, the past or the authority of the lineage. Of all the sixty or so *mhondoro* mediums with whom I came into contact or heard about between 1980 and 1982 only three were women. At possession rituals all the important and individualised actions were performed by men and observed by a crowd of de-individualised women. Their exclusion from participation is justified on the grounds of their 'ignorance'. They participate only as singers and as dancers but never individually, only as members of a group, never creatively, always repeating what has been repeated time after time in the past. When the *mhondoro* speaks, the men consult and banter with him, crowding round his medium at the edge of his mat. The women sit quietly in a group at a distance and observe. What they observe is men creating life through death.

When the *mhondoro* possess their mediums, biological life is explicitly rejected. It is rejected symbolically by the abhorrence of the colour red which represents blood and empirically by the exclusion of women from active participation in the rituals. The presence of women at the rituals is however obligatory. If the women stay at home, the statement that they are excluded from the especially interesting and important parts of social life cannot be made.[21]

But the avoidance by *mhondoro* mediums of people in the wet, soft condition is only one aspect of their avoidance of the biological processes of human life. They may have nothing to do with the creation of life but they may have as little to do with the ending of it. It is dangerous for mediums to see human corpses. They may not attend funerals. It is said of one medium that he may not even hear the sound of a rifle-shot that kills an animal. All these avoidances taken together make quite plain that biological life and biological death are outside and opposed to the domain of the *mhondoro*. They must be avoided by the mediums on pain of their own deaths.

The days of rest, the *zvisi*, are days on which men's work ceases and only women's work may be done. The most important of these rest days is *chiropa*. *Chiropa*, as I have said, is a word used to mean liver but the core meaning applies to this day of women's work as well as to the organ in which the body's blood is believed to accumulate. The day after the death of the moon is an 'unpleasant bloody thing'.

To string all this imagery together: on *chiropa* the moon is dead. It is the day of blood when the earth may not be cut into with a hoe nor may any other men's work such as hunting be done. Only women's work in the house or the gathering of wild plants is allowed. On *chiropa* there are no *mhondoro*, no spirits, none of the life after death, the re-emergence of the ancestors of the lineage made possible by the mediums and the men. There is only biological life, the life of the menstrual blood of wives, that is to say the life made possible by affines. On *chiropa* the ancestors of one's own lineage do no work. They are dead and the mediums cannot restore them to life, for *chiropa* is a day polluted by affinal blood.[22]

A little later, I will show how the gender symbolism activated by the rituals of possession relates to the symbolism of the myth of Mutota's journey from Guruuswa. But before I do that I want to say a little more about another set of symbols attached to these rituals.

When there is no moon in the sky the night is said to be either *usiku dema* meaning simply 'the night is dark or black', or *usiku hwakasviba*, which also implies darkness but in the sense of dirty or mucky. The notion of darkness is closely associated with three of the sources of authority which I have returned to time and again. In the past, the costume of chiefs was two black cloths. The medium indicates the member of the royal lineage he has chosen to be chief by placing a black cloth on his shoulders. A black cloth is placed on the body of a chief after he has died. And blackness or darkness is also intimately associated with rain and the bringing of rain, the ultimate expression of lineage authority. Mediums, who themselves wear black, are believed to be able to make rain appear by hanging out black cloths. The medium of Musuma, the most important rain-bringing *mhondoro*, completely covers his body in black cloth when he becomes possessed.

The association of rain with darkness is emphasised by the contrasting association of lightness or whiteness with lack of rain. This can be seen at the rituals of the *mhondoro* mediums which have nothing to do with rain (such as the protecting of the seeds described on pp. 46–8). At these times white cloths replace the mediums' customary black. Certain mediums are reported to hang out white cloths if they wish to stop the rain falling and so on.[23]

The word for whiteness or brightness (or cleanliness) is *chena*. But this is not the term that is used to refer to the moon when it is visible in the sky. The term used is *kupenya*. This intriguing word can be used as a noun to mean 'lightning', or as a verb meaning 'to be alive'. It is in fact derived from the noun *upenyu*, a common word meaning 'life'. Modern means of creating light are not described as *kupenya*. The light of a torch or of a motor car are expressed by the neologism *kushina*. The essence of the idea of *kupenya* is the appearance of light surrounded by darkness, such as lightning or the moon. To glow like the moon in the sky, to flash like lightning is to be alive. But what sort of life is this?

Black cloth worn by the *mhondoro* mediums represents the authority of the ancestors who in death produce rain. But white cloth is also an acceptable gift to a *mhondoro* medium. Indeed the costume of the *mhondoro* is constructed entirely out of black and white. The black cloths of the mediums are often trimmed with white and the multiple strings of beads that they wear may be black or white but never any other colour. In particular they may never be red.[24]

The ancestors control both life and death, both darkness and light. This is most clearly expressed when a person attempts to achieve possession for the first time. The special cloth called a *hungwe* that is placed over the head of the aspirant medium is made by stitching together two equal lengths of cloth. The one is black, the other white. Again darkness and light, death and life are brought together in opposition to the biological life achieved by being born of woman which is symbolised by the colour red. (See Plate 4, between pp. 118–19.)

This black-and-white life is the life of the ancestors achieved after death and controlled by men. And everything about this sort of life demonstrates that it is better than the life created by women out of blood. Ancestors are wiser and more powerful than people. They can cure sickness, they know everything that has happened in the past and that will happen in the future. They bring the rain and protect people against witches. And unlike people they live forever. Theirs is an authority and a power without end. The life of the ancestors is a dazzling luminosity in the sky. Although for some brief periods each month the *mhondoro* are unable to come alive to their descendants, this serves only to emphasise their triumph over death, for their absence is brief. The *mhondoro* always return.

For the Korekore, then, there are two kinds of life. There is the biological blood-drenched life associated with women as affines, and there is the social and intellectual life-in-death of the *mhondoro* controlled by men. Chiefs become *mhondoro* by passing from life into death and then back into life again. Of course, in reality it is the chiefs who are alive and the *mhondoro* who are dead but from the perspective of the perfect, permanent and unchanging *mhondoro*, human life is indistinguishable from human death.

Of the two kinds of life, the first is associated with affinity, the second with descent. The first is symbolised by blood, the second by rain. Of all substances blood is the most dangerous to the *mhondoro*. If blood falls on the ground drought follows. Blood is, as it were, anti-rain. By their ability to control the rain the *mhondoro*, the ancestors of the lineage, demonstrate that the only kind of fertility that is worth having is in their gift. As we pass from life to death to life again, we pass from corporeality to incorporeality, from ignorance to knowledge and from the world of blood to the world of rain, from the world of affinity to the world of descent, from a temporary and insubstantial world to a world that can never change and never end.

The central symbol of this transition from life into death into life is the moon. Among the Korekore, as in many other societies, the menstrual cycle is very closely associated with the cycles of the moon. This is explicitly recognised by the women. The phrase used to express the idea of menstruation is *kuenda kumwedzi*, to go to the moon. To fail to menstruate is *kudarika mwedzi*, to jump over the moon. It is no coincidence that precisely the same symbol is central to the expression of male, ancestral fertility. It is as if the symbolism of biological reproduction, in reality the most significant source of fertility and creativity, has been stolen by men to lend lustre to their own cheap-jack construction of cloth, beads, sticks and beer.

Without the moon the *mhondoro* cannot appear. Though it is not always in the sky it always returns. One of the songs sung frequently at funerals goes:

aenda-enda, achadzoka   (s) he has gone, (s) he will return
aenda-enda, achadzoka

The same sentence is repeated over and over again. Like the moon, we die and we come back to life and it is the creation of this second life, the life of the *mhondoro*, of the fertility of the earth, of rain and of the past that is achieved by men through the rituals of possession.

How the mhondoro *bring the rain*

There are many different ways in which a claim to own an area of land can be made. In some contexts the possession of title deeds which can be bought and sold is considered adequate. In other contexts the act of clearing the land or of using it may establish that one group rather than another has the right of ownership. Amongst the Shona the right of ownership in land is demonstrated and proved by the ability of a particular set of ancestors to control its fertility. The people whose ancestors bring the rain own the land.

This does not mean that in order to hold onto their backyards and fields every woman or man has to provide evidence that their ancestors sent the rain that made their maize or pumpkins grow. Ordinary people have the right to use the land they occupy because it was allocated to them or to their lineage by the chief. Up until very recently it was taken for granted that only a royal lineage can actually own land. The question 'who owns the land?' has always meant which royal lineage owns the land and the answer was 'the royal lineage whose ancestors bring the rain'. Or rather, this was part of the answer. As we have seen, each of the Korekore royal ancestors of Dande is responsible for bringing rain to his own spirit province. At the same time it is believed that only the most senior Korekore ancestor, Mutota, can bring the rain. And yet again it is believed that only the autochthon, Musuma, has this power. My analysis of the symbolism of Mutota's journey from Guruuswa and of the possession rituals puts us in a position where we can see what this contradiction means and how it is resolved.

To start with the possession ritual: the performance of this ritual implies that each royal lineage is able to produce its own rain with no help from wives or other affines. The biological reproduction of human life is symbolically associated with women and the statement is made that this sort of creativity is infinitely less important than the creativity of men through whose actions, the rituals of possession, the life of the ancestors is perpetuated. The evidence of the power of these ancestors is that they make the rain fall. When it falls this demonstrates that the royal lineage whose ancestors sent it owns the land that is watered by it. The possession rituals of *mhondoro* mediums are in a very important sense a claim by a royal lineage to be authochthons. They say: we own the land, we bring the rain.

Myths I to V, as I have shown, contain two opposed implications. Myths II to V make the claim that the Korekore own the land by right of conquest but they are content to leave ultimate control of the land and the power to bring rain in the hands of the autochthons Musuma, Chimombe and so on. The Mutota myth is more ambitious and claims ownership of Dande by right of conquest *and* by right of autochthonous rain-bringing power as well. The Mutota myth says in effect: we Korekore owe nothing to anybody, especially not to our affines, we are our own affines and everyone else owes their rain to us. The Mutota myth and the possession rituals therefore 'say' precisely the same thing while myths II to V 'say' the opposite. This contradiction is consistent with the information I collected about Nehanda and Mutota's rain-bringing powers. In some contexts they were said to bring rain and in others it was said that they do not. What we need to do now is define just what these contexts are.

Let me remind you that when the medium of the *mhondoro* of a spirit province receives requests for rain he passes the request and a portion of the gift up the hierarchy of Korekore ancestors until it reaches the senior *mhondoro*, either Mutota or Nyamapfeka. This senior ancestor will then refer the request to the senior local autochthonous *mhondoro* (Musuma in the case of Mutota; Musuma, Chimombe or Nyajore in the case of Nyamapfeka). Only those who live within the spirit province of an autochthon send their requests for rain directly to him.

This ritual combines both conceptions of the origin of rain. The passing of the requests for rain up the hierarchy of ancestors establishes the integrity of the Korekore lineage, treating each *mhondoro* as if he were an autochthon, an owner of the land. This is continued until the rain-bringing powers of the complete set of ancestors have been proclaimed and exercised. Only when this is accomplished and the desire of the Korekore to lay absolute claim to Dande has been taken as far as it will go is a concession made to the original owners of the land and offerings are made to them.

What this analysis makes clear is that these rituals are part of a political process, specifically a process of the centralisation of political and religious authority. Myths II to V represent separate political traditions, with each Korekore ancestor independently recognising the ultimate authority of the autochthons. The Mutota myth insists that the Korekore are the autochthons. The ritual of passing offerings up the genealogy links all the Korekore ancestors and their descendants into one religious community. When the integrity of the Korekore as a whole has been affirmed, when the offerings have reached the senior medium, then, having established his control over the Korekore, he may concede that ultimate authority belongs to the autochthons and make an offering to Musuma, Chimombe or whoever. But he may not. He may decide to make a statement of his own absolute authority and keep the offering for himself. It is precisely at the point where the offerings are transferred from one lineage to another that a stage is cleared on which current political manoeuverings are acted out. For example, throughout the 1950s and possibly for many years before, the medium of Mutota claimed that he had no need to make offerings to the autochthon Musuma because he himself was able to bring the rain. During my time in Dande, some six years after the death of this medium, the need to make offerings to Musuma was acknowledged by the medium of every Korekore *mhondoro* to whom I put this question.

Myth and ritual – the meaning of the journey from Guruuswa

My intention in this chapter has been to unpack the ideas of autochthony and conquest, of rain-making and of political authority. I have shown that the possession rituals are a source of ideological energy. They make an unequivocal statement. By contrast with women who give life to people, men give life to the *mhondoro* who bring the rain which confirms the ownership of the land by the *mhondoro's* descendants, the chiefs. The energy of this ritual can be used to charge a variety of different political systems. It provides the energy of the rain-making rituals of the autochthons as well as of those of the conquerors and it fires the claims that the royal lineages make to hold political power over the land. In Chapter 9, I will show that it fired the claims of the ZANLA guerrillas to be 'owners' of the land or autochthons in opposition to the 'conquering' white Rhodesians. It is in order to be able to explain the ritual prohibitions by which the guerrillas explained this opposition that the myths and rituals of Dande have been analysed at such length. However, before putting this analysis to one side, there are a few more questions that it would be useful to ask.

The first is this: Can the existence of the two sets of myths (I, and II to V), as well as the double origin of fertility and rain, be accounted for historically? The small amount of reliable evidence that we have allows a few suggestions to be made.

D. N. Beach has argued that the tradition of the journey from Guruuswa represented in the myth as a single journey with a single leader should be interpreted as a series of migrations by a number of separate lineages over some hundreds of years. If we accept this view it opens up the possibility that each of the *mhondoro* of the Korekore royal genealogies was the head of a lineage that arrived in the Zambezi Valley (or the north of the Plateau) and conquered a territory by driving out and/or absorbing its previous occupants. But when the Korekore lineage is considered as a whole (myth I) the peculiar relationships *between* the *mhondoro* as well as the practice of referring requests for rain up the lineage presents a problem. What historical reality can this correspond to?[25]

I have already suggested that the Mutota myth represents and expresses a concentration of political power, a drawing together of long-established individual lineages and traditions. Perhaps it is not dodging too many thorny questions to suggest that whereas II to V and the localised rain-makings are the legitimising myths and rituals of small-scale political units, myth I and the linking of all the rain-makings into a great chain of ritual interdependence are the legitimising apparatus of a state. The state in question is the semi-independent province of Dande, for centuries an integral part and eventually the last remnant of the kingdom of Mwene Mutapa.

At a time of the centralisation of a number of lineages to form a state or a state-like political unit, myth I will have dominance over myths II to V. Then Mutota will be presented as the ultimate source of the fertility of the land; conqueror and autochthon in one. At times (or in an area, or in a context) when the centralised authority is less strong, myths II to V and others similar to these will regain their significance and offerings will be made to the local autochthons for rain.

Let me make one more historical conjecture. The title by which the ruler of the Mutapa state was known has come down to us from Portuguese and other documents in a number of forms: Mwene Mutapa, Monomotapa, Munhumutapa and so on. Its meaning has been the subject of much debate. W. G. L. Randles suggests 'child of the country' (from *mwana* = child and *mutapwa* = captive). Donald Abraham offers 'master pillager' though he does not provide us with an explanation. Bhila prefers 'the person who explores'. However if we chose the form Mwene Mutapa, which is the one most commonly recorded, and translate *mutapa* not as Bhila does to mean 'explorer' but as 'one who seizes' or 'captor' as the *Standard Shona Dictionary* suggests, and if we give *mwene* its uncontested meaning of 'owner' then the meaning that emerges by putting the two words together contains precisely the same duality of political and ritual authority that my analysis attributed to Mutota and the political process he represents. He is owner/captor of the land whose fertility he supplies. He is autochthon and conqueror in one. No greater power can be claimed by a political or military leader than that he can conquer a territory and then himself become the source of the fertility on which that territory depends.[26]

This immediately raises a new problem. If the story of Mutota's journey from Guruuswa is a representation in mythic terms of the forging of a number of Korekore lineages into a state, then who is Mutota? Was he the leader of one of the lineages that settled in Dande? If so why is *he* regarded as senior ancestor rather than Chivere or Nyahuma or any of the other Korekore *mhondoro*?

It is important always to remember that there are traditions outside Dande that name Mutota as ancestor and yet others that claim Nebedza as their first chief. The tradition I am concerned with, myth I, is told by people *who live in Dande* as they contemplate and argue about who they are and where they come from. Before answering the questions I have raised, I would like you to think (or turn) back to the description of the geographical features of Dande that I gave in Chapter 2: the towering Escarpment, the flat plain leading down to the river, and standing in the Valley looking upwards, the streaming banks of clouds that flow over the cool and fertile Plateau and build up on the edge of the Escarpment before they fall into the hot, dry Valley below bringing rain.

The word *mutota* means 'the wet one' or 'he who became wet in the rain'. Mutota's son Nebedza is, as I have said, frequently referred to as Matope or as Matope Nebedza. *Matope* is the plural of the word *dope* which means mud. *Dope* is not *daga*, the firm moist mud used for building houses. It is the wet, sloppy mud that appears after rain and makes the paths impassable. From the point of view of Dande, the rain pours down onto the mountain top and the mud flows down the mountain side just as in myth I Mutota stood on the edge of the Escarpment looking out over Dande and his son Matope climbed down into the Valley. Matope's son is Nyahuma. This name does not continue the sequence from rain and water to mud. Like Nebedza which means 'owner of Bedza', a territory in Dande, Nyahuma is the name of a man.[27]

I can at last draw together all the strands of my argument and give a full account of Mutota's journey from Guruuswa.

Guruuswa, the starting point of the journey, is the origin of all life, the source of the rivers on which the subsistence of the Korekore in Dande depends. It is female, it is the vagina, it is the source of biological life within the lineage. It is the place where the notions of descent and of female fertility are combined to form the notion of maternal fertility or, more simply, 'mother'. It is the place of birth. It is wet. (The presence of the Zambezi River in the Valley is of no use to the Korekore who live miles away from it. The Valley soils are much drier and less fertile than those on the Plateau.) It is the origin also of social life, the place where the ancestors come from.

The Valley, the end of the journey, is the place of affines, of wives. It is dominated by wives' fathers who combine the principles of masculinity and affinity. It is hot and dry and it is the place where the salt comes from, for humans eat salt and the Valley is the place not of ancestors but of people, the descendants of Mutota, the Korekore.

The contrast between the Valley and the Plateau is very fully worked out in the myth. In Dande salt is categorised as 'hot' whereas the ancestors are 'cool' like the rain that they bring. In general everything to do with life and being alive (sex, sickness, dying) is 'hot'. During the burial ceremony water is poured over the newly dead person so that she or he can cool down and become an ancestor. So 'hot' salt is taken by Nyakatonje from the hot land of 'hot' living people up to the cool Plateau where the 'cool' ancestors live. There are few or no cattle in Dande because of tsetse fly whereas cattle thrive on the Plateau. The very close association between ancestors and cattle has been described by numerous writers for many Southern African societies including the Shona. It is not made explicit in the myth but it is reasonable to assume that the meat eaten by Mutota and salted by Nyakatonje in Guruuswa is the flesh of a cow, the beasts of the ancestors which live on the Plateau but not in the Valley below.[28]

The journey from Guruuswa is a journey from mother to wife but it is also a journey from birth to manhood. At birth we are wet, as we age we dry. Mutota in Guruuswa and on the edge of the Plateau is pure wetness. His son Matope is mud, a combination of water and dry sand which crosses the barrier of the Escarpment and flows down into the Valley. On the way down, the mud dries out entirely and becomes Nebedza, owner of Bedza, a dry adult male who owns and lives on dry sand and who is, most significantly, the first chief.

In Guruuswa, the home of the ancestors (myth I) there are rivers and rain and no affinity. But in the Valley (myths II to V) away from their original home, Korekore must live among affines. And here affinity is essential for rain. The central problem of life in the Valley is drought. For the Korekore this is the consequence of the fact that they no longer live in their ancestral home. If they were the owners of their present home, they would be able to make the rain fall.

Mutota never enters the Valley. He remains unpolluted by affinity and is forever fertile, an unceasing source of rain. But his fertility is useless. His descendants live in the Valley, not on the Escarpment or the Plateau where his rain falls. As the rivers which flow from Guruuswa containing the waters of maternity reach the edge of the Escarpment they are added to and strengthened by the rains of the father Mutota. But the water of rivers is not enough. People also need rain on their fields. It is this crucial problem of the Korekore, how to get access to rain in a strange land, how to gain control of their own rain, how to make it leave the Escarpment and move into the Valley and fall on their fields that the myth of Mutota attempts to resolve.

Between pure lineage fertility in Guruuswa and pure affinal fertility in Dande a compromise is reached. This compromise is the incestuous fertility that is created at the mid-point between the two regions, on the edge of the Escarpment. By the marriage of Nehanda to Nebedza, the pollution of affinity is banished, conqueror becomes autochthon, the Korekore lay claim to the ownership of Dande and the fertility of Mutota enters the Valley in triumph (see Figure 5.6).[29]

But for Mutota himself the journey has ended in failure. This failure can help us to resolve a few of the elements in the myth I have not yet accounted for. You will remember that the reason that Mutota cannot enter the Valley is that Nyakatonje fails to allow him enough time to do

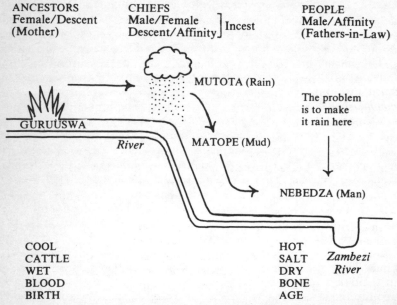

ANCESTORS	CHIEFS		PEOPLE
Female/Descent	Male/Female	Incest	Male/Affinity
(Mother)	Descent/Affinity		(Fathers-in-Law)

MUTOTA (Rain)

GURUUSWA

The problem is to make it rain here

River

MATOPE (Mud)

NEBEDZA (Man)

COOL	HOT	
CATTLE	SALT	*Zambezi*
WET	DRY	*River*
BLOOD	BONE	
BIRTH	AGE	

Figure 5.6   The journey from Guruuswa to Dande : 2

his magic (*kuita mapipi*) before they arrive at the Escarpment. What is this magic? Mutota never does it so we never find out. But we have two other references to *mapipi* or magic in the Dande traditions. The first is the magic performed by the autochthons Nyamakwere and Nyamazunzu when they fight off their Korekore adversaries by raising fogs and mists which are, of course, the sign of the autochthon, water, floating in the air.

The other doer of magic is a Korekore. This is Nyamapfeka who did not come from Guruuswa but was born after three years in the womb and emerged dressed in furs, armed with bow and arrow and was greeted as chief by his people. It seems that the point being made here is that founders of lineages are magical people. They are not born as the result of ordinary biological process. They are complete in themselves and in some manner powerful and strange. Mutota would have been just such a doer of magic but he fails to found his own lineage and so his magic is redundant and is never performed. It is Nebedza who founds the lineage and who becomes the first chief.[30]

But even now we have not reached the last level of meaning that the Guruuswa myth contains. I have devoted a great deal of space to showing that Mutota's journey from Guruuswa and the rituals of possession by *mhondoro* make the same statement about the ability of the lineage ancestors to bring rain to the land. But we can go one stage further than that. Not only do the myth and the ritual say the same thing but the myth is built up out of precisely the same elements as the ritual is. Indeed the myth virtually contains a description of how the possession ritual is done.

The messenger who travels from Dande to fetch Mutota from Guruuswa is Nyakatonje, whose name means assistant or *mutapi* of a spirit medium. He travels to Guruuswa with salt as a gift for the *mhondoro* and guides him back as far as the Escarpment. But Mutota can go no further. For the last time, why?

Guruuswa is the world of the ancestors. Dande is the world of men. Mutota cannot enter into Dande any further than *mhondoro* can *by themselves* enter into the lives of men. They cannot enter directly into men's lives because they have no bodies. Their knowledge, their power over rain is a product of their incorporeality but, paradoxically, without a body, without even a voice to make their will known, their knowledge and power are useless. At the Escarpment, the boundary between life and death, Mutota's journey comes to a stop.

But the *mhondoro* do acquire bodies. They acquire bodies of two kinds. They acquire the bodies of their descendants, the chiefs, who rule in their name the lands they ruled 'when they were alive' and they acquire the bodies of their mediums. As with *mhondoro* in the rituals of possession, so with Mutota in the mythology. Mutota when alive can go no further than the Escarpment. His son Nebedza continues the journey down into the Valley to become the first chief of the Korekore. But by means of their second kind of body, that of their mediums, the *mhondoro* are themselves able to enter the Valley and take part in the lives of their descendants.

Every time the possession rituals of the *mhondoro* mediums are performed, the *mutapi* travels back to the beginning of the world and fetches the ancestral spirit from its home in Guruuswa. At the Escarpment, the boundary between life and death, the original home and the new, the medium allows his body to be filled up with the ancestor of the present chiefs. Every time this ritual is performed, the right of the Korekore to live in Dande and their claim to be able to provide their own rain are asserted once again (see Figure 5.7).[31]

One final point. Nyakatonje carried the salt to Guruuswa. Ancestors never eat salt. Men, on the other hand, must eat salt to live. Mutota tries it, likes it and sets out for Dande to find more. The ingestion of salt by the *mhondoro* marks the beginning of his journey from the world of the spirit to the world of men. But he can never set foot in Dande. His power derives from his existence outside the social world. (He is not a *mudzimu* who is brought home to the village by the performance of a ritual, but a *mhondoro*, a lion whose home is the bush.) He can only participate in the lives of his descendants through the polluted bodies of the medium and the chief.

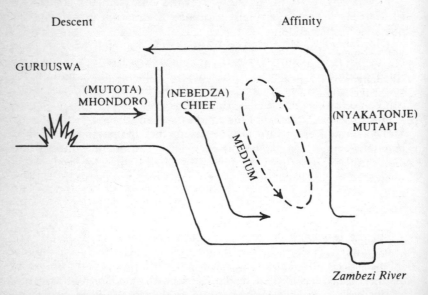

Figure 5.7   The journey from Guruuswa to Dande : 3

106

In the Guruuswa myth, Nyakatonje smacks his lips over the salted meat to persuade Mutota to try it just as, in the ritual, the *mutapi* claps his hands and entices the *mhondoro*, beseeching him to leave the world of the dead and return to the world of the living. By eating salt Mutota becomes a little more like a man. But he cannot become entirely a man. To do so would be to lose his purity, his rain-bringing power, which confers on his descendants the ownership of the Valley of affines, the country of blood.

NOTES

1 For the 1906 reference see File N 1/1/6 in National Archives, Harare, Zimbabwe.
2 Figure 5.1 was compiled using all the kin ties of which I was told by the *mhondoro*, by their mediums and by their assistants. Only the most senior of the mediums might be able to produce a similar diagram should he choose to do so. Most people know only those fragments which hold importance for the part of Dande where they live. However in compiling this total family tree, very few inconsistencies arose. In the cases where there were alternative linkings, I have given what I think is the majority view. No one spirit or medium ever linked *all* these ancestors together precisely in this way, though stretches were supplied to me numerous times by a variety of experts. By consulting this figure the *mhondoro* that are discussed in the chapters that follow can be placed in relation to all the rest.
3 Garbett's major work on Mutota is Garbett (1977).
4 A common description of Musuma given in Dande is that he is *yekudara*, meaning 'of the very old times' whereas the senior Tande *mhondoro* Bangomwe is thought to have lived 'more recently' at the time of the arrival of the Korekore. The reason that Bangomwe is placed at a specific time whereas Musuma is not is probably that Bangomwe has descendants living within Dande (the Matsiwo chieftaincy) whereas Musuma has none. Apart from the myths that involve Musuma, few people are able to say more about him than that he comes from Tsenga, north of the Zambezi River. According to traditions I collected in the far east of Dande, Musuma (also known as Nyamukokoko) is a son of Dzivaguru, the most famous Tavara ancestor, known throughout Zimbabwe as a rain-bringing *mhondoro*. When I encouraged people to speculate on historical sequence, I was told that Musuma came to Dande after Bangomwe but that before he came Bangomwe made his requests for rain to Musuma's father Dzivaguru. The Tande, Bangomwe's descendants, like the Korekore, have never been able to bring rain by themselves.
5 From the point of view of Dande, the term 'Korekore' does not refer to the more than one million people who speak a dialect of this name. The term is used in a more limited sense to refer to a collection of lineages living in

Dande and on the Plateau who are thought of as conquerors in opposition to the Tande and Tavara peoples who are thought of as the original owners of the land.

6 References to and/or discussions of this myth appear in every recent account of the history of northern Zimbabwe and the Mutapa state. With the exception of Beach (1980) all are heavily influenced by a series of articles published since 1959 by Donald Abraham. In these articles Abraham treats the narrative recounted in the myth as if it were a condensed account of real historical events. In my thesis I have described some of the effects of this and challenged Abraham's interpretation on the basis of the analysis which, with some modifications, I reproduce in this chapter. See Lan (1983, Ch. V). The earliest version of this myth is found in Pacheco (1883). Although this version is very sketchy it suggests that it has been told in the Valley for at least 150 years. As there are many versions of this myth, some of which do not mention Mutota, it is important to remember that my analysis is based on versions of the myth as it is told in Dande.

7 Beach (1980, p. 62).

8 Beach (1980, p. 63). For the Xhosa see Hodgson (1982, p. 18).

9 I owe this observation, as well as a number of others which have been silently incorporated, to Professor Maurice Bloch. Overall, this analysis owes a good deal to the theoretical innovations contained in the introduction by Bloch and Parry to the volume, *Death and the Regeneration of Life* as well as to some of the essays contained there. See Bloch and Parry (eds) (1982).

10 Pachecho (1883); Randles (1981 p. 18). The word used for *mutapi* among the eastern Korekore is *mutonje* (Bourdillon, 1971, p. 202n).

11 See Beach (1977, p. 47) and Randles (1981, p. 18) for the trade in salt. For saltless offerings to ancestors see also the accounts of the Tonga of the Zambezi Valley whose *basangu* ancestors are similar to and interrelate with the *mhondoro* of the Korekore (Weinrich, 1977, p. 43; Colson, 1977, p. 126).

12 For the location of the territory of Bedza see Beach (1980, pp. 69, 131). For the Nyamita aspect of Nehanda see Chigwedere (1980) and Edwards (1928). For Nyanehwe see for example Gelfand's account of a medium of a *mhondoro* of this name in the extreme north-east of Zimbabwe (Gelfand, 1962). For Nebedza see for example, Lancaster (1981, p. 18).

13 Myth II was recorded in the Chisunga chieftaincy. Another version is found in White (1971, p. 42). For more on Chimombe see Campbell (1957) and Beach (1980). Myth III was recorded in the Chitsungo chieftaincy. Myth IV was recorded by Kaschula (1965a, p. 16). Two versions of myth V were recorded by Kaschula (1965b, pp. 85, 92).

14 Note however that men are permitted to take wives from any lineage of which the women are not their mothers-in-law; they are not obliged to perpetuate the marriages of the past by marrying only those already designated as the daughters-in-law of their lineage.

15 The notion that the wife's father's lineage supplies the rain is in contrast to the general Southern African pattern as described in Kuper's comparative study. In these systems, rain-bringing is associated with semen and therefore with the husband's lineage. See Kuper (1982, p. 16). Although I argue that in the Mutota mythology and in the rituals of possession the claim is made that

the husband's lineage can produce rain, the force of this statement is that it contradicts what one might call the received wisdom which is that the opposite is true. However, I am dealing only with the Korekore and only with them as conquerors of Tavara territory. One would expect non-conquering Korekore (if such exist) to conform to the general rule.

Although other kin terms are available, the term *tezvara* can be used for any male member of the wife's lineage (the females are *mezvara* or *vamwene*). The 'rain-givers' are thought of as the wife's lineage as a whole. An incident from my field work illustrates this. While one version of myth III was being told me, an argument broke out about whether it was Musuma's daughter or his sister that Nyahuma had married. Those who argued for sister eventually fell in with those who backed the daughter, but that Nyahuma and Musuma might have been brothers-in-law was considered a possibility, even though it was rejected. These two versions of the myth make no difference to its essential point, that the wife's lineage provides the rain. And it is, perhaps, this view of the marriage exchange contained in the myths (rain exchanged for marriage payment or labour) which accounts for one of the prohibitions that occur during the month of *mbudzi* (November). *Mbudzi* is the month of the *mhondoro*, when they perform the rituals necessary to ensure that the rains will fall in December. During *mbudzi* no marriage payments may be made. It is as if this is the time for sons-in-law to keep their side of the bargain and supply the rain.

16 In myth II, Nyamapfeka's daughter is called Semwa. His daughter who possesses a medium in Dande today is called Chigua. According to my informants, Semwa is another name for Chigua. I suspect that historically the matter is more complex but for the sake of this analysis I treat the two daughters as one.

17 Bourdillon (1979, p. 242) writes of the relationship between the Korekore Nyombwe chieftaincy, descendants of the *mhondoro* Nyabapa (who is sometimes described as a 'brother' of Mutota) and the Tavara *mhondoro* Karuva as follows: 'The people of Nyombwe call Karuva the 'wife' of Nyabapa. In explanation they claim that Nyabapa is stronger than Karuva, that Nyabapa sends Karuva cloth as a man should give his wife cloth with which to clothe herself, and that Karuva supplies Nyabapa with rain as a woman fetches water for her husband. This subordinate position of Karuva is not, however, accepted by the people of Choma.'

My Korekore informants made similar statements about the Tavara *mhondoro* Musuma (a 'brother' of Karuva). I do not see these comments as explanations of the characterisation of the Tavara *mhondoro* as wives or women. Rather they are a commentary on, almost a trivialisation of the expression of claims to the ownership of land as a relationship between affines. That this commentary is made goes some way towards confirming my analysis while demonstrating the way in which this relationship is consciously perceived.

18 It is not only the two Korekore lineages of Dande that feature women as ultimate ancestors. Many others in the Zambezi Valley and on the Escarpment do so as well, e.g. Kotswa, *mhondoro* of the Chiruja chieftaincy; Nyahuwi, *mhondoro* of the Diwa chieftaincy; Anadondo, *mhondoro* of the

Rusambo chieftaincy etc. (Latham, 1965; Bourdillon, 1971).

19 Interview with Silver Guvamombe, a son of George Kupara, late medium of Mutota, 11 April 1982.

20 I am grateful to Janet Carsten for suggesting this formulation. Holleman (1953, p. 38) makes the same point quite explicitly: 'A child becomes dry after it has started cutting teeth'. I never heard anyone attribute the loss of their own teeth to eating a clan animal though people do jokingly claim it to be the cause of toothlessness in others.

21 The association of the colour red with blood is made quite explicitly. For example:

> *Question to a medium*: Why are you not allowed to see red?
> *Medium*: It is blood.
> (Interview with Silver Guvamombe, 11 April 1982).

22 In apparent contradiction of this analysis there is found in the villages of many mediums a woman who is thought of as the wife of the *mhondoro*. She is known by the archaic term for woman, *mukaranga*, which is also used to refer to the wife of a chief. She is said to have been selected by the *mhondoro* and paid for out of money collected from visitors to his shrine, money which may not be used by the medium to his own advantage. Her responsibilities are to care for the house of the spirit and for his possessions, the clothes, plates, sticks and other tools of the medium's trade. If female fertility is dangerous to the *mhondoro* how can they have wives? In fact, when the *mukaranga* 'marries' the *mhondoro* great care is taken to ensure that she is pre-pubescent and virgin. In some cases, when she begins to menstruate, the *mukaranga* is thought no longer fit to perform her function. If she continues, she may bear children by the medium who is obliged to pay a fine to the *mhondoro* for having seduced 'his' wife. The children of this marriage have an ambiguous status. From one point of view they are the children of the *mhondoro* and, at the death of the medium, should be inherited not by a member of his lineage but by the next medium of the *mhondoro* their 'father'. In practice though they are usually treated as members of the medium's own family. (I am grateful to Dr Garbett for assistance in resolving this point.)

23 The black/white; rain/no rain; death/lightning distinctions are also made by the Tonga of the Zambezi Valley. Colson (1977, p. 126) reports that animals sacrificed to the ancestors for rain must be black; any white on their skin would bring lightning with the rain. Different coloured beads are offered to the mediums depending on the service required. Black or blue beads are given for rain, white if a dry spell is required (Colson, 1969, p. 76). Weinrich (1977, p. 43) reports that the Tonga sacrifice black animals to their ancestors because 'black is the colour of rain clouds'.

24 Dark blue is categorised as 'dark' or as black. Thus dark-blue cloth or beads may also be worn.

25 Beach (1980, p. 60).

26 Randles (1981, p. 11); Abraham (1962, p. 12); Bhila (1974, p. 79).

27 The translation of these names is consistent with the principles laid out by Pongweni (1983).

28 For ancestors and cattle see Kuper (1982, p. 15); Bourdillon (1982, p. 222).
29 For an analysis of two Tavara (i.e. autochthonous) myths in similar terms see Lan (1983, p. 334, n. 15).
30 In the myths of many peoples of the Valley or the Plateau neighbouring on Dande, Nebedza is acknowledged as the conqueror of the autochthons. See Randles (1981, p. 11); Beach (1980, pp. 163, 173); Lancaster (1981, p. 18) etc. The tradition of the 'magical lineage founders' helps to explain the meaning of Matope Nebedza's third name Nyanehwe. In nineteenth-century records Nyanehwe is often rendered as Nhantègue (e.g. Pacheco, 1883). Nhantègue can be translated to mean 'the one of the hide or pelt' (personal communication from Dr S. I. Mudenge). Beach (1983) has remarked that Rozvi chiefs customarily wore hides whereas ordinary people wore cotton clothes. I have mentioned that the fur hat of the *mhondoro* mediums is said to represent the chieftaincy. The evidence is slight but if Nhanehwe can be translated as 'hide-owner' i.e. founder of the lineage (remember that Nyamapfeka, another lineage-founder, comes out of the womb dressed in furs) this would perhaps explain why there are so many unrelated Nyanehwe *mhondoro* in Dande and beyond whereas, with the exception of Nehanda, no other *mhondoro* has more than a single legitimate medium at any one time. This would also help to explain a usage which seemed mysterious to me until this line of thought began to evolve, namely that in Dande people would say to me *Nebedza, ndiNyanehwe* meaning 'Nebedza, he is Nyanehwe'. I am tempted to translate this to mean 'Nebedza is the hide-owner, the founder of our lineage.'
31 In his description of the eastern Korekore chieftaincy of Chiruja, Bourdillon (1971, p. 119) mentions the existence of a ritual officiant called Nyamvuri ('Owner of the shade' i.e. shadow) whose job it is to help build the roof of the *dendemaro* in which possessions by *mhondoro* take place. He was informed that in the mythology, it was the job of Nyamvuri 'to go ahead of the ancients on their way from Guruuswa looking for shade for them to rest in'. This is a further suggestion that the possession rituals and the Guruuswa myth 'say' the same thing.

6
The Country
of Kin

When the dim-sighted traveller first arrives in Dande and is confronted by mile upon mile of apparently empty bush, a scattering of mud huts, a few gravel paths and precious little else, amongst many other absences the one that seems most striking is the absence of a record of the past. Mud huts decay, the sites of abandoned villages are soon lost in the dust, the traces of ancient cultivation are ploughed over time and time again. But in the ritual of the bringing of the rain a powerful sense of history, of the relationship between the present and the past, suddenly appears. When requests for rain are carried from spirit province to spirit province and from more junior to more senior ancestor, it is as if the whole history of the land has come alive, linking the most recent to the most distant past and all inhabited parts of the spirit realm to each other. And there is not only one version of the past. The climax of the ritual is a battlefield on which rival historical claims fight for acceptance. When the request for rain reaches the senior Korekore ancestor he either passes it on to an autochthon or keeps it for himself thus claiming for his descendants the status of autochthons, of owners of the land. In the course of the ritual, each past age proclaims its contribution to the making of the present, every corner of the spirit realm declares itself to be an essential part of the country as a whole. And in this way is assured the one event without which all life, all history would come to an end: the coming of the rain.

When the ZANLA guerrillas came to Dande, they too claimed to be 'owners of the land', autochthons rather than conquerors. They arrived as highly trained, highly armed strangers. Many accounts of the first response of the peasants to the guerrillas make clear that, at first contact, their instructions were obeyed only because they were armed and the peasants were not. But within a very short space of time, in addition to this view of the guerrillas, another had emerged. In this

112

second view the guerrillas appeared not as hostile foreigners or strangers but as legitimate residents of the area, as people thoroughly 'at home'.

The detail of how this transformation occurred will be given in Chapter 9. The point I want to make here is that the techniques they used to establish themselves in this way were not invented by them. The guerrillas fitted themselves into a structure of authority that had existed before they arrived and which has survived their departure. This brief chapter is an account of the last aspect of political organisation that needs to be clear for the set of events described in the second half of this book to be seen for what they were: a remarkable feat of sustained co-operation between guerrillas and peasants, between politicians and mediums, between the leaders of the present and the long-dead leaders of the past. This final aspect of political organisation is the technique used by the many people in Dande who live away from their fathers' villages to create new alliances in their new homes.

In the first part of Mutota's journey from Guruuswa, Dande appears as a territory under the authority of affines or, more accurately, potential affines. It is a country owned by people of other clans and other marriageable lineages. In the second part of the myth, Nebedza establishes the authority of Mutota's descendants as the royal lineage of Dande, the rightful owners of all the land they occupy. In the symbolism of the myth, Nebedza replaces the chaos and pollution of affinity with the orderliness of descent which brings the rain. This is not the same rain that watered the fields of the earlier autochthonous owners of Dande. It is the rain of the Korekore controlled by their own ancestors. The title deeds to land are the power to ensure its fertility and this is demonstrated on two levels: first by the rituals that the medium of the senior *mhondoro*, the most distant ancestor, perform to provide rain for the entire spirit realm, and secondly by the rituals that each more junior *mhondoro* medium performs to provide rain for his own spirit province.

Now, within each chieftaincy and within each spirit province there live people who are not descended from these royal ancestors, who are not, as it were, entitled to the rain provided by them. These people are the 'strangers' I discussed in Chapter 2. They may have been allocated land by the chief because they had nowhere else to go but more commonly they are people, or the descendants of people, who at marriage came to live with the fathers of their wives. These strangers pose a threat to the resident royal lineages. This threat is that they will do precisely the same to the conquering royal lineages as the royals did to the autochthons who lived where they do before them.

As the history of Dande is expressed in myths II to V, the Korekore arrived, took the daughters of the autochthons as their wives and performed rituals to the ancestors of their fathers-in-laws to ensure the fertility of the land on which they now lived. But myth I and the possession rituals present a different story. According to these accounts, the Korekore actually own the land and perform their own rituals to their own *mhondoro* to provide themselves with their own rain. A royal Korekore lineage with their affines living amongst them in the spirit province of their ancestor would be aware that these affines stand in precisely the same relation to them as, in myths II to V, they stood towards the autochthons. Their affines take their daughters and make use of the fertility of their land. Their fear therefore must be that if these affines, who are by definition members of other clans and descendants of other *mhondoro*, arrive in sufficient numbers they will begin to perform *their* rituals to *their mhondoro*, their rain will come to them and the land of the royals will fall under the affines' control.

In what sense does this 'fear' correspond to a genuine possibility? Although the strangers outnumber the conquerors by approximately three to one, the real danger of a 'second conquest' is not great because the strangers are not all members of one lineage or one clan. They have allegiance to a variety of different *mhondoro* and chiefs. They have no lineage basis for uniting and mounting a campaign against their hosts. Nonetheless the royal lineages assert their dominance over the strangers and affines living in their midst by transforming them all into *vazukuru* or descendants of the *mhondoro* in whose spirit province they live.[1]

Two elements make up the personality of a *mhondoro*. Each is the ancestor of a royal lineage but also the ancestor of a specified territory. If you leave your father's village with peaceful intentions, if you travel to a territory not your own as an affine rather than a warrior, then you leave your own *mhondoro* behind you. From the moment that you arrive in the territory that you plan to make your home you treat the *mhondoro* of your hosts as if he were your own.

The kin term *vazukuru* (sing. *muzukuru*) groups together all descendants of all the generations below that of one's children and includes one's sister's children in the category as well. The reciprocal is *sekuru* for men and *ambuya* for women. These categories strictly exclude the notion of affinity. Sex with a *muzukuru* is incest. The relationship between *vazukuru* and their *ambuya* and *sekuru* is one of warmth and affection, of openness, of intimacy and relaxation in contrast to the greater formality that is regarded as proper between fathers and their children.

The particular function that male *vazukuru* fulfil for their elders is to organise their rituals for them. At all family rituals the *muzukuru* is, as it were, the master of ceremonies. Only he can intercede with the ancestors of the person for whom the ritual is held. Similarly, any *mudzimu* or lineage ancestor can be referred to and addressed as *sekuru* or *ambuya* and those who organise their rituals are thought of as their *vazukuru*.[2]

114

And the same is true of the relationship between the *mhondoro* and *his* master of ceremonies, the *mutapi*. The *mutapi* always fulfils at least one of two criteria. Either he is thought of as the first man to have lived in the spirit province or he is believed to be descended from the *mhondoro*. If for any reason the full-time *mutapi* is unable to carry out his duties these two principles work together to produce a schedule of deputies to act in his stead. In essence any *muzukuru* of the *mhondoro* can be called on to act as his *mutapi* but the first on the list is the *muzukuru* who has lived longest in the spirit province. The one that has lived there next longest is the second and so on. Ultimately any man who lives in the spirit province can be called on to serve his turn.

But it is not enough simply to live in the spirit province to become the *mhondoro's muzukuru*. When a newcomer arrives in a spirit province he must apply to the *mhondoro* for permission to live there and to plough his land. This request must be accompanied by a gift (*mukowho*). If you have not made the gift and received permission you can never be accepted as a *muzukuru* of the *mhondoro*, a legitimate resident in his territory and beneficiary of the fertility he provides. But even the making of this gift is not sufficient. To be a *muzukuru* you must also do the work of the ancestors. You must take part in the rituals of the agricultural cycle and in the rituals of possession. If any household head resident in the province fails to do so, this reduces the likelihood of the ritual achieving the desired affect. By doing these things strangers come to regard themselves and to be accepted as *vazukuru* of the *mhondoro*. In this way is the threat that they pose to the authority of the royal lineage dispelled.[3]

These *vazukuru*, these strangers-become-kinsmen are defined not in terms of lineage but of territory. The imagery that characterises them is geographic rather than historical. As I have stressed many times, social identity is a question of action not of essence. All the *vazukuru* of the *mhondoro* think of themselves and of others as such because they all live within the same spirit province, they all work the same land and they all take part in the same rituals that maintain its fertility.

This acquisition of a new identity can occur in both a strong and a weak form. In Chapter 2, I described how by working the same piece of land and performing the rituals of the same *mhondoro* for a long period of time, members of one clan can acquire membership of the clan associated with the territory where they work and live. It is probably by a similar process that the lineages of *vatapi* who have been associated with the same *mhondoro* for many generations, such as the Kwainona lineage described in Chapter 4, come to consider themselves as directly descended from the *mhondoro*. The change in affiliation that I have described here is a weaker version of the same process. It is weaker because it is more quickly achieved and because though it works a profound change on the way in which individual women and men think about themselves, it is reversible. If they return to their fathers' homes they may participate in the rituals of their original ancestors there. But while they live where they do they are regarded as the ritual descendants of the *mhondoro* who provides them with their rain.

For the Korekore, the ideal form of social organisation would allow each clan, and within each clan each lineage, to live within its own territory free of the pollution of affines producing its own rain. But this is impossible. A lineage on its own is sterile. People have to live with affines or die out, either as strangers in the territory of their father-in-law, or as 'owners' of the land challenged by the stranger husbands of their daughters and sisters.

If the ideal order is ever found, it is for the brief moment of the founding of a new community, a chieftaincy or a village, by a section of a lineage that desires to live on its own. For a short space of time the ideal order, pure descent, exists. But then the demands of social life, the prohibition on marrying within the clan, the need to live and work on the fields of the father of your wife, force some men out of the new community and bring in strangers. People no longer live 'at home' and the new community has to face all the old challenges to its ownership of the land.

It is only in ritual that the ideal of social organisation can be brought into being and maintained. In the possession rituals, the journey made by the *mhondoro* from the 'long grass', the source of all life, to the world of the living recreates the moment of undefiled descent at the birth of a new community. The successful performance of these rituals demonstrates the authority of the ruling lineage and the rain-bringing power of its ancestors. But it does more than this. The possession rituals construct an ideal alternative society which persists after the rituals have been completed, a society based on the ideal of 'one lineage, one territory', the ideal of pure descent in which any threat of change, any challenge to the ownership of the territory by 'strangers' is defused by transforming them into 'descendants' of the *mhondoro*, ancestor of the royal lineage and of the spirit province within which they live.

To conclude this part of the book I describe one last ritual which expresses with great subtlety and rigour the unity that is created by the descendants of the *mhondoro* out of the diversity of lineages found within each spirit province.

The pangolin or ant-eater (*haka*) is a creature that lives in the bush far from people and their villages. If, as occasionally happens, one is found by hunters, it does not run away like a truly wild animal. It curls up into a ball and waits to be taken to the *mhondoro* in whose spirit province it was found.[4]

A number of very stringent taboos surround the pangolin. If you catch one and eat it by yourself, you will go mad and die. It must be taken to the *mhondoro* who will give it to his *mutapi* to cook and share out so that everyone in the spirit province may eat a little of its reputedly excellent meat. When you bring it to the *mhondoro*, you may not speak a word until you have handed it over and been paid for it, either with money or a gift. This practice echoes that of the newly wed wife arriving at her husband's village. She may not speak until she has performed a number of menial tasks and been paid for them. This echo is not surprising, as the *haka* is regarded as a *mukaranga*, a ritual wife of the *mhondoro*. If you find a pangolin and do not take it to the *mhondoro*, he will berate you and demand to know why you have left his wife to live all alone in the bush. If you should find a pangolin so close to the border of two provinces that you cannot tell to whom it belongs, you may take it to either of the *mhondoro* who will discuss the problem with the other and decide whose it is. Like all good wives, the pangolin follows the *mhondoro* about. They live only where the *mhondoro* live which is why you will never come across a pangolin in the towns.

In those clans which are designated by the names of animals, members identify themselves by saying: *tinoera nzou*, we respect and abstain from eating elephant or monkey or whatever their clan animal happens to be. It is said of the pangolin: *inoerwa nevanhu vese*, it is respected and avoided by all people. While the pangolin found within a particular spirit province is being eaten, it is as if all those who live within that province become members of the pangolin clan.

Ordinary clans are constituted out of the principles of common substance and of descent. Within a spirit province live members of many different clans. The 'pangolin clan' combines the principle of common substance with the principle of territoriality to overcome the divisiveness inherent in the principle of descent. By the intervention of the *mhondoro* and his 'wife', the pangolin, self-identification in terms of individual lineage history is suppressed. By the conversion of the fruits of the wild from the property of individual lineages into a source of general benefit and delight, the consciousness of solidarity that is experienced by all those whose livelihood depends on the continued fertility of a single spirit province finds, if only for a moment, a ritual expression.

NOTES

1 For the proportion of strangers to royals in Dande see Garbett (1967, p. 314).
2 The only exception to this is the ritual of burial in which the *muzukuru* as a member of the lineage of the deceased may not participate and yields the

role of *dunzvi* or master of ceremonies to the *sawhira*, the ritual friend. In all other rituals the preferred *dunzvi* is the sister's son but either son's son or daughter's son can perform the necessary tasks if called on to do so. For women the preferred *dunzvi* is brother's son, or daughter's son if the first is not available. See Radcliffe-Brown (1950, p. 34) for a discussion of the mother's brother among the Shona, and Kuper (1982, p. 36) for a summary of the arguments about this relationship throughout Southern Africa.

3 The particular individuals at whom this ritual creation of *vazukuru* is aimed are the daughter's and the sister's husbands. No special effort is needed to bring second-generation affines into the category. Daughter's son and sister's are both *muzukuru* even though they are, in terms of succession and the inheritance of rights, property and jural status, members of their father's lineages.

4 There is apparently more than one species of pangolin. I do not know how many species are found in the Zambezi Valley or whether all, one or a few are treated in the way that I describe here.

Plate 1   Charwe, the medium of Nehanda (left), with the medium of Kagubi in prison. 1897.

Plate 2   A village committee chairman possessed by the hunting spirit, Kapori

Plate 3   Two village wives dancing while possessed by their recent ancestors (midzimu). *The woman on the left is holding a ceremonial axe* (gano. *see Plate 5*).

Plate 4   A young woman in trance wearing the ritual half-black, half-white cloth

Plate 5   Nationalist leaders Joshua Nkomo (left) and Robert Mugabe (second from left) being greeted at Salisbury airport in 1962 by a veteran of the 1896 uprising. The ceremonial axe with which they are being presented is identical to those used by spirit mediums and symbolises the legitimate ownership of the land (See Plate 3.)

Plate 6　The medium of the senior rain spirit, Musuma

Plate 7　The medium of Nyamapfeka, a senior Korekore ancestor

Plate 8　The medium of Chivere

Plate 9　The medium of Madzomba wearing his spectacles (see page 189)

PART III

The Sons of the Soil

It goes without saying that the Valley of the Zambezi has entered upon a prolonged, indeed, there is every reason to believe a permanent, state of peace. It is years since the last armed outbreak took place and as time goes on and the native comes more clearly to comprehend the advantages they derive from the European protection and teachings, any smouldering feeling of discontent, impatience or restraint will finally die away and disappear.

R. C. F. Maugham, *Zambezia* (1910), quoted in Isaacman and Isaacman, 1977.

7
The Coming
of the Guerrillas

The north-eastern district of Rhodesia is a hot, rugged area. The Matusadonha Mountains, with their caves and many hiding places, run along the Zambezi Escarpment, and adjoin Tribal Trust Land. The border with Mozambique is ill-defined, and Africans in the area have family links in the Portuguese territory. Inside Mozambique, the bush thickens out. Flying across hundreds of miles of this territory, you think: an army could hide there. In fact, an army is hiding there . . .

Extract from 'Rhodesia: What Smith really faces'
Peter Niesewand, April 1973.[1]

The occupation of the territory that was to become Rhodesia took place in 1890. The hope of the first settlers was that they would find gold deposits the equal of those which had produced such a massive expansion of wealth in the Transvaal Republic to the south. When this hope proved unfounded, the settlers transferred their interests to agriculture and took for themselves huge expanses of the most fertile land, allocating to the peoples whom they displaced at gunpoint ever-smaller and less fertile reserves. In all, over half the land in present-day Zimbabwe was taken into the hands of a tiny minority of the population.[2]

That these lands were lost was one cause of resistance to the succession of white regimes that ruled over the peoples of Zimbabwe. The imagery of dispossession, of loss, of landlessness, of longing for the 'lost lands' to be restored was a constant pulse in the literature, the oral tradition and the rhetoric of the nationalist movements. But the loss of the land was not the only cause nor was it sufficient to make the great, brave leap into armed resistance seem the only available option. Though people had had their lands heavily reduced, though many had been removed to distant places where they felt none of the intimacy that the Shona characteristically feel (or feel that they should feel) for the land on and by which they live, there was it seems a readiness to accept all this provided that they were able to exercise 'the peasant option'. If people were able to make good their losses by selling their surplus agricultural goods to the markets which the settler state had introduced, by and large they accepted the limitations on their political and economic freedoms.[3]

But the taking of the peasant option was not encouraged by the state. To explain why this was so is also to explain why the white farmers took for themselves so much more land than they were ever able to cultivate (roughly 3 per cent of land in white hands was put to productive use). Quite simply, the intention of successive governments was to prevent the black population from developing its agricultural production to the level where it would be able to support itself satisfactorily by this means alone.

The strategy refined by the state over the years was to maintain commercial agriculture, industry and the mines under exclusive white control while the black population was reduced to little more than a source of extremely cheap labour. The massive expulsion of blacks from their lands was designed not merely to make these lands available to white farmers but also to deny them to the blacks. That the reserves were too small, that their overcrowding became intolerable and their soils increasingly barren were not failures of the system but indications of the successful achievement of its aims: the transformation of the population of independent agricultural producers and traders into labourers dependent on the white-dominated markets.

To assist with this transformation, taxation in cash was imposed on all households. There were only two methods by which the money to pay this tax could be raised. The first was by increasing the production of agricultural goods. The second was wage labour. By providing subsidies to white farmers and, in some areas, closing markets to black produce, the state ensured that the second method, wage labour, became the only viable one. In 1900 70 per cent of black earnings came from the sale of agricultural produce. By the early 1920s this figure had fallen to around 20 per cent.[4]

But the secret of the extreme cheapness of labour in Rhodesian was that dispossession of land and the destruction of black agriculture was not allowed to go all the way. The continued farming of small, low-grade plots in the countryside was expected to provide the workers' families with all they needed for their subsistence. Thus salaries paid by commercial and industrial employers could be kept at a level just high enough to provide for the minimum needs of the workers themselves. The result was that the next generation of workers and the support of women and men past working age, as well as of the unemployed, was provided out of the sweat of the wives of the workers at no cost to the employers or the state. Under this system there was virtually no chance that either the workers in the commercial sector or their families in the countryside would ever accumulate more than they consumed, dragging on from one year to the next, if indeed they managed to do as well as that.

Even within the reserves allocated for subsistence farming, the black population was not allowed to go its own way. Government policies were designed to control and improve peasant agricultural techniques. All these policies must be seen within the context I have outlined. The population pressures in the reserves quickly resulted in the fragmentation of landholdings beyond a size where a subsistence could be easily produced. Land was overgrazed and overcultivated. It was brought back into use long before its fertility was restored, either naturally, as in the days before their confinement to reserves when shifting cultivation was common practice, or artificially by fertilizers which few peasants could afford.

From the point of view of the state it was essential to improve peasant agricultural production for, if the system collapsed completely and the reserves were no longer able to support the families of migrant workers, this burden would fall on their employers, causing a decline in their rate of profits, or on the state. Therefore the scattered villages were centralised so as to separate grazing from arable land; each adult man was allocated a fixed area, roughly 2.5 ha, and penalties were provided for not making substantial improvements to this land; the number of cattle in the reserves was drastically reduced so frequent dipping could take place, and so on.

This brief outline is sufficient to show that when resistance came it had three main sources. First, the loss of the lands. Secondly, the enforced restructuring of the black population, once independent agricultural producers and traders, now a labour force divided into two sectors: very low-paid male migrants flowing back and forwards between town and countryside and unpaid female subsistence producers in the reserves. Thirdly, the enforced disruption of long-established agricultural techniques in order to perpetuate a much-hated economic and political order.

In the imagery wrought out of the process of resistance, all these three sources reappear. Together they express two powerful desires: to regain the lost lands and to regain the control which the people had lost over their lives. Much of this imagery is fired by and forged out of memories of what life had been like, of how society had been organised, of the freedoms that had prevailed before the arrival of the British settlers. It is always important to remember that the colonisation of Zimbabwe lasted just short of ninety years. The first blows dealt by the new state were felt by the grandmothers and grandfathers of the guerrillas and peasants who finally broke its power.

By the early 1960s the Zimbabwe African People's Union (ZAPU) led by Joshua Nkomo was the leading nationalist party in the country. But in 1963, frustrated by the disinclination of the ZAPU leadership to take up armed struggle against the Rhodesian state, a small group of militants broke away and formed the Zimbabwe African National Union (ZANU) under the leadership of the Rev. Ndabaningi Sithole. The 'Battle of Sinoia' in 1966 was the first of a handful of armed attacks launched by ZANLA, ZANU's military wing. These early ZANLA guerrillas made little attempt to gain support from the local peasantry and this first attempt to regain the lost lands and the lost autonomy was, in the words of Cde Simbi Mubako, the first Minister of Justice in independent Zimbabwe:

> a defeat. We do not have to accept the figures of those killed or captured given by the Salisbury regime to come to that conclusion, for time has now shown that the gallant effort displayed by the pioneer band of freedom fighters was not and could not be sustained . . . Criticism . . . can be levelled, not against the cadres, but against the superiors who hastily threw them into battle apparently for short-term political gain rather than laying the groundwork for a protracted armed struggle.[5]

In a phrase that became popular in the 1970s, the attack had failed because the struggle had not been 'given to the people'. An urgent reassessment of strategy took place and the training of ZANLA guerrillas along lines developed by Frelimo in Mozambique was begun. As Robert Mugabe has described:

> There was a complete revision of our manner of carrying out the armed struggle. We began to realise that the armed struggle must be based on the support of the people . . . We worked with Frelimo for eighteen months in Tete province [in Mozambique]. It was there that we learned the true meaning of guerrilla war.[6]

Cde Josiah Tungamirai, second-in-command of ZANLA forces for much of the war, has recalled that:

> 1971 was the year we invaded Zimbabwe clandestinely for the politicisation of the masses in the Dande area. By then our strategy was mass political mobilization and building up of armed forces, i.e. massive recruitment and training of forces. By this time Smith's propaganda was portraying us as 'terrorists' from foreign countries like Mozambique, Tanzania and Zambia. I remember he called us 'misguided youngsters who have resorted to terrorism on behalf of our masters'.[7]

Of course, the guerrillas were not foreigners but the illusion that they were was strengthened by the fact that they were not deployed in their own home areas. It was feared that ties of kin or sentiment might distract them from carrying out their tasks impartially and with rigour. So they fought as strangers, their identities concealed behind *chimurenga* names. These evocative *noms de guerre* declared their bearers' intentions or boasted their military prowess. Thus Comrade Bvisai Mabunhu intended to Cast out the Boers (whites). Comrade Tichaona Freedom declared by her name that One Day We Shall All See Freedom in Zimbabwe. Some guerrillas chose simpler more forceful names such as Comrade Dracula, Comrade James Bond, Comrade Hokoyo (Danger). Comrade Tungamirai's name means simply Comrade Lead! And there were those whose names celebrated the success of the campaign such as Comrade Takawanda PaChipuriro or We [the guerrillas] Are Many at the Town of Chipuriro. How these nameless strangers were integrated into the social life of Dande is the subject of the next two chapters.

In 1980 and 1981, thirty residents of Dande recorded at my request some of their experience of the war as well as a range of other materials they wished to preserve. Translated extracts from their notebooks have already appeared in these pages.[8] For the rest of this chapter I shall draw on this uniquely valuable source to give an impression of the effect on the people of Dande of the coming of the guerrillas. To start with, here is an extract from a notebook kept by a young man who became a *mujiba*, one of the estimated 50 000 intermediaries who in all parts of the country carried supplies and information between the guerrillas in the bush and the adults who remained in the villages. Here he describes his first contact with the guerrillas as they advanced into Dande:

At the start of the war I was living at home. At that time we had no idea how much we would suffer in the course of the war.

When the Security Force soldiers spoke to us of the terrorists, they told us they were animals with tails and we believed this for a long time. Then one day people with guns came to the village. We did not know who they were. They said: Cook *sadza* [stiff porridge] and chickens. None of us eat vegetables, only meat. So all the people brought *sadza* out of fear of the guns.

The people were asked to sit down and one of these men came and stood in front of the adults. He said: Forward with ZANU! and told them that they should answer by saying: Forward. Then another came to the front and said: Forward with ZANU! Everyone answered: Forward! He said he wanted to talk to all the unmarried boys and girls. We stood up and went where we were told to go. He said: How are you, boys and girls? We answered: Fine. He said: Do you know us? We said no and he said: We are the terrorists who you heard about; and he turned round to show us that he did not have a tail.

They began to teach us politics. They said: We are called Comrades not terrorists. We came from Mozambique because the government of Rhodesia

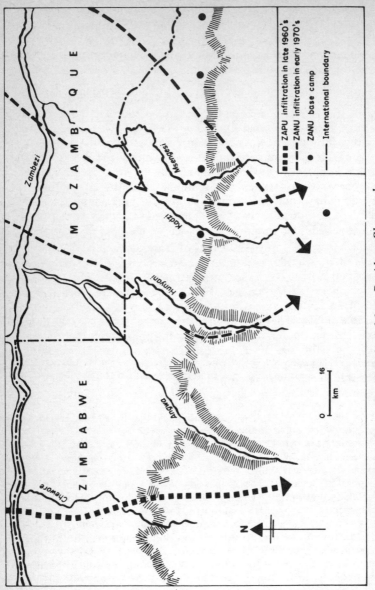

Map 7.1   Guerrilla infiltration into Dande (adapted from Davidson, Slovo and
Wilkinson, 1976; Maxey, 1975; Martin and Johnson, 1980)

does not treat everyone as equals. A white man works for a month and has enough money to buy a car. Can you people do the same as he can? We answered no.[9]

The guerrillas were organised into sections containing five people, each with special responsibilities:

First there is the commander. His job is to lead. Then comes the political commissar. His job is to introduce us to the masses and to instruct them in who we are, what we are going to do and why. Then there is the man in charge of security. He finds out who is on our side, who is for our cause and who are the sell-outs. The man in charge of logistics must ensure that there is enough food, transport, ammunition and everything that we need. The medical assistant who is also known as doctor sees that our health is taken care of and that everything is being kept quite clean.[10]

The guerrillas usually travelled four or five sections together. The *mujibas* were organised along similar lines, though with separate 'platoons' for the young women and men. Political education, talking to the villagers about 'who we are, what we are going to do and why' took place at rallies known as *morari* or *pungwe* held at night away from the main roads and out of the hearing of the security force encampments. *Mujibas* were stationed along the paths between these camps and the meeting places so as to deliver an immediate warning if the enemy was about to make a raid. This account of a rally was given by a young ex-guerrilla who had received his training in Mozambique:

When we came to a village, the first thing we would do is hold a rally. The Commander and the Political Commissar would go to the place where the rally was to be held. The rest of us would go to all the houses and make sure that everyone came. Some people would want to come, others would not but there was no choice about it. You had to come. We wanted everyone there because if anyone wasn't they could go off quietly and betray us.

First we would explain who we were. We were ZANLA. We were not ZANU. ZANU was a political organization. We were the military wing. It was ZANU's job to go to other countries, to talk and negotiate. We did not go to other countries. We did not need the help of soldiers from other countries. We were Zimbabweans in Zimbabwe. And we did not use talk, we used guns.

We explained the structures of the ZANU party. We then explained the structure of the army and told the masses about the army high command and described their duties. Next we explained national grievances, then colonialism, then neo-colonialism and capitalism. We explained that ours would be a socialist government and what that would mean to the masses.

The pattern of the meeting would be: talk for half an hour, then teaching the masses songs for an hour, then talking for another half hour and so on, so that people did not get bored.

While this rally was taking place, one of us would go on to the next village and quietly find out how much support we had there, whether it was safe for us to enter. He would look just like an ordinary person. There was no way you could tell he was a comrade.

At the end of the meeting we would say to the older people: 'Mothers and Fathers, go home now and sleep in peace. But children you must stay here The younger people would stay, and we would then say: 'What is our support here? Are people in favour of us, are people speaking against us and who is doing so?' Then they would tell us, for example, that some people were saying that they didn't have enough food to eat themselves without giving some to us. And many other complaints came out as well.[11]

Quite how much about 'colonialism, neo-colonialism and capitalism' the guerrillas actually taught is far from clear. Other accounts suggest that national grievances received the greater emphasis:

We would get into an area, study the problems in that particular area, and then teach those people about their problems, how we can solve them by fighting the enemy . . . Overall the land question was our major political weapon. The people responded to it. As for socialism versus capitalism, since the olden days of our ancestors our people used to work communally and live communally, which was almost the same as socialism.[12]

The other side of the question is just as important: how were the teachings of the guerrillas interpreted by the peasants? We can go some way towards understanding this by taking into account the particular physical circumstances in which the relationship between the peasants and the guerrillas evolved.

Given the terrain of the Valley and the relatively small size of the operational zone, it was impossible to establish training camps within Zimbabwe undetected by the army of the state. Trainee guerrillas were therefore sent to ZANU camps outside the country, either in the 'front-line' states of Mozambique and Tanzania or, in some cases, as far afield as North Korea and Eastern Europe. This pragmatic necessity was partially tranformed into a ritual practice. No one was considered a fully fledged guerrilla unless she or he had crossed the borders of Zimbabwe into another country for training before taking up arms. During the later stages of the war, the training of guerrillas became ever-more brief and superficial but the process of leaving the country, receiving training and returning was maintained.

This had the effect of placing a very sharp emphasis on the unusual qualities of the knowledge obtained by the guerrillas outside Zimbabwe. Quite apart from the powers they acquired from the mediums, guerrillas who had completed their training were believed to have exceptional skills of their own. The most remarkable of these was their ability to vanish into thin air whenever they wished. I have many times heard people describe this phenomenon and insist that there was no question of the guerrillas hiding behind trees or scuttling away into the high grass. The disappearance was magical and quite outside the bounds of ordinary experience. These skills, obtained by their esoteric training, transformed the young women and men of the countryside into figures of exceptional power and authority.[13] I discussed this with one of the guerrillas who had operated under Tungamirai in the north-east in 1972.

> Oh yes, we knew that the peasants believed that we could simply disappear. We knew that very well. This was a technique we had acquired during our training. There was nothing magical about it but we allowed the peasants to go on believing because it was to our advantage that they did so.[14]

This tension between the guerrilla's techniques of survival in the forest, how the peasants perceived them and how the guerrillas responded to this perception will emerge as a central theme as we proceed deeper into the relationship between the guerrillas and the peasantry. To disentangle this perception of the guerrillas from the perception of the political programme which the ZANU had instructed them to teach is extremely difficult. Much of it was challenging to the holders of power in Dande society, the adult men. How much was accepted simply because of the authority of the guerrillas and how much because it was considered a meaningful and practical contribution to the peasants' knowledge of their world can be estimated by considering the extent to which the innovations achieved during the war were retained when the guerrillas left the countryside. I will deal with some of these questions in later chapters.

There is however no doubt of the great success the guerrillas achieved in communicating one central aspect of ZANU's conception of the nature and goal of the struggle. It was clearly explained and understood that the return of the land could only be achieved by the victory of one class rather than of one ethnic group over another. The enemy was defined as racism and the structures of exploitation, rather than as individual members of the white population. Throughout my time in Dande I was never in any doubt that this argument had been very widely accepted.

People thought to be corrupted by racism were treated very harshly indeed. The following quotation is, I believe, an exaggerated generalisation but it makes its point:

> The prostitutes were killed because the comrades said: You are holding us back from winning our country. The comrades were saying: the country is ours, we blacks. People who were putting Ambi [skin-lightening cream] on their faces were killed.[15]

Those who continued to work for the state or on the commercial farms felt very vulnerable. A young man who had been working on the farms on the Plateau came to the Valley to get away from the fighting. Finding it just as bad there:

> I decided to go back to my job but it was difficult to return to the farm. I had to walk all the way back by night because the *mujibas* did not like those who return to take their jobs.[16]

A tailor who worked at a white-owned store in the Valley was accused by the *mujibas* of being a sell-out:

> They took me from my house to the black forest. They told me that I must be killed by the comrades. I answered them saying: What is the reason I am going to die? They replied with anger: You are a sell-out. Liberation soldiers are killed by the soldiers of Muzorewa because of you. When they had finished talking they went and cut a big stick. I had never been beaten by such a big stick in my life.[17]

The relationship that developed between the guerrillas and the 'unmarried boys and girls' who supported and worked alongside them was one of the most striking features of the war. The boy who wrote the next account was 15 when he attended his first late-night rally:

> They told us the work that we would do. They said 'You are ZANLA youth' which means we are the *mujibas*. We agreed with everything they said. We chose our leaders, one boy and one girl. Then we were dismissed. The next day we began to do our work, looking after all the people who were members of the party. The work of the girls was to wash and sew the clothes of the comrades, the boys' work was to guard the camps when the comrades had to sleep. All of us used to inform the comrades of who would support them in villages, who they could trust and who would sell them out.[18]

Not all recruitment took place at the *morari* as this account by a 16-year-old girl makes clear:

> I was fast asleep when the guerrillas came. They passed through our village. I asked the boys what they were looking for. They said that they were looking for girls. All the girls are wanted at the headman's village. When I arrived there they said: How are you, sister? I said: I am fine and how are you? They said: Do you not want to go where the others are going? I said: Truly, I am not going anywhere. They said: We are not playing games with you today. If you are so lucky that you haven't died before, today you are surely going to visit the cemetery. I started crying. They said: Come. You are going to cook for us. So I went.[19]

After some months of working with the guerrillas, many of these young people crossed into Mozambique for training. Conditions there were not always what they expected:

> As the war went on, many people were crying to go to Mozambique with the comrades. They wanted to get guns, get trained and come home to fight the enemy. Some went but had to come back again because in Mozambique

there was not enough food for all. The number of *mujibas* grew and grew because many of our schools were closed at that time. All the children who could not go to school lived in the bush with the comrades and helped them in the struggle.[20]

Many accounts express the delight these young people took in working alongside the guerrillas, freed from their daily chores and thrown into a world of adventure and excitement. But even for those less willing to risk their fortunes and their lives, it quickly became impossible to avoid taking sides:

The enemy began to beat young boys or even to take them for call-up. We did not want to go for call-up so we ran up into the mountains and watched how and when the enemy entered our villages. When we saw them we ran to tell the comrades at their base.[21]

And after having taken sides and become *mujibas*, the notebooks record many moments of deep unhappiness and doubt:

Many children went to Mr. Mugabe's side and they began to suffer. Some said: If I was at home I would be looking after the goats. Others said: This war is very bad. It would have been better if I hadn't come here. I am being bitten by lice and mosquitoes. But I can do nothing because this is what the ancestors wanted, that I should live here in the bush.[22]

When the guns start to fire you think: Why did I come here to die? But if you returned you might be killed so you had to go on. When I am silent I am troubled because really I don't know if this country is for blacks or if it is not. Why are all these guns being fired? I don't know the answer. Then it is quiet and I just hear the noise of the birds.[23]

But though the work was hard and the responsibilities heavy there were good times as well:

We would go on patrol from 5 pm to 7 am and then return and tell the comrades what we saw. We would carry things on our backs, heavy things like guns. We would dig trenches on the road so that if a car comes passed it falls in. We were cooking *sadza* [porridge] for the comrades at their base. When we were in the bush we were singing and saying slogans: Forward with war! Forward with being brave! These are some of the slogans that I know.[24]

And when they returned home, often to parents who had spent months not knowing if their children were alive or dead, they were greeted with praise and by an extraordinary inversion of the rituals of respect between generations:

The parents clapped to their children, thanking them for the work they had done. They were so happy at what we had done and they killed many goats for us to eat.[25]

The adults were not allowed to 'patrol in the bush' as their children did but they had their contribution to make as well. Adult men were appointed members of secret support committees whose duties were to organise the collection of food and clothing for the guerrillas. After the concentration camps were built, they found ways to smuggle out these supplies and leave them to be collected in previously selected corners of fields. At the end of the war these support committees were transformed into the Party Village Committees which took over responsibility for the administration of the countryside. Many of the men appointed to the earliest support committees survived to be elected to senior positions in the new administration. Adult women were required to cook for the guerrillas and to supply them with food. Their role in the war was frequently acknowledged and applauded at meetings. When slogans were shouted, following 'Forward with Robert Mugabe!' or 'Forward with ZANU!' you would also hear *'Pamberi nemugodhi'*, which means literally 'Forward with the stirring stick!' In other words:

Forward with those who cooked in the Chimurenga war![26]

During the war our parents cooked *sadza* for the comrades. They bought clothes for the comrades. Our parents were very brave. They cooked *sadza* while the rain was raining, they cooked even at midnight. That's why we say: Forward with Unity and Cooperation![27]

But despite the best efforts of these mothers, food was often very short:

When people grew crops and reaped them and put them in their granaries, soldiers would come and burn them down. So many people died of hunger. No matter. Nehanda and Kagubi looked after their children.[28]

And for those who fled their villages and lived with their children in the forest, life was unbearably hard:

The parents began to cry and we said: You must be brave like we are. The parents asked for food. We said: Do you think we grow anything while we are in the bush? They took bamboo shoots and gave them to the children. One woman complained: Do you call that food? And the comrade said: Woman, do you want to stay alive? And she kept quiet. Then she began to speak softly. She said: We people, we are now wild animals. Our children are now wild animals. Do you think we shall ever go back home and grow crops? And she began to cry again.[29]

The concentration camps were built so that the peasants would no longer be able to supply the guerrillas with food and other supplies. But the result was that the well-being of the peasants declined:

We were put in the 'keeps' [concentration camps] like cattle to be sent to the Cold Storage Commission to be killed. Our property such as radios, beds, chairs, and maize were all destroyed. Maize which we had harvested was burnt when our houses were destroyed. So we didn't get any food. If you complained you were hit. If you tried to run away you would just feel a bullet in your head. When we were in the keeps people could not sleep because of the guns sounding again and again. If we hadn't had our *mudzimus* looking after us, I think today there would have been nobody left walking here on earth.[30]

A confidential memorandum submitted to the Ministry of Internal Affairs in 1976 concerning camps in the nearby Chiweshe and Mount Darwin areas declares that:

It is now clear that the community is caught up in an uncontrolled collapsing sequence of events which, if not checked, will eventually lead to a degrading state of poverty where the people themselves will become so malnourished that both physical and mental degeneration will take place and we will have on our hands a huge national liability.[31]

And this of course hugely increased the support the guerrillas received:

Many places were now short of salt, meat, sugar. People suffered from various types of diseases. The comrades went and explained this to their leaders and they were given medicines to cure the people. This showed how friendly the comrades were towards us.[32]

Indeed as the war progressed these people, caught between two armed forces, suffering the most extreme deprivation and fear, came more and more to blame their fate on the government of Bishop Muzorewa and his auxiliary forces who, though sent into the countryside against the guerrillas, spent most of their energies attacking the peasants:

The auxiliaries were very bad people. They beat you even though you had done no crime. If they see you going to the fields carrying maize they say you are going to give the maize to the terrorists. They were afraid of the comrades but they just liked to beat the masses. When they held a meeting you hear them say: We are killing your children in the forest. They say: We want to be united. How can they be united when they beat the masses like that? Muzorewa was taking children to go to war. He gave them only three weeks training. Is that enough for a soldier? When the people were put in the keep the guns were sounding every day. The comrades said: Get out of the keep. The auxiliaries said: If you get out the jet bombers will kill you all. We could do nothing because everywhere we go is death.[33]

The next account written, like the last, by a woman, shows just as clearly the position of the peasants and their feelings towards the government of the day:

During the war it was a very bad time. If you hadn't fetched water before it got dark you were not going to get it because of the curfew. If you were late cooking for your children they just went to sleep hungry. If your relative died, if they lived far away you couldn't go there because of the war. Every family was unhappy because the war destroyed so many things. During that time a person could choose to die rather than to be alive. Many children were running away from their homes. It was a time of fear. They started holding meetings called *morari*. Boys and girls were patrolling. But the soldiers of Smith did not want to see a boy or a girl so we parents suffered. What were we going to do with our children in the bush suffering from hunger and thirst? Why did this war reach this place? It was caused by Muzorewa and his soldiers. We were hating him then because some children died and others were arrested. Others were beaten, some were put in the keep and others ran away. We thank the *midzimu* and God because we finally got what we suffered for. In some ways the war was good because we got our country.[34]

Three themes in the relationship between the guerrillas and the peasants which appear many times in the notebooks have not yet been discussed. The first is that the guerrillas were subject to certain laws while they were on active service inside Zimbabwe:

There were rules which the comrades were following in the war. They were not allowed to sleep with a girl, to shake hands with girls and not to be cruel to people . . . The comrades were not eating okra or vegetables or the intestines of any animals.[35]

The second is that the attack against sell-outs, those who betrayed the guerrillas, and the long-established fear and hatred of witches were somehow bound up together:

When the comrades arrived, we would give them food. If there were sell-outs there they would say: Down with sell-outs! If there were witches they would say: Down with discrimination! Forward with our Independence![36]

And finally, as is clear from many of the extracts already given, everywhere and in all circumstances peasants and guerrillas felt themselves in the presence and under the protection of their ancestors. In the following three chapters I will elaborate on these themes and explain some of the more puzzling aspects of these accounts of the war: that the peasants are said to have at first believed that the 'terrorists' were animals with tails, that the guerrillas selected only unmarried people as their go-betweens, that training took place only outside the borders of Zimbabwe, as well as the nature of the 'politicization' that the guerrillas practised on the peasantry. To a large extent, my commentary will draw on the analyses and descriptions presented in Part I and Part II of this book.

NOTES

1 Quoted in Windrich (1975, p. 296).
2 In 1941 a new Land Apportionment Act was passed. The final assignment of

land was 51 987 000 acres to the European areas, 41 900 000 acres to black areas, 3000 acres to forest areas and 57000 acres to undetermined areas. See Garbett (1963b, p. 189).

3 The quotes are from Ranger (1985) which contains an excellent and full-scale political and economic history of the causes of the war throughout Zimbabwe.

4 These paragraphs draw on Palmer and Parsons (eds) (1977), Arrighi (1973), Palmer (1977), Malaba (1980), Ranger (1985), Van Onselen (1976).

5 Quoted in Martin and Johnson (1981, p. 11).

6 Mugabe, Nkomo and Zvogbo (1978).

7 Mitchell (1982, p. 3).

8 All these notebooks have been deposited in the National Archives in Zimbabwe.

9 Notebook 4.

10 From an interview conducted by Nicholas Wright in Dande, 14 July 1981.

11 ibid.

12 Quoted in Frederickse (1984, p. 61).

13 Magical events of this kind appear almost invariably in accounts of battles of the past. The most common is the story of the warrior who, when forced into a corner from which he could not escape, flew up into the air and disappeared. This is told of well-known heroes of the past, but I have also heard people give accounts of the exploits of their grandfathers and other ancestors of equally recent vintage in very similar terms.

14 Interview with Cde Kenneth Gwindingwe in Harare, 17 January 1984.

15 Notebook 5.

16 Notebook 6.

17 Notebook 22.

18 Notebook 4.

19 Notebook 19.

20 Notebook 4.

21 Notebook 5.

22 Notebook 20.

23 Notebook 19.

24 ibid.

25 Notebook 4.

26 Notebook 5.

27 Notebook 20.

28 Notebook 5.

29 Notebook 19.

30 Notebook 24.

31 Copy placed in National Archives, Harare, Zimbabwe.

32 Notebook 5.

33 Notebook 13.

34 Notebook 7.

35 Notebook 19.

36 ibid.

8
The Legitimacy
of Resistance

We spoke to the old people who said that we must consult the mediums. We were taken to Nehanda . . . We told her 'We are the children of Zimbabwe, we want to liberate Zimbabwe'. She was very much interested.

The three questions that I try to answer in this chapter all flow from this extract from an interview with Cde Mayor Urimbo, the leader of one of the first groups of ZANLA guerrillas to operate in the Zambezi Valley. The first is: when the guerrillas explained their aims to the people who lived in the Valley, why were they led by them to the *mhondoro* mediums? The second is: when the guerrillas met these mediums, what persuaded them that they should try to win them to their side? The third question puts the first two from the mediums' point of view: when the mediums were confronted by the guerrillas, why did they agree to advise them in their struggle?

The answer to the first question, why the peasants led the guerrillas to the spirit mediums, is that the mediums had taken the place once held by the chiefs as the focus of political action within Dande. To show why this was so, I need to review very briefly the experience of the chiefs under the colonial state.

After the failure of the rebellion of 1896, the victorious white government set about a full-scale reorganisation of Shona society intending to squeeze out of it the last remaining drops of resistance. As the populations living on the lands claimed by the whites were cleared out and resettled, so chieftaincies were broken up and their members scattered. Large numbers of royal houses were abolished altogether. Others were amalgamated so as to streamline administration from the capital. Chiefs who had been loyal to the settlers during the rebellion were rewarded. Those who had resisted or were thought incapable of adjusting to modern conditions were removed from office and replaced with more pliable members of the royal lineages. In some cases non-royals were installed and their descendants given the right to succeed. The salaries (known as subsidies) paid to chiefs provided them with a higher standard of living than those categorised as their followers, as well as a reason for their continued loyalty to the state.

The effect of these measures within Dande was that the Korekore Kasekete Kamota chieftaincy which had ruled Dande for generations was divided into three. Chief Mzarabani who had welcomed fleeing rebels into Dande lost his position as leader of his house. His chieftaincy was reduced to a headmanship and made subservient to the newly created Kasekete chieftaincy with which a related lineage which had supported the state was rewarded. To undermine the authority of ex-chief Mzarabani still further, a branch of this house living some distance to the west of Kasekete was created an independent chieftaincy under the name of Chitsungo. A related house, the Chiweshe chieftaincy on the Plateau, was also demoted to a headmanship and placed under the authority of Kasekete.[1]

The process of restructuring the chieftaincies continued right up to the last years of the Rhodesian state. The chiefs who emerged from it had been transformed. In exchange for their political security and economic advancement, they were obliged to relinquish the greater part of the authority that their predecessors had held. The right to try criminal cases was put in the hands of native (later district) commissioners. As the area each peasant could farm was decreed by law, the chiefs were able to do no more than redistribute the scarce land in the reserves. The one function for which the chiefs and their headmen did have authority was the collection of taxes which forced the majority of young men out of their homes and into underpaid white employment. Headmen became known as *sabhuku*, owners of the tax book. By these means two of the most important communal rituals, the installation and the burial of chiefs, became moments of maximum penetration by the state into the depths of the countryside.

The cycle of ritual exchange which had for so long bound chief, ancestors and living men together in an unequal but flexible relationship finally broke apart. In the past, certain days of each month had been set aside for the followers of the chief to carry out agricultural tasks on his fields. This labour was given in return for access to land, the inalienable possession of the chief's ancestors. The grain that resulted from this labour was returned to those who had produced it either directly, in times of famine, or indirectly in the form of beer contributed by the chief for consumption during the annual rituals at which the royal ancestors were requested to provide the rain. Now three separate cycles emerged. In the first the state exchanged cash with the chiefs for their loyalty. In the second the chief's male followers, no longer able to rely on the royal granaries or on trade to support them in time of need, offered their labour power to the market in exchange for wages. And in the third exchange contributions of grain for the annual rain-bringing ceremonies were made, in Dande at least, not by the chief but by the heads of individual households.

All in all, the chiefs had become minor civil servants with the powers of constables. As such they were subject to the wishes of their masters, the native commissioners, and no longer to those of their ancestors, the *mhondoro*, or of their people. Their new status was symbolised by a uniform of red robes and a sola topi set off by a pair of sparkling handcuffs dangling from a leather band tied round the waist.

By the 1960s, the only one of the Dande-related royal houses that remained in opposition to the state was the Chiweshe headmanship which never relented in its attempts to regain its lost chiefly status. All the other houses, including the Tande Matsiwo and the Korekore Chisunga, had fallen under the rule of men prepared to co-operate, perhaps because they believed this best for their people, perhaps because they saw no alternative. However the majority of the *mhondoro* mediums associated with these chiefs opposed their co-operation. As a first step to understanding how and why, let us take a close look at the structure of the relationship between chiefs and mediums.

This relationship was discussed at some length in Chapter 4. Two points made there are relevant now. The first is that both chief and medium derive their authority from the *mhondoro* – the chief because he is descended from him, the medium because he is possessed by him. The second point is that the dynamic element in the tight circle of political authority running between chief, medium's assistant and *mhondoro* is the creativity of the medium. This creativity is generated but also concealed by ritual. Statements made by the mediums in trance are experienced by their listeners as if they were the truth as it was known and practised in the past. This allows the spirit mediums a great deal of unacknowledged political influence. The time has come to show how this unacknowledged influence can become effective in practice.

To begin with we need to examine a third point made in Chapter 4 in the light of evidence provided by two historians. I reported that chiefs and mediums whom I questioned agreed that the job of the chief is to rule while the job of the medium is to teach and advise. But in two instances at least we have accounts of mediums of the past who, if they did less than rule, certainly did a great deal more than advise. Dr S. I. Mudenge has described the mediums in the Zambezi Valley in the late eighteenth and early nineteenth centuries:

In the Zumbo region was found some of the most powerful *mhondoro* (spirit mediums) in the Zambezi Valley . . . These *mhondoro* wielded much political and social power over the peoples of the region. The documents on Zumbo covering the period 1770s to 1800 are full of examples of the roles played by the *mhondoro* as arbiters in matters of war and peace, trade disputes and political misunderstandings between the Portuguese at Zumbo and the neighbouring African rulers as well as among the rulers themselves. In the absence of a superior authority recognised by all the groups in the region, the senior spirit mediums acted like the final court of appeal.[2]

The best-known account of *mhondoro* mediums wielding 'political and social power' is Terence Ranger's history of the 1896 rebellion, *Revolt in Southern Rhodesia*. This book was the first major attempt to work out the consequences of the sharing of politico-religious authority between chiefs and mediums, the unique characteristic of the Shona peoples. Ranger's analysis is based on the premise that because the *mhondoro* mediums were possessed by spirits who were the ancestors of more than one chieftaincy, they had authority over territories wider than those of individual chiefs. They were therefore perfectly placed to organise the small scale independent chieftaincies into a co-ordinated fighting force.

The structural principles that underly the inter-chieftaincy authority of senior mediums are easy to understand if the argument in Figure 8.1 is followed. A, B, C, D and E are all *mhondoro*, the ancestors of the chieftaincy. If house E should split off and constitute itself as an independent chieftaincy, then *mhondoro* E will in time emerge as senior *mhondoro* of this new house. If the medium of *mhondoro* A or B is able to retain authority over the new chieftaincy, the medium of E will be obliged to refer his important decisions, such as the choice of successors to the chieftaincy, to them for confirmation. Should house E in turn

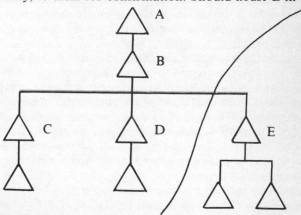

Figure 8.1   The fission of a royal lineage

divide into two separate chieftaincies, *mhondoro* E may retain authority over both, as may A and B. Whether or not this will happen, or whether an attempt by *mhondoro* C or D to exert their authority over chieftaincy E would succeed or fail is impossible to predict from the principles of the system alone. The reputations of the mediums, the desire of the new and old chieftaincies to maintain unity against a common enemy or any one of a dozen other factors could cause the claim to be accepted or rejected. The authority of the senior mediums will correspondingly increase or diminish. In time, claim and counter-claim will obscure the original historical relationships which are anyway no longer relevant.[3]

This explains how the sphere of one senior *mhondoro* medium can include the territories of more than one chief. It follows from this that, when both chiefs and mediums took up arms against the settlers in 1896 it was possible for one medium to co-ordinate the military operations of a number of apparently independent houses. But it does not explain why mediums should co-ordinate in this way, nor why they should be involved in military affairs in the first place. Moreover, in the modern case of the war for Independence, the extension of political authority which the mediums acquired was exercised not in conjunction with the chiefs but in their stead. How was *this* degree of political authority achieved?

As we shall see, it was not so much achieved by the mediums as thrust upon them. In the past, people who were dissatisfied with the chief in whose territory they lived were free to leave and establish a new relationship with another. But when dissatisfaction with the chiefs of Dande raised its head, there were no preferable chiefs to whom to turn. All were caught up in the same ties of obligation to the state. What followed from this is that the people of Dande shifted their political allegiance from the chiefs of the present to the chiefs of the past, the *mhondoro*, who could, of course, only be made available to them by their mediums.

The first thing to notice about this extraordinary development is that it was an explicit rejection of the authority of the colonial state. The second, and from this the rest of my argument will flow, is that the motivation for this shift was a change in the attitudes and the actions of the ordinary people and not of the religious or political specialists. The structure of political authority remained within an unchanged framework of ancestors, lineage and land, but it was made to work to the advantage of the peasants rather than of the state by being turned quite upside down.

It is now impossible to reconstruct when this inversion, this appeal from the present to the past first took place. But I can say that in the most recent past it has not been the chiefs of Dande who have allocated land either to their own people or to strangers. It has been the *mhondoro* mediums. It was, and it continues to be, the medium and not the chief who performs the ceremony that restores the social and natural order following a case of incest. It is the mediums to whom a fine must be paid as reparation for murder. Mediums rather than chiefs are charged with identifying and judging witches. And whereas in the past a pangolin was 'a delicacy which may be eaten only by an independent and lawful chief', today it is eaten by the *mhondoro* medium. It is not obligatory for people to work on the fields of the *mhondoro* mediums but neither do they any longer work on those of the chief. But they build huts for the medium's use during possession and on occasion they tend his yard and do other household tasks for him as well. All in all, the gifts, offerings and payments that indicate acceptance of political authority are no longer made to the chief but to the *mhondoro* medium.[4]

If a medium takes on the responsibilities associated with a chief, if he is treated by his followers as one would expect them to treat the living head of the royal lineage, a possible interpretation of this behaviour is that the medium is acting as a chief or even pretending to be a chief. This has the implication that it is in some sense illegitimate for a 'religious' leader to participate in 'politics'. This, as we shall see, was the attitude taken (or affected) by certain district commissioners. But the people of Dande do not see things in these terms.

'The real owner of the land,' wrote Charles Bullock in 1928, 'is on the spiritual plane'. The same can be said of the other expressions of political authority as well. The 'real' enforcer of fines for murder or incest is the *mhondoro* just as it is he to whom the offering of the pangolin is made. Both mediums and chief owe their status to the fact that they are the legitimate representatives of the *mhondoro* on the 'material plane', the medium possessed by him, the chief descended from and selected by him. What varies from one version of political organisation to another is the conception of which of these two representatives of the *mhondoro* is the most suitable to perform the rituals that protect the land from drought, the potentially fatal consequences of immorality and crime. As long as it is believed that both medium and chief are legitimate representatives of the *mhondoro*, either or both may be the recipients of the ritual offerings which are, in reality, directed to the *mhondoro*. But if legitimacy is lost, the flow of payments and gifts will stop or be redirected to the legitimate representative of the *mhondoro*, chief or medium, that remains.[5]

The loss of legitimacy did not precipitate a total loss of authority by the chiefs. The size of the royal lineages, their 'subsidies' and the support of the district commissioners allowed them to continue to dominate the lineages living in their territories. But two factors crucially altered the content of the authority which they held.

The first was that they were no longer selected by the *mhondoro*.

Although a medium might be persuaded to endorse the commissioner's decision, it was well known that chiefs were in office by courtesy of the state and that 'unprogressive' candidates would be passed over. The second alteration to established ritual practice related to the new system of state-controlled justice which was harsh both in what it did and in what it left undone. In what it did it was inflexible and authoritarian. What it left undone was the prosecution of witches.

The pre-colonial conception of major crimes such as murder, arson, theft, rape and so on coincided more or less with those of the Rhodesian state. Some benefit may have been perceived in the new judicial system in so far as it dealt with these crimes. But the one crime on which there could be no agreement was witchcraft. In the view of the people of Dande the practice of witchcraft was terrifying and widespread. In the view of the state it simply did not exist. The Witchcraft Suppression Act drawn up in 1899 was designed to eradicate witchcraft altogether. Under the terms of this Act, to accuse someone of practising witchcraft is as great an offence as attempting to practise it yourself.

To legislate against terror, however unfounded it may seem, does not cause it to disappear. The fear and anxiety that cause and are caused by witchcraft accusation, the disruption that might in the past have been resolved by the chief at his court, all the powerful and deep-seated emotions that can rip families and villages apart, all this the law forced below the surface of social life.

One solution that presented itself to people who believed that they or their children were at risk of death from witches was to kill those whom they suspected. Numerous accounts of such murders appear in Zimbabwean newspapers to this day. That victim and culprit are frequently members of the same family makes these cases especially appalling and the law that continues to prevent the hearing of witchcraft accusations in open court is in urgent need of reform. But taking the law into one's own hands was not the only solution. An alternative was to refer witchcraft cases to the *mhondoro* medium. In Dande this course was very frequently taken.[6]

It was neither coincidence nor simple expedient that the *mhondoro* mediums were required to judge witches. The opposition between *mhondoro* and witch stands at the very heart of the moral order. As I described in Chapter 3, the opposition between ancestral spirits and witch spirits finds its basic expression in kinship terms. Ancestors are inside the lineage and benign. Witches may also be found inside the lineage but are profoundly malevolent. The contrast between the two types of spirit is very fully worked out. Ancestors protect the lineage, witches long to devour human bodies and thus prevent the dead from becoming ancestors. Ancestors promote health, fertility and continuity. Witches promote sickness, death and cessation. Whatever is good for *mhondoro* is bad for witches. If there is no one to protect the world from

142

witches the life of every honest woman or man is at risk.

We are touching here on a very crucial point, one that we will carry with us to the end of the book. It was not necessary for the *mhondoro* mediums to hold any particular political view or to follow any particular course of action for them to become the focus of the combined religious and political attentions of the people of Dande. Though one set of representatives of the *mhondoro*, the chiefs, had failed them, their belief that the *mhondoro* would support them through thick and thin was unshaken. So they turned their loyalty towards the *mhondoro* themselves which meant, in effect, towards their mediums. By doing this they initiated the process whereby as the prestige and authority of the chiefs fell so that of the mediums went through the roof.[7]

But the mediums did not remain passive while this process took place. Many of them did a great deal to encourage and reinforce the shift of allegiance towards them. The most extreme examples were those who supported the nationalist parties. But whether they went this far or not and whatever their political beliefs and affiliations happened to be, all mediums expressed a powerful distaste for the economic innovations introduced by the state throughout this century.

This distaste was expressed in a variety of ways. Some mediums objected to the new techniques of agricultural production, especially to the use of fertilizer on the grounds that their spirits dislike the smell it gives 'their earth'. The medium of Musuma spent many months trying to prevent the clearing of fields for a government irrigation scheme. It is well known in Dande that when the baobab trees on this site were felled they cried out: 'Why are we being destroyed? Why do you pull us down for no good reason?' From east of Dande come reports of mediums who opposed the construction of dams which would flood sacred pools. But the most conspicuous way in which the antipathy of these mediums towards the new order was expressed was, as you might have expected, by the observation of a set of ritual prohibitions. These prohibitions, the third set I have dealt with so far, draw a very clear line between the world of the ancestors, including the techniques of agricultural production under their control, and the world of industrial production and exchange which was under the control of the whites and in which their followers laboured with so little reward.[8]

Throughout this period it was believed that it was dangerous for mediums to wear Western-style clothes or eat factory-produced foods, to smoke cigarettes or to use Western medicines. The smell of a clinic or a hospital was harmful to them. So were the smells of petrol and of tar. For this reason they could not ride in cars, buses or tractors or even walk along tarred roads. They ate only off wooden plates and drank from dried gourds. To use metal utensils was forbidden. In short, any goods produced by white technology were so objectionable and dangerous to the *mhondoro* that if their mediums came into contact with them the *mhondoro* would kill them. The reason given for the death of the medium of Mutota is that he was unable to protect himself from the fumes of the vehicles of the police sent to guard him at his home.[9]

The mediums did not object to their followers selling their surpluses of maize or sorghum on the market but the seeds of crops such as cotton or soya beans which were grown exclusively for cash sale were not added to the baskets they sprinkled each year with ancestral medicine. Nor were samples from the first harvest of these crops taken to the *mhondoro*'s shrine as a thanksgiving. They were outside the realm of the ancestors who refused to give them their protection.

It is important to understand that these restrictions express the antipathy felt by the ancestors, not that of the mediums. It is the forces of nature themselves that are put at risk by the economic domination of the whites. Many spirit provinces contain pools of water sacred to the ancestors and protected by lions. These pools will run dry if a tin mug so much as touches their waters. Only a gourd or a wooden bowl may be used to draw water from them. Such is the advance of white society into Dande that many pools which in the past were full even in the driest of dry seasons are today merely depressions in the sand. But though it is the *mhondoro* who reject the artefacts of white society, as always it is the mediums who express this rejection. The ritual prohibitions I have described were enforced when the mediums were in a state of trance as well as when they went about their day-to-day activities.

The last of this set of prohibitions is so powerful that it was observed by only the most rigorous of the mediums. This was that they might have no contact with any white people at all, neither to see nor be seen by them. The explanation given for this prohibition supplies an interpretation for them all. As whites were not in the country when the *mhondoro* were alive, it was dangerous for *mhondoro* to see them when they returned to take part in the lives of their descendants once again.[10]

A possible interpretation of these prohibitions is that they indicate the inherent conservativism of the mediums. In this view, the mediums protect their 'traditional' authority by isolating themselves. Thus their inability to provide their followers with as much and as good as the whites is concealed. But it is not only in relation to whites that restrictions of this kind are practised. They also occur between the *mhondoro* mediums themselves. For example, the medium of the autochthon Musuma is not permitted to have contact with the mediums of any Korekore *mhondoro*. This is explained on the basis of the myth recounted in Chapter 5 which tells how, 'long ago', the Korekore killed Musuma and gained the benefit of his rain-making powers. The present-day antagonism between the medium of Musuma and those of the Korekore *mhondoro* is an expression of the deep-seated opposition between the conquering Korekore and the autochthonous Tavara. The basis of this opposition is their conflicting claims to rights over territory.[11]

The refusal of *mhondoro* mediums to have contact with whites and the artefacts of white society is an expression of another deeply rooted opposition which also arises from conflicting claims to land. And in this case the opposition was strengthened by the effects of the military defeat of the 1890s, the destruction of the chieftaincies, the forced labour, the taxation, in general, by the peasants' experience of lost control over their lives. By their refusal to act as their descendants must act, by expressing the view that white society is a source of pollution that can kill, the ancestors add the final element to the spectacle of the past. With great eloquence these restrictions convey their belief that the dead world of the *mhondoro* is infinitely superior to the world of the present in which by their ill-fortune their descendants are condemned to live.[12]

Within the context of colonialism, the only context that any living medium had known, to become a *mhondoro* medium is to take a stand in opposition to white society. The profession of the medium is inherently radical. Though this radicalism comes in a range of intensities, from refusing to drink Coca-Cola to guiding columns of rifle-bearing porters through the depths of the Valley, it is part of the make-up of every modern *mhondoro* medium. This interpretation is given some weight by the fact that during the war the only mediums who did not observe this set of prohibitions, who for example ate factory-produced foods off enamel plates, were those few who gave their support to the District Administration. The consequence of their negligence in exposing their *mhondoro* to these dangerous substances was that their authenticity as mediums was very quickly cast into doubt.[13]

In sum, by observing the conventional restrictions on their behaviour, the mediums imitate the chiefs who held undisputed authority before the coming of the whites. They express an explicit rejection of the subservience of Shona society. They assert the significance and the integrity of its past and demonstrate a commitment to protect its central institutions from further humiliation and disruption. The emergence of the great spectacle of the past into the full light of the present as a source of inspiration and leadership in mounting resistance to the state was a result of two interacting factors. The first was the need of the people to find a source of legitimate authority free of the constraints by which the chiefs had been bound, an authority which could provide just resolutions of their disputes, assuage their fears of witchcraft and legitimise their growing antipathy towards chief, District Administration and all other local employees of the state. The second factor, quite simply, was the belief that the *mhondoro* belong to the past. This allowed the less attractive aspects of the present to be characterised as 'opposed to the *mhondoro*' and therefore as immoral, as dangerous, as pollutant, as needing to be got rid of by all possible means, with all possible speed.

By accepting their lowly position in the government hierarchy, the chiefs had acquired the authority to receive a monthly salary, to collect taxes, to wear a flamboyant uniform and to little else. Their followers were left with no authority but to do what the government required of them. The shift of ancestral political authority from the chiefs to the mediums over whom the state had no hold provided the thousands of deeply discontented villagers in Dande with the authority to do what the ancestors required of them. They received the authority to resist (see Figure 8.2 and compare with Figure 4.2, p. 59).

I have answered my first question and explained why, when the ZANLA guerrillas entered Dande for the first time, 'the old people said

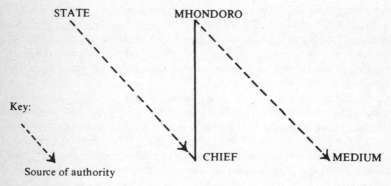

Figure 8.2   Post-colonial sources of authority in the relationship between chief, medium and mhondoro

that we should consult the mediums'. But having consulted them, why did the guerrillas decide that they needed their support? And why did the mediums agree to give it?

The guerrillas in Dande were not the first to consider the advantages of co-operating with spirit mediums. One of the guerrillas who fought the first battle of the war in 1966 at Sinoia made an attempt to contact a spirit medium named Gumbachuma who lived in the Zvimba area. His interest in this medium was sparked by the belief that the mediums knew where rifles used during the 1896 rebellion had been stored. To the weapon-starved guerrillas this information would have been a major contribution to the struggle. The belief that the *mhondoro* could supply the guerrillas with weapons and perhaps also reveal the location of the caves in which the rebels had concealed themselves during the 'first war of Independence' emerged at various periods of the war in widely scattered parts of the country. It demonstrates very powerfully how a continuous tradition of resistance was attributed to the mediums. The medium of Gumbachuma is said to have been delighted by the interest shown in him but before the relationship had time to ripen into trust, the attack took place and the guerrillas were annihilated. After this abortive campaign, I know of no further ZANLA contact with mediums until the meeting between Urimbo's group and the medium of Nehanda five years later.[14]

It is important to set out how the relationship between the mediums and the guerrillas of the 1970s developed. In their search for the support of the people of Dande the guerrilla commanders were pragmatic. Their intention was to lay down a durable foundation for long-term co-operation with the peasants. They were prepared to work with whoever they could trust. Certainly they knew of the part played by the medium of Nehanda and other mediums in the rebellion of 1896. This had been a source of nationalist propaganda throughout the 1960s. But they did not enter Dande with the intention of recruiting the mediums. It was only after they discovered the authority that the mediums held among the peasantry that they made efforts to persuade them to join them.

Terence Ranger has described the background shared by many of these early guerrilla leaders:

> Most of these recruits during the 1960s were young men from Zimbabwean families in Zambia. None of them had any direct experience of the spirit mediums or of the part they played in peasant consciousness inside Zimbabwe. Many Zimbabwean farmers inside Zambia, indeed, were members of Independent churches and ascribed their striking economic success to their freedom from antiquated tradition. Young men from this background who had then gone on to political education somewhere in the Socialist bloc were hardly likely to be very sympathetic to the idea that the mediums might have a crucial role to play in guerrilla war.[15]

But sympathetic to this idea many very quickly became. Many who started the war as sceptics were believers before the end. Some, though they did not believe, saw the success of the strategy and did not interfere. I will deal with the political and ideological questions raised by this pragmatism in Part IV. For the moment what matters is this. The reason that the deal with the spirit mediums was sought and that once struck was perpetuated year after year was that the mediums could deliver the goods. And the goods in this case were the people. As Cde Josiah Tungamirai, who held many senior positions within ZANLA including that of Chief Political Commissar, put it:

> When we started the war the spirit mediums helped with recruitment. In the villages they are so powerful. If they tell their children they shouldn't go and join us they won't. When we wanted to go and open a new operational zone we would have to approach the mediums first. Mbuya Nehanda was the most

important and influential recruit in those early days. Once the children, the boys and the girls in the area, knew that Nehanda had joined the war, they came in large numbers.[16]

As the relationship between guerrillas and mediums deepened, it brought many other advantages to the guerrillas as well. The *mhondoro* mediums knew the land intimately and could guide guerrillas, porters and new recruits through terrain that was physically dangerous because of wild animals and dense forest and through territories that held spiritual dangers as well. I will deal with this at length in Chapter 9, but the point I want to stress here is that none of these advantages, crucial though they proved to be, were anticipated by the guerrillas. The mediums could supply recruits and on that basis the relationship began.

Why were the mediums who ruled supreme in the countryside willing partners in this relationship? What was in it for them? Some of the mediums of Dande had been committed to support of the nationalist parties and to the liberation of Zimbabwe before the guerrillas arrived. For example, the medium of Chiwawa who in his youth had been a so-called '*daga* boy', a labourer on a building site, was a long time supporter of ZAPU, shifting his allegiance to ZANU when it broke away under Sithole in 1963. The medium of Chiodzamamera had been a school teacher in the town of Banket until he was struck by the sickness that heralded his possession. He too was committed to ZANU's political programme. But, as I have shown, whether they had had direct exposure to party politics or not, the profession of mediumship predisposed its practitioners to an antagonistic view of the state.

The factor that persuaded the majority of the mediums to convert their symbolic resistance into practice was the undertaking given by the guerrillas that if their efforts should succeed they would reverse all the legislation that limited the development and freedom of the peasantry. Of all the promised reforms the most important for forging unity between guerrillas and mediums was the undertaking to free the land from the grasp of the whites, to return it to the peasants who had barely enough to keep their families alive.

The single most important duty of the spirit mediums is to protect the land. From the grave, from the depths of the forest, from the body of a lion or of their mediums, the *mhondoro* control in perpetuity the land they conquered during their lives. Under the rule of the whites their land had lost its fertility. Sacred places had been fenced off and ruled out of bounds. The guerrillas offered land as renewed fertility and as restored tradition. They offered a Zimbabwe returned to its original and rightful owners. From the shared aim of guerrilla and medium to regain the land, to renew its fertility and the people's lost wealth, from this profound well of common hope and desire, the sharing of ritual and weapons, symbolism and strategy, the union of

148

the mystical power of the ancestors with the military strength of the guerrillas was to flow.

When the guerrillas declared their right to all the land in Zimbabwe in the name of the people and of the past, they began a process which culminated in the establishment of themselves as the successors of the chiefs. Indeed they may be called the chiefs' legitimate successors because, like all legitimate rulers, they were installed by the *mhondoro*. Apart from their recruiting of the peasantry to the resistance, the legitimisation of this succession was the most important contribution the *mhondoro* mediums made to the war. A demonstration of how it was achieved is the subject of Chapter 9. But before we move on to it there is a second set of three questions to be answered, though at rather less length than the first.

First, you will have noticed that of all the political and economic innovations described in Chapter 7, the only one that did not affect Dande directly was loss of land. The dry soils, the very high temperatures and the absence of cattle all made the Valley unconducive to commercial exploitation. Except for two state-run irrigation schemes and a few small areas commandeered to resettle people from the Plateau, no land was forcibly taken from those who held it by ancestral rights.

This did not mean that the number of migrant labourers pouring into the wage-earning areas from Dande was any the less. As the border between Portuguese and British territories was drawn and enforced, trade that had been conducted for centuries along the Zambezi River fell away. The only alternative source of an income to supplement the unreliable returns from the land was migrant labour. Once contracts on mines and farms and later in industry were taken up in large numbers, the restructuring of Dande by the ungentle forces of capitalism could begin. In 1961, for example, 72.3 per cent of the men in the territory adjoining Dande to the east were employed away from home. It is safe to assume that a similar number were away from Dande.[17]

But though those born within Dande did not experience loss of land directly, this factor was added to the groundswell of feeling there by the resettled peasants who found it quite as unattractive as the white commercial farmers but who had no choice of other places to live in. These settlers came as individuals, as whole villages, such as the village of the medium of Mutota who was thrown off his lands in 1957, and even as whole chieftaincies such as that of Chief Whata who was removed from the Chiweshe Tribal Trust Land to an area just east of Dande in 1961. The guerrillas drew on the resentment of these people as well as tempting their long-established neighbours with promises of better land and healthier living conditions if they could only win the war. As one commander who operated in the north-east has explained:

You see, in the north east where I was operating many people were far away from the good farming areas, so we told them that their land was very poor, since it is usually very hot and the soil is non-productive. So we would tell them, 'It's you, the people of Zimbabwe, of this area, who should have been in the areas where there are those farmers who are getting a lot from the rich land. They've thrown you out of the rich land so that you don't get anything,' and of course then the people would like very much to have the land which they did not have.[18]

Secondly, what of the Christians? The majority of members of the Evangelical Alliance Mission and of the Apostolic Church of John Marange had spent a number of years out of Dande in relatively well paid employment in the towns and had accumulated small amounts of capital. The congregations of the churches were, roughly speaking, the limits of the moral obligation they felt to share with their neighbours and kin and on the whole they had established a rather better standard of living for themselves. But for all that, they were no less willing to participate in the struggle in the ways that the guerrillas encouraged. Members of all the churches were represented on the secret committees that organised support for the guerrillas during the war.

But what of their response to the increase of authority that the *mhondoro* mediums achieved? From the evidence I have it is clear that Evangelicals and Apostolics did not turn to the mediums for the resolution of their problems in the way that the majority of the peasants had. Disputes between members of each Church were resolved by Church leaders. The Apostolics were especially resolute in this, refusing to take domestic or civil disputes either to the chiefs' courts or to any but their own. The Evangelicals dealt with cases of suspected witchcraft by prayer, the Apostolics by exorcism. The Catholics on the other hand, economically undifferentiated from the rest of the peasants, are among the most fervent participants in ancestral rituals as I described in Part I. Amongst them are *vatapi* and other leading ritual experts.

When the guerrillas entered Dande their attitude to all the churches was hostile. There were only two large brick church buildings in Dande and both were destroyed. Attending Evangelical or Catholic services was equated with hostility to nationalism and the Catholic priests who had held services fairly regularly in Dande found it impossible to continue. The official position of the Apostolics was that they could have no involvement in politics either in support of the guerrillas or of the state. Despite this, some senior members actively supported the guerrillas. Apart from the charge of collaboration made against the rest, a further objection raised by the guerrillas concerned the Apostolics' refusal to use either Western or traditional medicines and to rely entirely on prayer to cure sickness. The guerrillas considered this backward and foolhardy and the children of Apostolics were frequently treated by ZANLA medical officers despite the protests of their parents.

Children of Christian families who joined the nationalists either as *mujibas* or as guerrillas abandoned the ritual practices of their fathers and few took them up again when they returned home after the war.

For the Apostolics, compromise with ancestral spirits is impossible. They do not deny the miraculous feats that the mediums perform but, as a leading member put it: 'I must believe that the *mhondoro* are true but I cannot pray to them'. For many Evangelicals however the experience of the war brought the ancestors whom they had rejected back into their lives with very great force. During the years in the camps possession accompanied by ancestral song and dance took place day after day. One of the women whose recollections I quoted earlier is a member of this Church. She expresses a very typical emotion when she ends her account by stating that 'we thank the *midzimu* and God because we finally got what we suffered for.'[19]

The third question requires a more elaborate answer. A constant refrain of my analysis of the myths and possession rituals of Dande in Chapter 5 was that water or rain is in some profound way opposed to blood. The spilling of blood on the ground causes drought. The rain-bringing mediums are put in grave danger if they come into contact with people who are at critical moments of the biological life cycle. They must avoid birth and menstrual blood but they must also avoid death and the blood of the dead. How then can these mediums have allowed themselves so close an alliance with the ZANLA guerrillas who were, amongst other things, trained and efficient killers?

According to one frequently repeated story, when the guerrillas first approached the *mhondoro* mediums they admitted that their campaign would be the cause of much death. They were determined to kill as many of their enemies as possible. At first, so it is said, the mediums refused to give their permission for this. But when it was explained to them that the intention of the guerrillas was to liberate Zimbabwe they agreed, though they insisted that the killing be kept to a minimum, 'We don't want a lot of blood,' they said, 'don't just kill people for nothing'. What this semi-mythological account is intended to illustrate is the distinction between homicide and murder, between legitimate and illegitimate killing.

From the point of view of the *mhondoro*, killing can be defined in two ways. Firstly there is the secret killing of a member of one's own lineage. This is witchcraft and is always forbidden. Secondly there is the acknowledged killing of either a member of one's own or of another lineage. This is also extremely dangerous and causes drought but its effect can be counteracted if a fine is paid to the *mhondoro*. *Mhondoro* are able to remove from the act of killing the threat it carries to the society as a whole, just as they can for the act of incest, provided that the specified fine is paid and the appropriate ritual performed. One way of seeing the arrangement arrived at between guerrillas and mediums therefore is as an agreement in a good cause to condone the necessary killing and waive the fine. But we can go further still.

If you turn back to the myths in Chapter 5 you may notice a striking contradiction in my interpretation which I have left unresolved until now. In flat defiance of the belief that killing causes drought, in these myths killing is presented as a source of fertility and of rain. In myth III Nyahuma kills his father-in-law Musuma by tricking him into seeing a red cloth, which stands for blood and thus gets access to rain. In myth II when Chimombe's throat is slit, his blood pours out onto the ground and is transformed into the source of a river. Similarly in myth I the committing of incest, which in theory should bring drought in its wake as inevitably as killing, actually provides the descendants of the incestuous couple with all the rain they need.

The reason for this contradiction is quite simply that chiefs and ordinary people are profoundly different from each other. The crimes of ordinary people pollute the earth. The crimes of the chief purify it. Or, more accurately, what is a crime for a commoner is no crime for a chief, a point of view which is not altogether uncommon. This is clearly expressed in the terminology used. Incest committed by ordinary people is called *makunakuna*. Incest committed by royals is referred to as *kupinga pasi* which means 'the protection of the earth'.[20]

At their deaths chiefs become *mhondoro*. The royal lineage is the source of the soil's fertility. Or rather each dead chief is the source of the fertility of his own spirit province. In other words, dead chiefs are the source of the fertility of the territory they are believed to have conquered when alive. By their very nature *mhondoro* are conquerors, warriors, killers. It is through their violence that the fertility of the earth is made available to their descendants.

All *mhondoro* were responsible for a great deal of killing while they were alive though always in a good cause, indeed in the best of all possible causes: the establishment of the territory within which their descendants now live. And therefore all *mhondoro* know a great deal about war. Very frequently ex-guerrillas explained to me that the reason they had worked so well with the *mhondoro* mediums was that they know *zvinhu zvese zvezvohondo*, everything there is to know about the art of war. Amongst the Shona, soldiers do not form a separate section of the population. All men are potentially warriors, chiefs are the military leaders of the present, *mhondoro* were the military leaders of the past. If you think of the ZANLA guerrillas as the warriors of the past returned in new guise, their alliance with the *mhondoro* mediums seems neither innovatory nor surprising. No more does the desire of the guerrillas to gain their permission for, or better, their legitimisation of the killing which they knew would ensue.

Illegitimate killing, murder by witchcraft (and any illegitimate killing is regarded as witchcraft) is anathema to the *mhondoro*. But killing in defence of their descendants or their territory is a long-established ancestral tradition. One way in which this is expressed is by the ritual axe or *gano* which all *mhondoro* mediums carry. The present-day version has a blunted edge but in its original practical form it was a battle axe, a weapon of war.[21]

By way of conclusion to this chapter, Alan Isaacman's pioneering study, *The Tradition of Resistance in Mozambique* provides an historical perspective. This history of the Zambezi Valley in the late nineteenth and early twentieth centuries contains account after account of *mhondoro* spirit mediums deep in the thick of battle against the Portuguese colonial forces leading, planning and advising:

> Besides their involvement in the decision-making process, the religious authorities played an important role in organizing the rebellions. In Makanga, for example, Chicango [a medium] helped plan the strategy of the insurgents and persuaded a number of Chewa *afumu* to participate in the uprising . . . The *svikiro* [medium] of Chaminuka, for example, precipitated the abortive 1904 uprising, and Mbuya, earthly medium of Kabudu Kagoro spearheaded the 1919 rebellion.[22]

The main leaders of these rebellions were the chiefs but where the chiefs sided with the colonial power then, in precisely the manner of their successors of the 1970s, the spirit mediums moved to the front line:

> While the prime concern of the religious leaders was to legitimate the authority of the secular rulers, they sometimes felt compelled to divorce themselves from specific rulers whom the Europeans had coopted . . . When Kageo [a chief] publicly refused to join the 1901 Shona insurrection, the spirit mediums successfully appealed to the local population to disregard his pronouncements.[23]

It is entirely consistent with their role as conquerors of land and as warriors in the anti-colonial struggles of the past that when the ZANLA guerrillas approached the spirit mediums of Dande they should have agreed to the spilling of blood in a just cause and joined them in their struggle against the Rhodesian colonial state.

NOTES

1 This account is based on information collected in Dande and on scattered references in the Government Per 5 files (Ministry of Local Government Archives, Harare) for the three chieftaincies. See, for example, Per 5

Kasekete letter dated 9 June 1947. Also records of the recent reconstitution of the Chiweshe house in Per 5 Chiweshe have been consulted. For the history of the chieftancies throughout Zimbabwe see Garbett (1966b, p. 118); Bourdillon (1971, p. 5); Holleman (1969); Weinrich (1971); Ranger (1982b, 1985).

2 Mudenge (1976, p. 34).

3 One of D. N. Beach's contributions to the historiography of the 1896 rebellion has been to cut the spirit mediums down to size. His research in the western districts persuaded him that the chiefs had been far less united than Ranger's reading of the evidence had suggested. If this was so the need to explain the co-ordination of the chiefs by the spirit mediums, and to discuss the whole question of the ambiguous power relations between them, falls away. But having trumped some of Ranger's best tricks, Beach overplays his hand. He asserts that spirit mediums have authority *only* within the territory of the chiefs descended from them, ignoring the distinction between the political realm and the spirit realm controlled by the mediums. He ignores, that is, the ability of the senior mediums to accumulate a following based on the descendants of their *mhondoro* but including many others attracted by their personality, their curing skills, their predictive powers and so on. Note, however, that Ranger's original account of the structural relationship between chief and medium was not based on the analysis I have given but on the works of Michael Gelfand which describe the hierarchies of *mhondoro* in the same terms as the mediums themselves do, as virtually nationwide permanent records of the chiefly genealogies of the past. I have criticised this interpretation of the royal genealogies elsewhere, showing how they reflect the political realities of the present rather than of the past and how, within certain limits, they can be restructured by the mediums. See Beach (1979); Ranger (1967); Gelfand (1959, 1962), Lan (1983, Chs VII and VIII).

4 On the pangolin see Holleman (1952, p. 34).

5 For Garbett's account see Garbett (1963, 1966a, 1967).

6 Throughout Zimbabwe, one established means of dealing with witchcraft accusation, village fission, was made impossible by the acute land shortage in the Tribal Trust Lands. This was a less significant factor in Dande but even here fertile land along the banks of the rivers was a scarce asset.

7 George Balandier (1970, p. 160) has provided a general account of the processes I describe here:

   Within the framework of the colonial situation real political life was expressed partly in a clandestine way . . . the doubling of the administratively recognised authorities by the effective, though unseen authorities. Politically significant reactions also operated in an indirect way and appeared where they could find expression, notably in the new religious movements and prophetic and messianic churches or under cover of an apparently unpolitical traditionalism and neo-traditionalism. The colonized peoples often used, with great strategic skill, the cultural gap that separated them from the colonizers.

8 For examples from the east of Dande see Bourdillon (1971, p. 261). See also Gelfand (1977, p. 134).

9 Other reasons given for the death of Mutota's medium are the smell of onions

eaten by the soldiers, and that the sight of the weapons the soldiers carried was offensive to the *mhondoro*.

10 This point was clearly made in a conversation between myself, the *mhondoro* Chivere (i.e. the medium in trance) and Chivere's *mutapi*:

Chivere: Ask him, if he sees a lion is he going to shoot it with his gun?
Mutapi: If you see a lion will you shoot it?
Me: No, I will not shoot.
Chivere: Tell him that his relatives were killing plenty. Your relatives, if they saw us they shot us. Do you understand what I'm saying? That's why we have a prohibition (*muko*) that we mustn't see you.

11 There are many other examples of *mhondoro* mediums not being permitted to see each other for reasons of murders and defeats said to have taken place in the past. Nyamasoka may not see his father Nyamapfeka because he killed his mother, Nyamapfeka's wife; Nyatseru may not see his father Chidyamauyu, etc.

12 In Albino Pacheco's account of Dande, written in 1861, although he records that the mediums were 'barred from seeing arms and weapons of war and also anything that is red', he makes no reference to the mediums being forbidden to have contact with the Western-produced commodities available at that time. In fact the contrary is true, for the most significant imported commodities, cloth and beads, are precisely those which were worn by the *mhondoro* mediums to identify themselves and their profession.

13 I will give some detail of the lives of the collaborator mediums in Chapter 10 below. Ranger (1982b) has described the career of another, Muchetera, the medium of the Zezuru *mhondoro* Chaminuka. This aspect of the relationship between mediums and guerrillas is mentioned in an interview with Comrade Zeppelin, a ZANLA political commissar who was active in the north-east. 'Most of the spirit mediums,' he pointed out, 'did support the struggle . . . You could see sometimes with those few spirit mediums who did not support the struggle, the spirits would vanish from such people. They would just end up a normal human being, and not get possessed again.' (Frederikse, 1984, p. 131).

The argument that mediums in their everyday lives enact their conception of the lives of the chiefs of the past is supported by the evidence of the Chikunda mediums who live on the banks of the Zambezi River near Kanyemba. These mediums do not observe any of the restrictions to which the Korekore and the Tavara mediums are subject except the avoidance of blood, menstrual or otherwise, which is the central symbol of mediumship, the triumph of life-through-possession over life-through-birth. The reason they give for this absence of restriction is that their ancestors, their *mhondoro*, were Portuguese, that is whites, who wore boots and shirts, carried guns, lived in European style houses and so on. Chikunda mediums dress in ordinary clothes. Only a few ritual items, such as beads and snuff boxes, distinguish them from non-mediums. As the Chikunda ancestors were white, or at least not perceived as opposed to whites, the set of symbols elaborated by Korekore and Tavara mediums, deriving from their notions of how *their* ancestors lived in the pre-white past, has no power for the

Chikunda. This should not be taken to imply that Chikunda mediums were not committed to opposition to the authority of the governments of Rhodesia and Portuguese East Africa. What it does mean is that they were not able to express their opposition by means of the same symbolic materials as those used by the Korekore and the Tavara.

14 This account is based on an interview with Henry Hamadziripi in Harare in January 1984. Ranger (1985, p. 203) has described an incident of contact between mediums and guerrillas of the ZAPU/South African ANC Alliance in the early 1960s. He also refers to the anticipation that the mediums would supply the guerrillas with guns.

15 Ranger (1985, p. 203).

16 Martin and Johnson (1981, p. 77/78).

17 The national average in 1961 was 65.4 per cent (Garbett, 1963, p. 18).

18 Frederikse (1984, p. 131).

19 The ease with which the Evangelicals accepted the authority of the ancestors may be in part a consequence of their very low numbers in Dande and therefore untypical. Ranger (1985) has described in great detail the consistency of the support for the nationalists across barriers of class and religion throughout Zimbabwe until the 'internal settlement' of 1978.

20 The phrase is also used in a number of other contexts, for instance, the placing of protective medicines around a new home or the erection of military fortifications.

21 An axe of precisely the shape of the *gano* carried by *mhondoro* mediums in Dande is identified as a battle axe or *cheyonangomby* by Richard Thornton, the nineteenth-century explorer of the Zambezi River (Thornton, 1963, Vol. I, p. 150).

22 Isaacman (1976, pp. 129, 193).

23 ibid., p. 129.

9
From Chiefs to Guerrillas

For some months now these terrorists have been operating in this area, quietly and methodically undermining the local population. They have done this in a number of ways. Firstly, through intimidation at the point of a gun; secondly they found a few witchdoctors of doubtful character and of little substance, and succeeded in bribing them to their side. These were then used to good effect in misleading local tribesmen into accepting that the terrorists were worthy of their support. I am sure that I do not have to inform you how easy it is to mislead these simple gullible people who still believe in witchcraft and the throwing of bones.

Broadcast by Ian Smith, Prime Minister of Rhodesia, 18 January 1973[1]

Quite apart from their skills at 'misleading local tribesmen', the 'witchdoctors' of Dande had a range of other abilities which they put at the disposal of the ZANLA guerrillas. They shared with them their intimate knowledge of the countryside, guiding them by little-used paths out of sight of the gravel roads patrolled by the Security Forces. They led columns of weapon bearers in and out of the country and showed them the most secure places where these weapons could be concealed.

But they did a great deal more than this too. Their most spectacular contribution to the guerrillas' success was their instruction in how to interpret certain signs displayed by animals in the bush. As the following quotes from three ex-guerrillas testify, with the use of the information revealed by these signs, the guerrillas were able to protect themselves from the dangers of the forest and even to predict the outcome of their actions:

The spirit mediums gave us many good ideas. The *chipungu* (eagle) was a very important sign. If we saw them we would take off our shoes and our hats. If they flew down and made a great deal of noise, we knew there was trouble coming and would leave that place. If they flew round peacefully we knew we were safe.[2]

If you saw two eagles fighting in the sky that meant that the bomber planes were coming. In March 1979 we saw two eagles fighting near Gonono. We made off. The planes came and bombed but no one was hurt.
    If an eagle should fly over our base in the forest we all take off our hats. If anyone refuses there is no doubt they will die.[3]

You had to watch out for the *chipungu*. If it twice makes a noise, that is very dangerous. If you see a tortoise in the path you will have a good journey for at least two or three days. But if you find a snake, that is bad. Turn back. The enemy is near.[4]

Protective techniques that the mediums had practised before the war were made available to the guerrillas. One recalled that the mediums 'gave us some snuff which they call *bute* which we rub on our foreheads. This means that the enemy is quite unable to see us wherever we may go.' The belief that the guerrillas, especially those trained in the early years of the war, were able to disappear into thin air was very widespread. So was the belief that *bute*, the *mhondoro*'s patent cure-all, a source of general good health and fortune, could protect them from the bullets of the enemy. But the powers of *bute* would fail and the guerrillas would lose their ability to interpret the signs unless they observed a complex set of restrictions which the mediums imposed on them. The first of these restrictions prohibited the guerrillas, both female and male, from having sex while on active duty, either with each other or with the peasants whose villages they passed through:

Though there were many women with us, fighting with rifles, you could not sleep with one or even shake her hand. If a man and a woman fell in love, they could tell each other but then they had to tell the Commander of the Platoon and he would write it down so that after the war they would live up to their promise to marry. But to sleep together during the struggle was forbidden.[5]

A young *mujiba* recounted that 'our forces didn't make love to girls but Muzorewa's forces did this very much. If our forces had done this, our country would never have been taken by the blacks.'[6] It was especially dangerous for the guerrillas to come into physical contact with women during menstruation or to eat food cooked by them while in this condition:

The women were sent into the operational areas for only short periods at a time and their leaders were women who took the danger of even shaking hands with a man while having a period very seriously. Some boys even used to keep records of when the women's periods were because if you made a mistake you could get killed. We never did this but I know some who did. Also it is dangerous to eat food cooked by a woman with a young child or while pregnant. The best is the food cooked by old women or young girls who don't know anything.[7]

Another account describes the consequences of disobeying this restriction in the most extreme terms remarking that: 'Even at the time of the elections we did not want to see a pregnant woman. If a pregnant woman came to one of our camps, sure that camp will be destroyed.'[8] You will have recognised at once that these restrictions are similar to those observed by the spirit mediums themselves. In addition the guerrillas observed a number of others as well:

> The comrades were never allowed to kill the wild animals in the bush. Especially elephants and baboons were forbidden but also any other kind. If they did this they would quickly go mad. The foods the comrades could not eat were okra, beans, groundnuts and all vegetables. Of animals they could not eat intestines, lungs, heart and all things found in the abdominal cavity. Even the heads and limbs of animals were not allowed.[9]

If the guerrillas killed a goat (so an old man who lived in Dande throughout the war told me) they would always give the intestines and the head to a civilian supporter. And, finally, although salt was not explicitly prohibited, the guerrillas were encouraged not to eat it or to eat as little as possible.

In a moment I will have something to say about the extent to which all these prohibitions, especially those relating to sex, were consistently observed. But there is no doubt that the guerrillas and the *mujiba*, young unmarried women and men living for months on end in the depths of the forest, believed very firmly that these prohibitions ought to be observed. Only those who remained in the villages, the married people, the parents, were exempt, as two such parents recall:

> These were the rules which the comrades followed during the war. If one of them broke a law, when he is next on contact [i.e. in action] his gun will never let the bullet out or else he will be beaten to the worst degree. If the *mujibas* break these laws they are to be killed straight away. Only parents were allowed to do just as they please.[10]

> During the war many people were patrolling in the bush but we who were married we did not patrol. But we were on the look-out for the enemies if they should come. We did this to help the freedom fighters.[11]

Why were these prohibitions imposed? What did they mean? Long before the guerrillas set foot in Dande, some of these prohibitions had been observed by hunters. The historical record concerning Shona warriors of past ages is thin, but there is some evidence to suggest that before the most recent war these prohibitions applied to warriors as well. In order to demonstrate the coherence of this random seeming set of prohibitions, I need to treat the three typical male occupations (hunter, warrior, *mhondoro* medium) together and in some detail. Proceeding in this way will also allow me to suggest a possible explanation of the fourth and last set of prohibitions observed by the mediums: their refusal to eat pepper, onions and to use strong-smelling soap.

Hunters and warriors

Mhondoro and warrior are at once opposed to and identified with each other. What matters is whether the warrior carries out his characteristic activity, killing, with or without the approval of the *mhondoro*; whether he is fighting to defend the territory of the *mhondoro* or to capture it from him. A very similar account can be given of the relationship between *mhondoro* and hunter.

The power of the *mhondoro* to transcend life and death is marked by their abhorrence of blood. Any kind of dead body is dangerous to them. Hunters on the other hand, are practised killers. They shed the blood of animals and provide their dead bodies to be eaten. But the opposition goes deeper still. All things that grow wild in the bush, both game and uncultivated plants, are under the protection of the *mhondoro*. Indeed, as their name implies, *mhondoro are* wild animals. They are lions. When a royal ancestral spirit is not in the body of its medium it lives in the body of a lion. If you kill a lion you take the chance of killing the temporary home of a royal ancestor.

The *shave* spirit that possesses and assists hunters is known as Kapori. This is not an animal *shave*. The Kapori were 'so-called hunters . . . possibly survivors of Early Iron Age Sinoia culture'. Over time, the memory of these hunting people of the past has been converted into a possessing *shave* spirit which confers the talent to hunt exceptionally well. The colour of the beads the Kapori mediums wear on their wrists is red, the colour abhorred by the *mhondoro*. According to hunters I questioned, these red beads symbolise the blood of the animals they kill. They seem to imply the following set of oppositions. The bush is the place of the incorporeal, unpolluted, deathless ancestral spirits. Into the bush stride the human, death-dealing hunters. The *mhondoro* are wild animals of the bush. The Kapori hunters are men who kill wild animals. The *mhondoro* hate blood. The Kapori hunters display blood on their wrists as a sign of their identity.[12]

Ancestors are the essence of all that is good. Following the logic of these oppositions it would seem that hunters must be 'bad'. But of all foods, meat is the most highly prized. If hunters were forbidden to practise their skills it would be impossible for people to eat it. As the prime duty of the *mhondoro* is to care for their descendants and provide them with all they desire or deserve, a compromise with the hunters must be struck. If hunters observe certain restrictions they will be permitted to catch game. The most important of these is that they abstain from sex on the night before they go out hunting. By doing so the hunters symbolically allow the bush to remain free of the pollution of biological reproduction. In return the *mhondoro* allow a sufficient number of animals to be caught. In addition, for every animal killed an offering must be made to the *mhondoro* who controls the spirit province within which it was caught.

With hunters as with warriors, killing is permitted if the *mhondoro* agrees. Strangers or newcomers must ask permission to hunt before they set out and, as we saw in the account given in Chapter 3, if they so wish, the *mhondoro* may make it especially easy for them to catch game. Game 'given' in this way by the *mhondoro* is known as *huku* or chickens, the customary gift to visitors. What all this information adds up to is that if the *mhondoro* decides to he can make it extremely easy for those he protects to live on the best of terms with the forest and the creatures that live there. If you consider how complex and hard won are the skills of the hunter and how frequenty he encounters danger, you will realise how desirable it is to have the local *mhondoro* lending his invisible but powerful support. If he does you will find game aplenty and return home in safety to the praises of your household.

Hunters say that they do not eat pepper or onions or use soap because each of these has a smell that announces their presence to the animals they stalk. But there is more to it than this. Pepper and onions are classified as 'hot' foods and are therefore antipathetic to the *mhondoro* who are associated with the cooling qualities of water or of rain. It may also be relevant that the colour of the pepper pod is bright red.

As far as soap is concerned, it is said that in the past, before the introduction of soap by the whites, people used to cleanse themselves by rubbing their skins with little bits of bark. In those days people had unlimited power over animals and could see many extraordinary things in the bush. Today people use soap and all these skills have been lost. The only people who retain some of these powers, so one of the people who gave me this information continued, are lion tamers (described as 'power men') such as the one my informant had seen when a travelling circus came to the town on the Plateau where she lived long ago. Lion tamers, she insisted, do not use soap when they wash. If they did they would lose the power to make animals obey their commands. To add some weight to this explanation, turn back to the description of the medium of Ambuya Nehanda given by the guerrilla leader Mayor Urimbo on page 4. Amongst many other details, he mentioned that she did not bathe. Perhaps the reason why mediums cultivate this reputation is in order to stress their at-oneness with the bush, their identity as wild animals.

The avoidance of okra (*derere*) is a different matter. A number of different wild plants are referred to by this name. Common to all is that they are never cultivated, that they exude a highly glutinous substance when boiled and that they are avoided by those whose work or reputation depends on physical strength such as hunters. The association between okra and weakness is so strong that it is given as an example of the use of the word in the *Standard Shona Dictionary*. A less explicit reason for the avoidance of okra is that it is considered to be the least desirable of foods. It is only eaten as a relish when no other is available. It is associated with failed hunting, lack of control over animals, disfavour from the *mhondoro*.[13]

If this information about hunters is applied to the restrictions placed on the guerrillas, another class of human death-dealers, their coherence and meaning become clear. It was precisely the hunter's ability to live at one with the forest that the guerrillas desired. They achieved it as the hunters and the mediums do by pleasing the *mhondoro*, by obeying their commands and, implicitly, by praising their bodiless but eternal life by keeping themselves free of the polluting power of female sexuality. Ancestors are thought never to eat salt. The guerrillas' disinclination to add it to their food was another means of making themselves more like the ancestors, less subject to the dangers inherent in having a body. Meanwhile the killing that, in the cause of the struggle, the guerrillas inflicted on their enemies was legitimated and purified by the *mhondoro*. It is these techniques of placing yourself under the protection of the ancestors when your life is threatened that are shared by the *mhondoro* medium, the hunter, the warrior and the guerrilla. If you observe these restrictions you become, like the *mhondoro*, at one with the bush, part of the life of the forest and therefore able to live there at ease and to communicate freely with the wild animals with which the forest is shared.

Having agreed to support the guerrillas, the *mhondoro*, who have overcome life and death, taught them how to preserve their own lives, how to avoid their own deaths. As the medium of Kavhinga told me:

> You know in the bush there are wild animals, very dangerous ones. There are plenty of snakes in the bush and many elephants. But not a single comrade was chased by elephants. Not a single comrade was bitten by a snake. They just went their own way without harm.

The forest, a potential hindrance to the guerrillas, had been transformed into a resource which they could draw on in time of danger or need:

> If you were separated from your comrades after a battle, you would find that a hare would guide you straight back to your camp. One time we were sleeping in the bush. During the night a herd of elephants made a circle round our camp. At 3:00 a.m. they made a noise and woke us. Then they began to

move away. We followed them and when we looked back through binoculars we saw we had been sleeping right next to a camp of Security Force soldiers.[14]

This explains the final restriction, that on killing wild animals. These, like the guerrillas, were under the protection of the *mhondoro*. In effect the guerrillas had *become* wild animals. As one lady diarist recorded in her notebook:

In 1974 I started hearing people talk about the *vakomana*. Some are saying they are terrorists, others freedom fighters. Some were saying they were animals. They've got tails. They can't talk. So I was curious to see them. So I travelled for a long distance looking for firewood and I just saw darkness. I lifted up my head and I thought I saw Rhodesian forces so I continued looking for firewood. One of them came to me and said: How are you grandmother? I said: I am fine, my child. He said: Why have you come so far from home for firewood or were you sent to look for us? I was shocked by these words and I wanted to run away but he had spoken to me politely so I took them home and cooked them some food.[15]

This courageous woman had discovered for herself that, though the ZANLA guerrillas lived like animals, they did not in fact have tails. They could speak and even speak politely. But the belief that these extraordinary people who lived in the bush did have some animal characteristics was so persistent that demonstrations that they did not were a feature of many of the early meetings between peasants and guerrillas. The guerrillas, one account noted, said 'do you know us? We said no and he said: We are the terrorists you heard about, and he turned round to show us that he did not have a tail.'[16] And even after the human-ness of the guerrillas had been firmly established they were frequently referred to as *magandanga*, meaning 'wild people who live in the bush'. For the Security Forces, who took up and spread the story that the guerrillas had tails, this was a term of abuse. For the peasants it was not. It expressed a complex perception of people who lived in their territory but not in their villages, who were strangers but who claimed to be ready to risk their lives on behalf of people they hardly knew.[17]

This analysis of the symbolic power of the restrictions imposed by the mediums does not rule out other explanations of the same actions. For example, the prohibition on the shooting of wild animals conserved scarce ammunition and made the guerrillas reliant on local villagers for their food supplies, so drawing them into the resistance. The prohibition on sex, insofar as it was effective (and there is a good deal of evidence that it was less than universally observed) offered some protection to women from the attentions of the large number of strange men who had come to live among them. But whether or not all these restrictions were obeyed in all circumstances the demand that they should be obeyed was an expression by the spirit mediums of their approval of the goals of the guerrillas as well as a means of protecting them from the dangers to which they had committed their lives.

But it was also more than this. The policy of the ZANLA commanders was that guerrillas should not be deployed in their home areas. Guerrillas were frequently involved in the punishment or the execution of villagers. To minimise the strain of divided loyalties they were sent into areas where they had no or few kin ties. The result of this policy was that, in terms of the classification I outlined in Chapter 2, wherever they were stationed the guerrillas were 'strangers'. In other words, they were not descendants of the royal ancestors who 'owned' the land, either as members of the royal lineage itself or of any of the commoner lineages which held rights in land but whose members could not succeed to the chieftaincy. Therefore, in terms of the established techniques for the expression of political authority these strangers, the guerrillas, held no political authority at all. They spoke, of course, with the authority of ZANU but ZANU had no organisational base in Dande. Its policies and and its structures no doubt held many attractions but, for all that, in the first instance they were challenging, alien and odd. The guerrillas themselves were an alarming presence whether because of their symbolic tails or their rather less imaginary guns.

But despite their lack of political authority, the guerrillas claimed the land – all the land in Dande, all the land in the whole territory of Zimbabwe. They stressed this claim in their speeches and songs and they demonstrated in action their determination to make their claim good.

It is possible that the spirit mediums and the guerrillas might have found themselves irrevocably opposed to each other, the guerrillas claiming the land and political authority on the grounds of their allegiance to the programme of ZANU, the mediums making just the same claims in the name of the royal ancestors. But their broadly similar goals – the retrieval of the lost lands and lost autonomy – brought about the alliance that I have described. And the effect of this alliance was that political authority was conferred on the guerrillas. And this authority was legitimate because it was conferred according to certain long-established techniques. By observing the ancestral prohibitions the guerrillas were transformed from 'strangers' into 'royals', from members of lineages resident in other parts of Zimbabwe, into descendants of the local *mhondoro* with rights to land. They had become 'at home' in Dande.

Let me be clear about what I am suggesting. There is no reason to believe that had the guerrillas been rejected by the mediums they would have failed to establish themselves in the countryside. If the peasants had supported the guerrillas and the mediums had not, I am quite certain that the mediums' advice would have been rejected. This certainty derives from the few cases where mediums did side with the state. Their credibility and authority fell away. Nor is it convincing to argue that the peasants were incapable of perceiving the advantages and disadvantages the guerrillas offered without the mediation of the mediums. Certainly the backing of the mediums brought the guerrillas more advantages than I have outlined so far. Speaking in trance they declared the legitimacy of the resistance. The instruction to support the guerrillas thus acquired the force of absolute truth characteristic of all statements made by the dead. This is not to say that these instructions were universally obeyed but once they had been issued, political allegiance could no longer be regarded as a purely individual choice nor as a pragmatic one. The intervention of the *mhondoro* made unavoidable the public, social and moral implications of the choice every individual had perforce to make. And the need to choose should not be dismissed lightly. The propaganda dispensed by the state was powerful and unrelenting. Huge rewards were offered for betrayal. Up to $5000 could be paid out for information leading to the death or capture of a 'senior terrorist leader'. The authority of the mediums and the claims of loyalty to the community they represented were powerful arguments against cupidity and treachery. But, in the end, each individual peasant had her or his own cause for discontent, her or his own reason for siding with or against the guerrilla army.[18]

The point I am making is quite specific. The contribution of the *mhondoro* mediums to the guerrilla war was that they made the acceptance of the guerrillas easier, quicker, more binding and more profound by allowing this new feature in the experience of the peasantry to be assimilated to established symbolic categories. This was achieved by the imposition on the guerrillas of the set of restrictions I have described but also, and this is the other side of the argument, by the participation of the guerrillas in the possession rituals of the *mhondoro*. By these means the authority of the ancestors was tapped to provide legitimacy to armed resistance and violent insurrection and the pact betwen guerrillas and peasants was struck at such great depth that the peasants began invariably and unthinkingly to refer to the guerrillas as *vasikana* and *vakomana*, our daughters and our sons.

In Chapter 2 I described how some lineages alter their clan affiliation from that of the area from which they derive to that of the area they have made their home. To do this takes generations of work on the land in the territory where they live and years of participation in the rituals of the local *mhondoro*. There is also a less profound means of assimilating a stranger which I described in Chapter 6. Affines and others who no longer live in their fathers' homes can retain membership of their own clan and yet become *vazukuru* or descendants of the *mhondoro* who controls the territory where they live. This does not take years, like the transference from one clan to another, but is accomplished as soon as a

165

stranger makes himself known to the local *mhondoro*, receives permission to farm, plants his crops and begins to participate in the possession rituals.

The guerrillas were never allocated plots by the *mhondoro* nor did they ever wish to farm. But this was made up for by the fact that the *mhondoro* allocated to them, in a sense, the whole territory of Dande or indeed of Zimbabwe. The second requirement, participation in ritual, the guerrillas fulfilled in full measure. They observed the prohibitions that shrouded them in ancestral benediction. They attended the possession rituals which demonstrate that the ancestors, and therefore their descendants are the owners of the land. They sang the songs of the ancestors, they danced their dances. They ensured that the rituals of the agricultural cycle were properly carried out and universally attended. When I arrived in Dande, some nine months after the guerrillas had departed, it was still widely believed that if you defied the *mhondoro* and worked in your fields on the *chisi* rest days you would be fined, beaten or perhaps even killed by the guerrillas. Many guerrillas wore the black bead wristlets associated with the ancestors. For some this indicated that they themselves had become mediums of their own lineage ancestors. For the rest it served to identify them with the local source of political authority which had adopted and endorsed them, the *mhondoro*.

From chiefs to guerrillas

Establishing themselves as descendants of the *mhondoro* was a considerable achievement. If the guerrillas had accomplished no more than this they would have accumulated all the authority they needed to command the allegiance of the peasantry for the length of the war. But in fact this was only the beginning. Once this first step had been taken, the next became inevitable. This second step was the displacement by the guerrillas of those other descendants of the *mhondoro*, the chiefs.

This step was inevitable as far as the guerrillas were concerned, but for the mediums it did not come before time. If the creativity of the mediums is to remain concealed, their intervention in the political realm must be sparing and carefully judged. Though the distinction between medium and *mhondoro* is habitually blurred, the impotence and ignorance of the mediums must be stressed from time to time if the unimpeachable authority of the *mhondoro* is to be felt with its full weight. In practice the mediums do a great deal more than merely 'advise and teach', the limits they ascribe to themselves, but by the nature of their profession they are not well suited to 'rule'. They took the opportunity provided by the guerrillas to unload this responsibility. Needless to say, the guerrillas were only too willing to accept it.

Four factors contributed to the achievement of this status by the guerrillas. The most conspicuous was the active antagonism which they displayed towards the chiefs. Extreme examples of this were assassinations of chiefs and of loyal headmen, but other measures were taken as well. Where villages lay near the boundaries of two chieftaincies, the secret support committees established all over Dande were set up so as to include people categorised as followers of both chiefs. The new forms of political organisation projected for the future thus had their beginning during the struggle itself.

The authority of the chiefs had been based on allocation of land, the organisation of the ritual cycles of exchange and the administration of law. The guerrillas could not allocate individual plots to their followers but they did promise that land would be given them and these promises were underwritten with their lives. The old cycles of labour for the chiefs in return for access to land and security in famine which had been broken up by taxation, wage labour and the salaries paid to chiefs were replaced with new cycles. Food, labour and shelter were supplied to the guerrillas in return for guarantees of access to land, of an end to taxation and of restored political and economic autonomy. But perhaps the most significant factor is the last of the three, that the guerrillas took over the administration of law. They demanded that all disputes should be brought to them for arbitration. In this way they challenged the authority and competence of the state-controlled chiefs' courts to resolve the disruptions brought about by war as well as by the less exceptional calamities of everyday life.

The clearest evidence of the guerrillas' assumption of the role of the chiefs can be drawn from the attitude taken by them to the most inveterate cause of calamity, the witch. Witch-finding was perhaps the most controversial of the techniques used by the guerrillas to gain support. It is certainly wide open to misinterpretation. It is only once the existence of a fundamental moral opposition between witch and *mhondoro* has been perceived, and the incorporation of the guerrillas into Dande as descendants of the *mhondoro* is understood that a just evaluation can be made.

To start with, there can be no doubt that witch-finding took place. One resident of Dande recorded that:

> When the comrades arrived they said: there are sellouts and witches in this village. They called a certain woman and said: let us see the human flesh you are concealing. The woman fell down and began to cry. They said: tell your children to come here and see. She called them. The comrades said: Your mother is a witch. The children began to cry. Some of them said: If there had been no war our mother would still be alive.[19]

According to one ex-guerrilla, it was left to the villagers to report cases of witchcraft to them:

> When we entered a village we didn't ask people where the witches are. We waited until people complained about a person and then we went to interrogate them. If that person continued to deny he was a witch we left him alone. But if he admitted it we asked the people what sort of punishment he should be given and we carried it out. He could be set free if this is what they wanted but also he could be killed.

The guerrillas also took action against traditional healers (*n'anga*) if they suspected them of practising witchcraft:

> The comrades hate the witches and the *n'anga* who kill people. If they find a *n'anga* they tell him to eat his own medicine. If he does so, well and good but if he refuses they destroy his medicines and warn him to stop practising. Or they kill him and leave his body by the bridge where everyone can see it.

In their campaign against the witches the guerrillas were assisted by the *mhondoro* mediums:

> The guerrillas got special magic [*mushonga*] from [the *mhondoro*] Musuma. They put it round the outside of the keep [concentration camp]. The next morning many witches came there crying and the guerrillas beat them.

Or as another ex-*mujiba* told me, 'During the war ZANU used to travel round with that medium called Chivere. He told them who all the witches are. It's very very good to kill those witches.'

When I arrived in Dande, faith in the ability of the ZANLA guerrillas to deal with witches was still strong. Some people maintained that there were fewer witches than ever before because of the good work the guerrillas had done. Others feared that now the guerrillas had left them the witches would return. It is extremely important to pinpoint as closely as we can who the witches dealt with by the guerrillas were.

Inevitably some of the people accused of being witches were participants in the tensions and hostilities that follow from unexplained death and misfortune. No doubt on more than a few occasions the guerrillas won support by judging in favour of the side with the greatest numbers. But the fact that the guerrillas had become imbued with the authority of the *mhondoro* meant that another group of people came to be included within the category 'witch' as well.

The *mhondoro* typify the ideology of descent. Witches are typically members of one's own *rudzi* who wish you harm, *rudzi* being interpreted as 'type' or 'kind of person', as lineage or clan depending on context. As the guerrillas were the representatives of the *mhondoro*, those who opposed them and allied themselves to the white government were thought of as traitors to their own people, their own *rudzi*. In effect, they had taken sides against the *mhondoro* and the only person who would do such a thing is a witch:

The two things that comrades like best were ancestors and beer. Many times the ancestors saved us when we were in the bush. If there were no ancestors we would surely have died. So many times we went to see the *mhondoro* Musuma who was staying at Mushumbi Pools. This *mhondoro* helped us a lot. He told us who all the sell-outs were. And this was very important. Many people died just because they had been betrayed.[20]

There can be little doubt that some of the individuals named as sell-outs (*vatengesi*) were innocent people identified for reasons of malice. But it is clear that many of those identified *to the guerrillas* as witches were people believed to be politically untrustworthy or treacherous, those believed to be acting against the interests of the

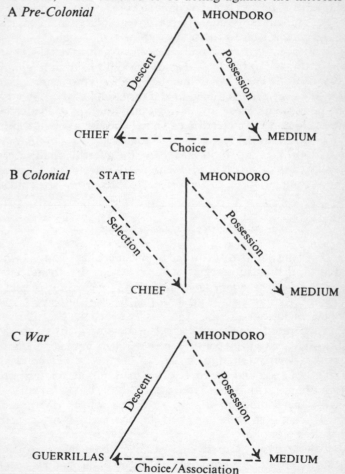

Figure 9.1   *The changing sources of political authority in Dande*

169

peasants as a whole. This does not mean that the people of Dande are unable to differentiate between people who use poisons, people who fly through the air in winnowing baskets, as witches are believed to do, and members of rival political parties. The point is that all these categories of people have one element in common: they are all opposed to the arbiters of the moral order, the *mhondoro*. That sell-outs were called witches is not evidence of the 'backwardness' of the rural populations and their unreadiness to participate in democracy as some Zimbabwean politicians claim to believe. What it demonstrates is the profound degree to which the guerrillas, and by extension the nationalist politicians, had become identified with the *mhondoro*. Anyone who opposed the altruistic and benevolent *mhondoro* and their protegés the guerrillas for selfishly individualistic reasons was placed in the category to which the ancestors are structurally opposed, the witch.[21]

The guerrillas' explicit and aggressive policy against witches was the final turn of the key in the lock. The doorway to legitimate political authority was opened wide. With the spirit mediums mounting a guard of honour, the guerrillas marched in and took hold of the symbols of their new power. The loose and tactical affiliation of individuals to chieftaincies, long a characteristic of Shona society, allowed a transference of political loyalty from chiefs to guerrillas with a minimum of anxiety. With the blessing of the *mhondoro*, the guerrillas had successfully established their succession. (Figure 9.1 illustrates the transition from the pre-colonial, through the colonial to the wartime structures of authority.)

The sons of the soil

To understand the authority acquired by the guerrillas, many of whom were barely more than adolescents, it was necessary first to understand the authority held by the *mhondoro* mediums. This was the reason for the inclusion of Chapters 3 and 4 in this book. Chapters 2 and 6 provided the background to the processes by which the guerrillas were ritually incorporated into Dande society, processes which had operated long before they arrived and continue now that they have gone. Chapter 1 was simply a description of the guerrillas' coming into Dande and of their taking Nehanda and the three other mediums across the border into Mozambique with some reference to the attitude taken to the mediums by the Rhodesian state. This theme will be elaborated in Chapter 10. What then of the long and complex analysis in Chapter 5? What was the point of all that?

Firstly, the analysis of myth and ritual enabled me to explain a number of the prohibitions imposed on the mediums and also on the guerrillas, above all the achievement of permanent (or at least, more permanent) life by the avoidance of female sexuality. But in Chapter 5 we explored a number of other categories which are relevant now. We have not yet reached the bottom layer of incorporation which the guerrillas achieved.

As we discussed in Chapter 5, ownership rights in a territory are expressed as the ability to contol the fertility of its soil. He whose ancestors bring the rain owns the land. This is precisely the statement made by the guerrillas' observation of the restrictions imposed on them, by their attendance at the rituals of the spirit mediums, by their incorporation as descendants of the *mhondoro*. What the guerrillas have learned to say is: 'our ancestors bring the rain therefore we own the land.' In other words they have become autochthons. And they are autochthons of a very extreme kind. They live deep in the forest like wild semi-human creatures, so profoundly at one with nature and all the wild animals that live there that they are able to perceive the secret meanings contained in their behaviour. These animals were not sent by the ancestors or the mediums to convey messages to the guerrillas. Of their own volition they gave their support to the guerrillas either actively, like the hares and elephants who led the guerrillas through the bush and the birds, tortoises and snakes that gave advance warning of the outcome of their missions, or passively like the lions and snakes who allowed the guerrillas free, untroubled passage through the forest. This extreme identification of the guerrillas with the land is made transparently clear in a song recorded by Terence Ranger in the Makoni District. Here is a prose translation:

> One day the District Commissioner gathered all the people in the village and amongst them was a ZANU comrade. The D.C. said 'We need to talk about these terrorists. A terrorist is a bad person' . . . The comrade stood up, the child of the soil, and began to question: 'What does this terrorist say he wants?' 'He wants the land' . . . 'O.K. oppressor, listen to what I have to say. I have some questions to ask'. The comrade goes and stands beside the *msasa* tree and asks: 'Are not the tree and I similar in appearance?' The oppressor answers 'Yes'. Then the comrade stretches himself out in the grass, under the *mutondo* and *mupfuti* trees, and again they are similar. 'O.K., oppressor, I ask you to do exactly what I have done.' The oppressor goes and stands against the tree and the contrast is obvious. Therefore the answer is 'No – you do not belong to this land as we do.'[22]

Despite their function as soldiers, the guerrillas were not conceived of as conquerors. Within the symbolic framework in operation this would imply that they were *not* the true owners of the land. Rather they were thought of as autochthons, or rather as super-autochthons, as the military vanguard of a nation of autochthons, of all the original displaced but authentic owners of the land. In opposition to the conquerors, the white population of Rhodesia, all Zimbabweans were regarded (and largely regarded themselves) as autochthons or, less pedantically, as 'sons of the soil'. An early ZANU leader expressed this idea with great clarity and force:

> The black man belongs to the soil. It claimed him. He and millions of others to come belonged to the Soil which had given birth to millions of his kind stretching back well beyond the human memory and lost in antiquity . . . To deprive him of it was to rob him of his birthright and his death-right . . . He is of the Soil in life and death – '*Mwana we Vu*', Child of the Soil . . . But of course '*Vana Vevu*', 'Children of the Soil', was more than a designation for all the black people of Zimbabwe. It was a clarion call to all those who were denied their full rights and freedoms in their own native land. It was a rallying-point. It was political through and through. It was a political doctrine of self-realization, of self-assertion, of determination, of hope, of resolve to be free of the heavy yoke of white supremacy which the white man fastened on the necks of all the blacks of Zimbabwe nearly a hundred years ago. Hence '*Vana Vevu*' carried with it the militant message: 'Sons of the Soil! Arise and fight!' To divorce it from its militancy, or its militancy from it, would be to miss its true meaning and relevance.[23]

The mediums who taught the ritual techniques to the guerrillas and transformed them into autochthons were not drawn from any one ethnic group. They included the Korekore Chiwawa and the Tavara Musuma. The guerrillas, all the residents of Dande – Korekore, Tande, Chikunda and Dema – the poorest peasants and those who farmed about fifteen hectares, the schoolteachers, the shopkeepers, the mothers, the young women who disappeared from their homes and returned as armed fighters, the widows, the youngest children organised in their *mujiba* platoons, the elders, the headmen, the healers, the mediums – all of these and all of their ancestors, in opposition to the conquering whites, were placed in one category: children of the soil, rain-makers, landowners, autochthons. In this most recent formulation of an ancient set of symbols all the local populations are grouped together in opposition to those lineages whose home territories are, ultimately, not within Zimbabwe, but in another land, on another continent, in Europe.

I have described the processes whereby strangers (e.g. affines or guerrillas) and even conquerors (e.g. the Korekore) are assimilated into Dande (and more generally Shona) society. To a large extent the reason why the whites were not assimilated in these ways is obvious. They did not wish to be. They had their own spirits, their own gods, their own ancestors. But this refusal had certain implications which are worth drawing out to complete this discussion of the power of the symbolism of the land.

Strangers gain access to land in two ways. They are awarded it or they conquer it. The second was the technique adopted by the whites.

Typically, over a period of time conquerors accept that the ultimate owners of the land are the autochthons, its previous owners, and they participate in the rituals that ensure the continuation of its fertility. Even non-Shona conquerors tend to follow this pattern. An example is the Ndebele who took control of parts of the west of Zimbabwe in the 1850s. Gradually they assimilated themselves to the local indigenous religion and made offerings at the long-established Shona shrines.[24]

But for the whole of the period that they held political power in Zimbabwe, the white conquerors refused to accept the supremacy of the autochthonous ancestors, either as owners of the land or as bringers of the rain. The Shona religious leaders were 'witchdoctors of doubtful character and little substance' who misled their followers, a 'simple, gullible people'.

The tribulations brought upon the Shona by the conquest might have been borne had it at least brought them prosperity and fertility. But although they claimed absolute ownership of the land for themselves, the whites proved unable to guarantee its fertility, its freedom from drought. Indeed, the lands allocated to the black farmers by a series of acts of parliament were the least fertile of all. Overcrowded and overworked, such fertility as they had rapidly declined. And no mechanism existed by means of which the Shona might transfer their allegiance to another set of whites whose ancestors might have greater success in bringing the rains.

In the pre-colonial ideology of Dande which persisted, though in a weakened form, right up to the period of the war, the authority of the chiefs was perpetuated by the belief that their deaths were the source of the fertility of the land. The death of a chief is the birth of a *mhondoro*. Thus a potential discontinuity in the authority of the royal lineage, the death of a ruler, was transformed into the source of the persistence of the society as a whole, while the authority of the chiefs was presented as a natural rather than a social phenomenon. Amongst the Chikunda in the north of Dande, the eighteenth- and nineteenth-century white Portuguese landholders took full political power into their hands just as the British in Rhodesia were to do. But the Portuguese intermarried with the local peoples. They participated in all aspects of the society that surrounded them and they made offerings to the autochthonous shrines. Their behaviour was a source of never-ending dismay to their superiors in Lisbon but it brought them undreamed of rewards, unmeasurable in ivory or gold. At their deaths many of these land holders became *mhondoro* (or *póndoro* as the Chikunda call them) a source of power and fertility to their descendants for all time to come. The British landholders in Rhodesia kept themselves to themselves. They broke apart the structures of authority that they found, took power into their hands and gave back precious little in return. The death of a district commissioner adds nothing to the fertility of the earth.[25]

It is perfectly logical then that the predominant expression of opposition to white rule stressed the powers of perpetual fertility held by the *mhondoro*, the true owners of the land. And it was inevitable that in conformity with their traditional role as installers of the chiefs, the mediums of these *mhondoro* would declare the guerrillas, the champions of the autochthons, to be the new chiefs who would restore natural fertility and social justice for all. It was no surprise to the spirit mediums that the harvest of 1980–81, the first after Independence and the victory of the autochthons, was one of the most bounteous in living memory.[26]

NOTES

1 Cited in Martin and Johnson (1981, p. 74).
2 From an interview with Comrade Mayor Urimbo in Harare, 7 January 1981. The unattributed quotations are from my field notes.
3 Notebook 19.
4 From an interview with Comrade Mayor Urimbo in Harare, 7 January 1981.
5 From an interview conducted by Nicholas Wright in Dande, 14 July 1981.
6 Notebook 19.
7 From an interview conducted by Nicholas Wright in Dande, 14 July 1981.
8 Notebook 20.
9 Notebook 19.
10 Notebook 5.
11 Notebook 29.
12 The quotation is from Beach (1980, p 73). See also the *simorongo* hunting *shave* of the Korekore Dotito chieftaincy to the east of Dande. Their mediums wear red ribbons on their chests and red and white spotted cloths (Gelfand 1962, p. 88).
13 The dictionary is Hannan (1974). A reference made to the Korekore Matope chieftaincy of Mount Darwin in Hodza and Fortune's study of praise poetry is pertinent. They wrote that 'Kakona as a *gamba* (heroic warrior) never allowed himself to eat food cooked by *vanhu vaziza*' (literally, 'women who had matured'). (Hodza and Fortune 1979, p. 280). Describing the game *mahumwe* (keeping house) Hodza writes '[The boy] will try to hunt or trap mice, birds and even hares. If he is unsuccessful . . . the family will have to fall back on "wild spinach" (*derere*) or other vegetables collected by the girl for the relish that goes with the stiff porridge (*sadza*)' (1979, p. 289).
14 From an interview conducted by Nicholas Wright in Dande, 14 July 1981.
15 Notebook 37.
16 Notebook 4.
17 Other restrictions were on eating the leaves of bean and pumpkin plants. These are foods of a status as low as *derere* and are possibly avoided for the

same reason. Groundnuts or *nyimo* were also taboo. I can offer no explanation of this. I can only suggest that, as in the Maji Maji uprising in Tanzania, 1905–7, they may have been associated with bullets and were therefore not allowed to enter the body (Gwassa, 1972, p. 135). I was told that the avoidance of the internal organs of animals by guerrillas made it less likely that bullets would enter their own bodies. This seems to be a separate magic, independent of any symbolism pertaining to hunters and *mhondoro*.

18 Maxey (1975, p. 133).

19 Notebook 19.

20 ibid.

21 As late as 1981, members of rival political parties, especially Muzorewa's UANC, were described to me by people in Dande as witches. They claimed that if they were to attend their rallies, they risked being poisoned.

22 Ranger (1985, p. 170).

23 Sithole (1977, p. 18).

24 For the Ndebele use of Shona shrines see Daneel (1970); Bhebe (1979, p. 287).

25 For the Machikunda Portuguese *póndoro* see Newitt (1973, pp. 169f).

26 Beyond the scope of this book but of great interest will be the reactions of the *mhondoro* mediums and their followers to the three years of drought (1982–4) that followed.

10
The Politics
of Tradition

'*Mutota is the great spirit of the Korekore. Chiwawa has* no *say in the selection of a new chief*'.

Note added by a district commissioner to records of the genealogy of the Chitsungo chieftaincy.[1]

In Chapter 7 I laid out the political and economic causes of the war throughout Zimbabwe and then described some of its effects on the people of Dande. In Chapter 8 I described how the spirit mediums achieved their pre-eminence over the chiefs in the countryside and explained why they and the guerrillas anticipated mutual advantage from their co-operation in the war against the state. Chapter 9 was an account of how the guerrillas achieved their status as legitimate leaders in succession to the chiefs who had been absorbed by the state and had forfeited their ancestral authority.

This chapter is an account of the relationship between two mediums and of their complex and contrasting attitudes to the chiefs, the state and the guerrillas. The first of these mediums is Enosi Pondai who was possessed by the *mhondoro* Chiwawa. The second is George Kupara who was possessed by the most senior of all Korekore *mhondoro*, Mutota. I will refer to them as Chiwawa/Pondai and Mutota/Kupara. (See Plates 13 and 14, between pp. 204–5.)

One way of describing the relationship between them is as a series of oppositions. These oppositions can be categorised as structural, historical and personal. Over the twenty years between the first possession of Pondai by Chiwawa in 1954 and the death of George Kupara these oppositions gradually worked themselves out. But as they did so the centres of political authority shifted beneath their feet. In the end they found themselves thrown onto opposite sides of the war of liberation; Chiwawa/Pondai a close ally of the guerrillas, Mutota/ Kupara a pawn in a campaign of 'psychological warfare' carried out by the army of the state.

My account of this history is drawn from a number of sources: interviews with some of the participants (the surviving mediums, district administrators, relatives of the chiefs), records found in the District Administration files and earlier accounts of the relationship between the two mediums. It remains partial and tentative but it is worth telling not only for its inherent fascination but because it sums up a great deal of the argument of this book so far and takes it one stage further.

One consequence of the events I describe was an extraordinary innovation in the rituals carried out at Chiwawa's shrine. This innovation severed the connections between the political and the spiritual spheres of Dande as represented by the chieftaincies on the one hand and of the spirit provinces on the other. A central theme of the previous chapters has been the ritual prohibitions taught to the ZANLA guerrillas by the mediums. These prohibitions will be seen in an entirely new light when I have shown how, unknown to themselves, the ZANLA guerrillas walked straight into this rupture between the political and the spiritual wrought by Chiwawa at the moment that they set foot in Dande.

Mutota vs Chiwawa

On 22 February 1974 the medium of Mutota died. In 1982 I asked the medium's son, also a medium though of a lesser spirit, to tell me about the events leading up to his father's death:

My father is the one who had the *mhondoro* called Mutota. Throughout his life he used to heal the people and he was the one who caused the rain to fall. You ask what caused his death? Well, one day the war started. Mutota was asked to explain what was going to happen. He said: I don't want blood in this country. We want to stay as we are. All whites and blacks are the children of this country. So the white people made a tape recording of what he said and they went away. Then they came back and said: Alright, Mutota, this is what we will do. We will send children who will live with you here. Then 12 soldiers came. When they were here they used to count the people who entered the *zumba* [*mhondoro*'s hut] to be healed and they asked the people why they had come there. Then Mutota realised that he was no longer happy. The boys [guerrillas] were wanting him and the soldiers were also wanting him. Now Mutota saw that his medium might be shot as an enemy by either side. So one night he came [the *mhondoro* took possession of the medium]. He spent the whole night talking from 2 a.m. until 7 a.m. Then he said farewell to his *mutapi* and went out of the house. He walked into the bush outside the village and suddenly he fell down. A white soldier came and saw what had happened. He called to us his children and said: We don't know what has happened to the *mambo* [chief/medium]. By the time we got there he had been lying on the ground for 5 minutes and we saw that our father was dead.

That Mutota/Kupara should have made the statement: 'I don't want blood in this country' is consistent with everything I have said about *mhondoro* mediums so far. But nothing has prepared us for the way he continued. For a *mhondoro* medium to have been of the opinion that 'We want to stày as we are. All whites and blacks are the children of this country', seems to contradict a good deal of the last three chapters. I have argued that the profession of the *mhondoro* medium is inherently radical, inevitably opposed to the colonial state. Here is a medium lending it his support at least so far as to declare his preferences for the way things were rather than for any of the changes that were pressing all around. Even taking into account that in those very volatile times mediums, and anyone else for that matter, might have expressed rather different opinions to different audiences, these statements still require some explanation if my main argument is to survive.

Both Mutota and Chiwawa are senior Korekore ancestors but their seniority is expressed in different ways. Mutota's importance is the more conspicuous. He stands at the head of the royal genealogy of the royal ancestors of Dande and of a number of other Korekore royal genealogies as well, both in the Valley and on the Plateau. He is the earliest ancestor, the one who made the long journey from Guruuswa, the distant land thought of as the earliest home of the Korekore. He is the father of those *mhondoro* who climbed down into the Valley and 'conquered' the Tande and Tavara peoples, the previous owners of the land. Within the Korekore lineage of rain-bringing ancestors, Mutota is the ultimate source of the rain. Standing at this most senior position, Mutota receives requests to resolve the political and personal difficulties of his direct descendants, the members of the royal lineage. In addition he is the last resort of members of all the other lineages who live within his spirit realm whose problems have not been resolved by the mediums of the spirit province within which they live. As the senior *mhondoro*, Mutota is the senior tester of new mediums. Many of the mediums operating in Dande today were tested and installed by him (see Figure 10.1).[2]

The authority of Chiwawa is also impressive. For the Korekore within Dande, Chiwawa is experienced as a more immediate, a more highly characterised individual than Mutota. Although Mutota is the ultimate, the original ancestor, there is a sense in which Chiwawa is thought of as the actual progenitor and protector of the Korekore

The Descendants of Mutota

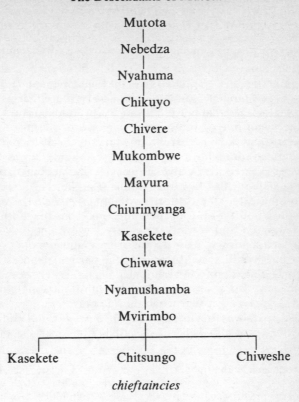

Mutota
|
Nebedza
|
Nyahuma
|
Chikuyo
|
Chivere
|
Mukombwe
|
Mavura
|
Chiurinyanga
|
Kasekete
|
Chiwawa
|
Nyamushamba
|
Mvirimbo

Kasekete   Chitsungo   Chiweshe

chieftaincies

Figure 10.1 The descendants of Mutota

people. When reciting the genealogy of their ancestors, people quite commonly get as far as Chiwawa and conclude 'and then come all the Korekore'. Whereas most *mhondoro* control only one spirit province, Chiwawa controls two and they are vast. Both stretch from some miles south of the Escarpment down the mountainside and north into the Valley. As the spirit provinces of today are thought to be territories conquered by the *mhondoro* when they were alive, Chiwawa's reputation as a warrior and conqueror is very great. He claims the land between these two provinces as well and, though this claim is disputed, if all this territory had ever been under the authority of one ruler as the claim implies, all communication and trade between the Plateau and Dande would have been under his control. Indeed, a major trade route operated by the Portuguese for many centuries ran directly through where one of his provinces is found today.

Altogether the personality of the *mhondoro* Chiwawa has a strong feeling of historical reality, hard as it is to pin down. In the early 1900s the Korekore Chiweshe chieftaincy claimed Chiwawa was 'the first chief to rule the tribe'. On the genealogy of the Dande Korekore houses it is after the name of Chiwawa's 'son' that the different houses split off. Each of his 'grandsons' is thought of as the founder of a separate house. This sense of an actual personality is felt also by the Tande people who have long maintained that it was Chiwawa who attacked and conquered them rather than one of the more distant Korekore ancestors. And indeed even today a ruined stone building on the Escarpment overlooking Dande is thought of by local people as a military fortification and firmly associated with Chiwawa just as a similar ruin on the Valley floor is associated with Chiwawa's 'father' Kasekete.[3]

Thus to some extent the authorities of the two *mhondoro* overlap and contradict each other: Mutota the more senior but the more shady, a source of wisdom and fertility to a very large number of lineages; Chiwawa less shadowy, also a rain-bringer and conqueror like all *mhondoro* but with a special status as the particular ancestor of the Chitsungo, Kasekete and Chiweshe chieftaincies. When the mediums of these *mhondoro* work in harmony, the contradiction remains unexpressed. The reverse is true when they do not.

George Kupara was first possessed by his *mhondoro* in 1919. Kingsley Garbett who knew him well has described him as a man of striking appearance:

> He was tall, lean, with bright piercing eyes and an expressive face. Like other mediums, he dressed simply but distinctively, in a black cloth worn, toga fashion, around his waist and drawn over the left shoulder. Around his neck he wore a thick, elaborate plait of fine black beads and on his wrists, black bangles of horn. He had a sharp mind, an extensive knowledge of herbal remedies and a phenomenal ability to retain genealogical detail and the minutiae of diverse myths of origin. His obvious charismatic qualities were revealed particularly through the drama of the seance . . . He would be fierce and terrifying with the sceptical and recalcitrant; gentle, playful, grandfatherly, with the awed and the afraid.[4]

He dominated the religious life of the northern Plateau and the Valley beyond for more than fifty years.

Enosi Pondai, still the medium of Chiwawa today, is also an imposing figure. Tall and broadly built with the air of a consul, a man born to command, he is nonetheless capable of great delicacy, warmth and charm. One indication of the strength of his personality and of his will is that he managed to establish his reputation as Chiwawa's medium and to maintain it over thirty turbulent years despite the drawback that, uniquely among established mediums, he has never passed the conventional testing that all *mhondoro* mediums are supposed to undergo. In 1954 when he belived himself ready, he presented himself to Mutota/Kupara to be tested. He was rejected and sent away. In every other case that I know, rejected aspirant mediums have accepted the judgment passed on them, perhaps to try again in a few years time, perhaps to abandon their belief in their powers. But Enosi Pondai is an exception and a well-known one. By the early 1960s he had built up a large following and was frequently consulted by chiefs descended from his *mhondoro*. From the very start of his career, therefore, Chiwawa/Pondai was in opposition to Mutota/Kupara. As long as he continued to practise and to receive support he constituted a challenge to Mutota/Kupara's authority.

And Mutota/Kupara took up this challenge. Garbett has told me of a conversation he had with Mutota/Kupara in 1964. Kupara was describing his own testing by the medium of Nehanda in 1919:

> He described how he went to a pool with Chigede who, so he said, was then Chiwawa's medium and who was also being tested. The pool was called Asanya and was filled with crocodiles and hippos. The object of the test was to enter the water, stay there unharmed for some lengthy period and then come out with a pillow or head-rest, i.e. a croc. Kupara described how he and Chigede passed the test and procured their 'head rests' and then went on to remark that Enosi Pondai had not yet secured his head rest. He said 'I am really surprised by that young man who is saying, "I am possessed by Chiwawa" for he has not yet gone into the pool to take his pillow. Now how can we know that he is really possessed by Chiwawa? I do not believe that the spirit of Chiwawa is in him. Is it not surprising that Enosi is now ten years with the spirit without entering the pool?'[5]

The contradictory authorities of these two mediums was sharply emphasised by a crucial incident that took place in 1957. A large area of land including part of Mutota's spirit province on the Plateau, previously designated as a 'Tribal Trust Land', was requisitioned by the government as a 'Native Purchase Area', one of the few areas of land in the country which could be bought by black farmers. Mutota/Kupara was among those who were forced to find new homes. Together with many of his followers and assistants, he moved down from the Plateau into Dande and took up residence in Chiwawa's spirit province near the Kadzi River.

Chiwawa/Pondai objected to this very strongly indeed. It may be that his complaint contained an element of hostility towards a medium who had rejected his claim to possession, but he had two far more powerful reasons as well. He argued that, according to established practice, Mutota had no right to enter the Valley and that another medium living within his spirit province placed his life in extreme danger. As Mutota/Kupara did not believe in Pondai's possession, this objection was a matter of indifference to him. But for Pondai to downplay the danger in which he felt he had been placed would have been to invite support for Kupara's scepticism about his authenticity. He had to protest.

Once again I quote Garbett who lived in Dande shortly after these events took place:

> Chiwawa argued that Mutota's medium had now placed him in mortal danger. The senior medium (Kupara) countered this by arguing that since the whole region was Mutota's, he could settle wherever he chose. Eventually, after a protracted dispute, Chiwawa's medium moved in 1962 to take up residence at a site said to be sacred to Chiwawa within the small spirit province of Chuzu. (See Map 3.1.)[6]

On what grounds could Mutota/Kupara have claimed that the whole territory of Dande was his? The most obvious are that the spirit provinces of most of his 'children' are found there. But Chiwawa/Pondai argued that Dande belongs not to Mutota but to his 'children', his descendants, alone and this is supported by many other mediums within Dande. It is also supported by the Guruuswa myth (see myth I, p. 75 above) which tells how at the end of his journey from the south, Mutota was unable to enter the Valley and had to remain on the Plateau where, in fact, his own spirit province is found today.

According to Garbett, despite the success that Mutota/Kupara achieved at attracting supplicants and visitors to his new shrine, 'at almost every seance and in public at every gathering, he expressed a desire to return to the Plateau'. As soon as he was able to, he left the Valley for good. But even so he continued to exert enormous influence over the people who lived there, an influence which Chiwawa/Pondai was determined to counter.

One way in which he could do this was to back his own candidates for chiefly succession against those supported by Mutota/Kupara. The most thoroughly documented example of this is the battle that took place between 1966 and 1972 over the selection of the new chief Chitsungo.

The Chitsungo succession, 1966–72

In theory a chieftaincy should not be left vacant for more than a year. If the contest between the various branches is intense, two or even three years may go by before a new chief is in place. It took six years to install a new chief Chitsungo. And they were six critical years. The chief died in the year of the Battle of Sinoia, the first armed attack of the war. By the time his successor was finally installed, the ZANLA guerrillas were well established in the forests of the Valley.

One reason that the succession took so long to resolve was that one of the two competing branches had the medium of Nyahuma and, at his death, Mutota/Kupara to argue the legitimacy of their claim while the other had the backing of Chiwawa/Pondai. A second reason was the part taken at a late stage by the local District Administration.

At least twice before, Chiwawa/Pondai had fielded a candidate for a vacant chieftaincy. In the early 1960s he had challenged the appointment of a chief made by a district commissioner but failed to dislodge him. In 1967 he opposed Mutota/Kupara's candidate for the Kasekete chieftaincy but ultimately accepted the senior *mhondoro*'s choice and paid a fine of $1.00. In retrospect these seem like preparatory skirmishes for the full-scale battle over Chitsungo.[7]

According to established practice each of the three houses descended from the original Chitsungo should provide a chief in turn. The *mhondoro* Nyahuma was charged with making the choice which had to be confirmed by Mutota. At the chief's death, Lazarus, a man of the same house as the chief, was appointed acting chief to serve until Nyahuma had selected a successor. For reasons which are unclear the medium, who was well into his seventies, delayed until 1969 and then named his choice. Immediately charges of bias and malpractice were made. A rival candidate wrote to the district commissioner:

> The trouble is with the *mhondoro* who takes a person who does not belong to the clan. I have never seen any *mhondoro* selling a chieftaincy before. This man who wants to buy the chieftaincy has been at the *mhondoro* Nyahuma's kraal for five months.[8]

The levelling of a charge of corruption against a *mhondoro* medium by unsuccessful candidates is standard practice. In this case the charge came to nothing for, shortly after being chosen, the candidate died of sleeping sickness. The medium of Nyahuma made another choice from the same house. At this a man named Kindo, a rival from the second of the two houses who considered themselves eligible, travelled across Dande to the Msengezi River where Chiwawa/Pondai was living and put his case to him. Chiwawa/Pondai agreed that he was the legitimate successor and indicated this by presenting him with a black cloth telling him to take it to Nyahuma and announce that he, Chiwawa, had appointed the new Chitsungo.[9]

The medium of Nyahuma's response came winging back. 'Chiwawa cannot rule in my area,' he is reported to have said, 'I refuse to be ruled by my *muzukuru* (descendant)'. In reply, Chiwawa/Pondai sent an emissary to see the district commissioner. He informed him that a chief had been chosen and that Kindo was the man. The result was that all the mediums and elders of the Chitsungo chieftaincy were summoned by the district commissioner to an official meeting at the village of Nyahuma's medium.

At this meeting Chiwawa's candidate Kindo received overwhelming support and the district commissioner, apparently satisfied that the chief had been chosen according to proper and traditional practice, agreed to forward his name to the government ministry for approval. Kindo himself felt that he was too old to rule well but recommended that his brother's son serve in his place. Chiwawa approved and this man was appointed. Within three months he was dead.

The cause of this second death of a candidate for the chieftaincy was officially recorded as cancer but some of his potential successors were afraid that other factors were involved. One wrote to the district commissioner:

> Now please do not give this portfolio to us again. We have left very few. We are afraid otherwise we may all die a ruthless death.

And another:

> Never in Rhodesia has such things happened . . . Once he is appointed chief, it won't be long before he dies. Now please . . . it's wise of you not to select anybody from our family to be a chief. It's better to give it to those who may wish to.[10]

Kindo however was unperturbed by such fears. He was selected acting chief with the backing of all three branches of the chieftaincy. Although the question who the chief would be had still not been settled, it must have seemed to Chiwawa/Pondai that, despite the powerful opposition of Nyahuma who had the backing of Mutota, his right to appoint the Chitsungo chief had been successfully established.

But if he did feel this way, his joy did not have long to run. For at this time, the broader, swifter flow of national events began to cut across the history being played out in the backwaters of the Zambezi Valley.

In the first round of attempts to find a new Chitsungo, Chiwawa/Pondai's authority to name a candidate had been accepted by the local administration. Indeed, the district commissioner had attended a meeting at which Chiwawa's choice had been universally accepted and he had approved this succession. But in the second round less than a year later, the district commissioner's attitude had swung a full 180 degrees. Now he was adamant that Chiwawa had no rights over the Chitsungo chieftaincy whatsoever. What had happened to cause this radical change of mind?

District commissioners and spirit realms

What had happened was that almost overnight the ritual by which chiefs were selected had become a matter of very great concern to the district commissioners and to the state.

In the early years of the century the government attitude to the chiefs was that they were simply a tool to be used to enforce their policies. If a chief refused to co-operate he should be got rid of and, to prevent future disobedience, perhaps the chieftaincy itself should be disbanded at the same time. When it was observed that the chiefs who remained had lost the respect of their followers, the response was to provide them with an exceptionally broad range of powers. As Terence Ranger has recorded, in 1926 the Solicitor General remarked that: '"There is a growing disobedience . . . an increase of disrespect". It was therefore proposed that "an order given by a Native Commissioner, chief or headman shall be deemed to be lawful and reasonable under native law and custom."'[11]

As we have seen, far from having any connection with 'native law and custom', this legislation was far more authoritarian than any that had guided the behaviour of any Shona chief in the past. The 'increase of disrespect' from which the chiefs suffered was the result of their loss of power to distribute land and to underwrite the political and economic autonomy of their followers. The only powers which they had left to them were those they acquired from the state. But if they used these powers, they forfeited even more respect for they had only been granted them to make easier the collection of taxes and the recruiting of labour gangs (*chibaro*) to build roads and do other unpaid tasks for the state. On the other hand, if the chiefs did not make use of their state-granted powers they were left high and dry with nothing to justify their status at all.

By the 1960s it had become apparent that this heaping of the authority of the state on the shoulders of the chiefs was counter-productive. It had passed a powerful advantage to the African nationalist parties that were rapidly gaining strength. If the chiefs were either ineffective old buffers or strong-arm tyrants, then the way was wide open for the nationalists to present themselves as the only legitimate representatives of the aspirations of the people. To counter this unexpected outcome, it became necessary for the district commissioners to think a little more deeply about what 'in native eyes' a chief ought to be. They concluded that for the chiefs to remain effective tools of the state they must be assisted to regain the 'traditional legitimacy' they had lost.[12]

The reason that this perception seemed to contain such a great deal of force was that throughout this period the administration believed that whatever impenetrable mysteries 'native tradition and custom' might hold, the one thing certain about them was that real traditions are binding and unchanging. Change was conceived of only as corruption, as loss of authenticity and therefore as loss of authority. It was assumed that if chiefs were installed according to their original, undiluted traditions the peasants would, in some inexpressible way, feel themselves obliged to obey them. Thus if large numbers of peasants should come under the sway of the nationalists, a truly legitimate chief would need only to condemn this and, all at once, the nationalists would find it impossible to exercise political control.

By a remarkable historical irony, the contempt expressed for the Shona (as well as the Ndebele) view of the world in the past, now gave way to the intention, under the African Affairs Amendment Act of 1966, to 'give more dignity and power to the chiefs . . . the people through whom (in the main) Government's power will be channelled.' To quote Ranger once again:

> It was emphasized in debate that the Rhodesian Front's predecessors had erred 'in not sufficiently recognising the virtue of African tradition and customs'. Section 3 of the Act laid down that in appointing chiefs the head of state 'shall give consideration to the customary principles of succession'. Chiefs were . . . made responsible for overriding nationalist opposition to agricultural rules. They were also drawn into the increasingly elaborate structures designed to provide a 'tribal government' as an alternative to the nationalist political programme.[13]

Even more remarkable was that the district commissioners came to see themselves as the custodians of Shona tradition, a bulwark against the 'communist-inspired' agitators who were dedicated to tearing down the hallowed customs of the people.[14]

Two subjects caught the particular interest of the district commissioners. The first was the genealogies of the chiefs. Each of the government files in which the records of the chiefs of Dande are stored contains a whole series of genealogies along with increasingly despairing attempts to fit all these versions together into one master genealogy. The belief was that if the original and true genealogy could be distilled from all the apparently self-serving and biased accounts that the district commissioner had collected, no illegitimate and therefore unpopular appointment of a chief need ever be made. In effect, the district commissioners set themselves up as substitute spirit mediums, attempting to choose from the many possible candidates the one who would be both legitimate and acceptable. If anything, the district commissioners had the more difficult task, for 'acceptable' in their terms meant acceptable to them, to the state and to the members of the chieftaincy as well.

The second object of the district commissioners' researches was the spirit mediums themselves. The two most relevant pieces of information that emerged had both been around for a long time. The first was that some spirit mediums had played a leading part in the 1896 rebellion. It was believed that it was only after the mediums had been captured that it had finally been possible to put the rebellion down. The second was quite simply that the mediums were responsible for legitimising the chiefs. It was concluded from this that to gain effective control of the chiefs you had first to gain effective control of the mediums. Although, as one ex-assistant commissioner, reflecting on his own experience of the mediums, put it to me: 'Try as you might, you'll never get to the bottom of the buggers', sociological research had become a patriotic duty and they had no option but to try. But how to do it? Where to start?

For the Dande area, one source of information was readily available. In the late 1950s, the historian Donald Abraham had conducted a number of interviews with Mutota/Kupara at his home in the Valley near the Kadzi River. In a series of closely argued articles, Abraham combined the Guruuswa mythology with a number of detailed genealogies that emerged from his conversations with Mutota/Kupara and arrived at an interpretation which has had a profound effect on Zimbabwean historiography. He concluded that the Guruuswa myth was an accurate if condensed summary of specific events that had actually occurred in the past. His most startling achievement was to present Mutota as an actual Korekore chief who had led an historical exodus from the fifteenth-century Karanga state centred on Great Zimbabwe, 400 km south of the Zambezi Escarpment. According to Abraham, when Mutota arrived in the north he founded the Mutapa state of which he was the first ruler, his son Nebedza the second and so on. Elaborate correlations with Portuguese records were supplied to buoy up the credibility of this interpretation.[15]

Few of Abraham's claims for Mutota survive close examination but that is another story. Their importance for this one is that they provided the local district administration, who 'regarded Abraham as an oracle', with precisely what they needed. Having learnt that Mutota was the first 'Emperor' of the Monomotapa state, they concluded that all the more junior mediums, the mediums of the more recent 'Emperors', would be under his direct control. If they could persuade this most prestigious of mediums to back their cause against the nationalists, all the others would surely follow. District commissioners and their assistants fell into the habit of stopping off at Mutota/Kupara's village either simply to butter him up or to make enquiries about native customs which they had not yet quite got the hang of. They sent gifts to his rituals, flattered him with their confidences and before long they were satisfied that they had the living remains of the first emperor of the Monomatapa state 'in their pocket'.[16]

You may remember Kupara's son's report of white men making tape recordings of his father's opinions of the war. This is not a reference to the anthropologists or historians who visited Kupara (at least three

187

have published accounts deriving directly from him). They were members of the Psychological Operations unit of the Rhodesian armed forces who used Mutota's name to forge a link between the state and the mediums and to claim that, as far as the peasants were concerned, the chiefs were the only legitimate political authority in the land.

During the early years of the war, recordings made by Mutota/Kupara were broadcast from aeroplanes circling over the operational zones. Thousands of leaflets were scattered containing variations on this central theme:

> TO YOU TERRORISTS   As the district commissioner of this area it is my work to see that all the mediums are respected so that my people can be protected from the hardships you are bringing them . . . You took the medium of Nehanda from her home which is not allowed by the spirit which caused the death of Nehanda . . . Now you must know that you are living in the country of Nehanda's father Mutota. He does not agree at all with the bloodshed. All spirits are very angry with your evil deeds . . . They will only bring you death. It will be the cause of the death of your mothers, your fathers and all your children . . . You can only get away from this punishment by the spirits if you . . . put down your weapons and give yourself up . . . If you don't listen all you will get is death.[17]

But was Mutota/Kupara really perched as cosily in the district commissioner's pocket as these statements would lead us to believe? 'All whites and blacks are the children of this country', his son reported him to have said and this is consistent with the government line. In January 1984 I interviewed a civil servant who had been responsible for collating information on spirit mediums received from all over the country throughout the war. Sitting in his office in the Earl Grey building in Harare he had no hesitation in saying of Mutota/Kupara: 'He was on our side'. But two hours later I was at 88 Manica Road, the ZANU/PF Party headquarters, discussing the war with an ex-commander of a ZANLA platoon that had been based in the north-east. He described Mutota/Kupara using the very same words: 'He was on our side'.

There is no doubt that Kupara had developed the skills required to play one side off against the other to a very high level indeed. He was consistent in claiming *all* Korekore as his descendants whether they were government employees, members of the security forces or nationalists. Considering this ambivalence it is remarkable that it was never suggested to me that Mutota/Kupara had betrayed the nationalist cause, that he was a sell-out. How did he manage to please so many masters and yet preserve this immaculate reputation? From the analysis made in the previous two chapters I can suggest an answer to this which will also explain, I believe, his eventual downfall.

The authenticity of the mediums is constantly displayed by their adherence to various sets of ritual prohibitions imposed on them by the *mhondoro*. The opposition of the *mhondoro* to white society, and especially to the sorry consequences for the Shona of their involvement with the capitalist economy, are symbolised by the mediums' refusal to have any contact with industrially produced goods which are available only on the white-dominated markets. Despite his long-standing intimacy with the white administration, Mutota/Kupara never weakened his observance of these restrictions. In this he contrasts sharply with the medium of Madzomba whose political sensitivity was rather less finely tuned.

The medium of Madzomba lived in a village on the side of one of the gravel roads frequently patrolled by the district assistants and the police. These officers of the state were instructed to behave respectfully towards the medium in order to demonstrate the government's support for the 'traditional' leaders of the people. They frequently visited Madzomba's village, clapped to him and presented him with expensive gifts including a number of cattle. They persuaded him to accept rides in motor cars and to eat and drink Western foods using Western utensils. For some years he had suffered from cataracts in both eyes. After some hesitation he accepted the district commissioner's offer to go to the capital and have them removed. 'This is an extremely important person in this district', wrote the district commissioner to the doctor who performed the operation, 'despite his somewhat disreputable appearance'. To this day this medium wears the spectacles that were issued to him at the district commissioner's expense.[18] (See Plate 9, between pp. 118–19.)

But the very success of these attempts to gain the medium's support made him virtually useless to the district commissioner. The result of his relaxation of the ritual prohibitions was that he became well known, first, as a sell-out but also, and this is the important point, as a fake. It was said that perhaps he had been possessed in the past but any medium who behaved as he did would surely be abandoned by his *mhondoro*. On a number of occasions the medium of Madzomba had to be taken out of the Valley and kept at the District centre behind barbed wire to protect him from the guerrillas. Although he returned to Dande when peace came, his reputation has still not recovered.[19]

Thus that a few mediums did collaborate with the state does no damage to my argument that the profession of mediumship was in itself inherently opposed to the colonial state. Certain minimum demands, the observation of the restrictions that express opposition, had to be obeyed. Provided that they were, mediums such as Mutota/Kupara had a degree of freedom to negotiate with the district commissioner or his assistants a strategy for protecting their interests. But if these demands were neglected and the medium appeared to be milking the state to sweeten his personal life style, all at once belief in his authenticity ran dry. In the very few cases that mediums were accused of collaboration, it was universally agreed that the medium had betrayed his *mhondoro*. The possibility that the *mhondoro* himself could lend support to the state was not entertained for an instant. And it was in the context of this unshakeable belief that the tape recordings sounding out of the heavens were listened to and the sky-scattered pamphlets were read. People knew full well that if the ancestors had something to tell them, the technology of aeroplanes and printing presses was the very last means of communication they would use. They had only to select a human medium and all would be simply conveyed. If one medium betrayed them, this was no cause for despair, for the medium is merely the vessel of the spirit. He is no more than flesh and blood, as susceptible to corruption as any other mortal. Another more reliable medium would be found by the *mhondoro* with no trouble at all.

Whether or not Madzomba actually did give active assistance to the district commissioner is hard to say but he abandoned his symbolic resistance to the state and this was enough to give the impression that he had. Mutota/Kupara, on the other hand, rigorously maintained the restrictions that express the underlying opposition between the two sources of legitimacy, ancestors and state, and was thus able to keep both sides convinced that basically he was on their side despite the compromises he might be forced into making with the other. And of course the symbolic statement of resistance made by the ritual restrictions was comprehensible only to the peasants.

The apparent compliance of Mutota/Kupara appeared to the District Administration to offer precisely what he was after, a means of providing 'traditional legitimacy' to the chiefs and hence gaining control of the local population. As a result an increasingly dim view was taken of any medium who challenged Mutota's authority over the chiefs of Dande and of the Plateau. As we have seen, the medium who most consistently challenged this authority was Chiwawa/Pondai.

Let us return to the battle over Chief Chitsungo. 'Mutota, Nyahuma and Chikuyo rule in Chitsungo's territory. Chiwawa has nothing to do with appointing chiefs here.' So runs a memo in the district commissioner's files. It is hard to think who else this information might have come from if not Mutota/Kupara, the district commissioner's main informant on 'local custom'. Kupara had spent years attempting to impose his authority over the untested Chiwawa/Pondai and he was now in a position to do so.

One year before, Kindo, Chiwawa's candidate, had been accepted as chief by popular acclaim and approved by the district commissioner. His brother's son had ruled in his place. But now Kindo's attempts to be accepted as chief in his own right were dismissed out of hand:

> Undoubtedly Chiwawa has been bribed by Kindo to put his spoke in the wheel . . . [I am] sick and tired of Kindo holding beer parties, giving money

and gifts . . . [he is] weak . . . against development . . . been going to see *mhondoro* all over the place and greasing palms.[20]

The candidate whom the district commissioner favoured was Lazarus, who had been appointed acting chief at the start of this saga in 1966. The medium of Nyahuma had died in 1971 and so the case was taken to Mutota/Kupara. Predictably he chose Lazarus. That this man was the favourite of the district commissioner and of no one else the minutes in the government file make almost painfully clear. The (black) district assistant who filed a report on the ceremony at which the chief was chosen reported that 'The people hope that Lazarus will not be too hard', to which the district commissioner added the comment, 'They will no doubt feel the beneficial effects of having a chief who cannot be twisted round their little fingers'.

Kindo determined to take the district commissioner to court and went as far as to instruct a firm of solicitors. But after one exchange of letters the case was dropped for good. Thus the district commissioner had achieved precisely what he had been after, a chief chosen by a spirit medium and hence 'legitimate' but a 'progressive', a man keen to implement government policy and to take a strong line against the nationalists.

In a letter of 21 September 1970, the district commissioner had stressed the importance of Chief Chitsungo's succession because 'although the chieftaincy is a minor one, it is important from a security point of view.' And indeed it was. For some months, incursions by guerrillas had been reported from various parts of the north-east. In many areas, government security officers had been able to do deals with headmen and chiefs and even with some mediums (Mutota/Kupara and Madzomba being the prime examples) promising that their followers would not be placed in the so-called 'protected villages' if all contact with guerrillas were reported. Most of these deals quickly proved un-workable and the camps were built anyway, but in Chiwawa's eastern provinces where he was living at the time, deals of this kind were never made at all. Here the discipline of the peasantry was rigorous. No information about guerrilla activity ever reached the police or the district administration whose officers were afraid even to enter the area. Those who did seldom returned.

The first armed attack of the second and ultimately successful phase of the war took place within Chiwawa's spirit province on the Plateau. The medium had kept a passage through the Valley clear of security forces and guided the weapon-bearing porters and guerrillas up the Escarpment towards Altena Farm near the town of Centenary where the attack was launched. It had an immediate and very wide-ranging effect. Perhaps part of its significance for Chiwawa/Pondai was that it provided a means of continuing his opposition to the local district commissioner and the new Chief Chitsungo by more radical means than those available to him in the past.[21]

Less than a month later, in January 1973, Chiwawa/Pondai was arrested and charged with three offences. He pleaded not guilty on all counts and his trial was held *in camera*. On the first charge of recruiting an African for terrorist training he received ten years' hard labour. On the second, that 'being a spirit medium by repute he had accompanied, encouraged and purported to protect terrorists and porters by means of his supposed supernatural powers', he received twenty-five years hard labour. On the third charge of 'failing within 72 hours or as soon as reasonably practicable to report the presence of terrorists to the police' he received a further five years hard labour. All sentences were to run concurrently. A reference to this case in Parliament a few days later acknowledged the success that mediums such as Chiwawa/Pondai had achieved:

> Some spirit mediums were abducted forcibly into Mozambique and others subverted to the terrorist cause. Through exploitation of the spirit mediums the terrorists were able to achieve a spiritual hold over primitive tribesmen. As a result no information was being volunteered to any government agency.[22]

Virtually overnight, the official attitude to the mediums was transformed. The collection of information about them was no longer simply a matter of securing legitimate political authority for co-operative chiefs. It had become a vital weapon in counter-insurgency.

Information already available on Shona religion was summarised, stamped 'Secret', and circulated to military and police commanders. Two early articles by Terence Ranger, the acknowledged expert on the mediums' role in the 1869 rebellion, were made available to all district commissioners, while supplies of his full-scale study, 'temporarily exhausted', were replenished. Academics were commissioned to write pieces on the history and religious organisation of the Shona. Government experts on native custom prepared lectures and talks and programmes on television. 'This,' so one such expert records, 'was what the military and the para-military wanted of me . . . to talk to the men on the ground so they could assess the social life of the people.'[23]

Every single medium at every level of seniority was to be interviewed. Standardised questionnaires were prepared. The tone of the instruction circulated in February 1973 among the district assistants who were charged with assembling information on the mediums in the north-east suggests how the attitude to the mediums had hardened. If any medium proved unresponsive, the instructions were quite clear:

> arrest him. All *swikiros* [mediums] etc. must be warned – and you must make this absolutely clear –

1.   That he is a subject of the chief.
2.   The chief holds the power of the government who will support him to the full.
3.   That any *swikiro* who goes against the chief cannot be a true *swikiro*.
4.   Ensure that each and everyone understands [that] those misguided *swikiros* [mediums] who have assisted terrorists or who operate with them will be destroyed. There is no place in any society for people such as these and they, having been severely punished or killed, as the case may be, will be responsible for their *Mhondoros* remaining dormant for all times . . . The European will if necessary, use the spirits of his mighty ancestors to fight terrorists and those who assist them. If this comes about the results for the Africans will be disastrous . . . Any complaint by Chiefs that *swikiros* are not toeing the line will result in immediate retribution upon the *swikiro* concerned.

Mediums known to be recalcitrant were threatened by name:

> In particular tell Johane, the medium of Chingowo, that the pretence of his not being allowed to see Europeans will need to be thought about by him carefully and if necessary he will be brought into camp. If he is sensible he will co-operate with the government.[24]

The issuing of this instruction was the final twist in the long and complex tale of the interplay between the state and the political ideology of Dande. Before this the district commissioners had been attempting to rebuild the authority of the chiefs by persuading the mediums to endorse and hence legitimise them. The objective had been to keep 'traditional custom' and hence the traditional authority of the chiefs alive. In so far as this attempt was successful at all, it was consistent with established practice. But it relied on the willingness of the mediums to let themselves be persuaded. Chiwawa's treachery had shown that the attempt to gain control of the mediums was not enough. In order to legitimise their authoritarian system of political control in the eyes of the people, the state needed the direct support of the ancestors themselves.

This presented a problem. The only way to approach the ancestors is through the mediums. But in no time at all the logic of the system became clear to the district commissioners just as it had to the autonomous chiefs of the past.

In the example I described in Chapter 4, when the chiefs and the mediums fell out, the chiefs would emphasise their authority as descendants of the *mhondoro* in order to substantiate their challenge to the mediums whose opinions they disagreed with. Now precisely the same process occurred. The district commissioners insisted that any medium who opposed the state was going against the wishes of the ancestors and on those grounds alone must be considered a fraud.

If the mediums refused to co-operate with the state or indeed if they chose to back the wrong side, the district commissioners had two choices open to them. One course of action would be to kill the mediums, leaving the *mhondoro* without a voice with which to oppose them, and there is evidence that this course of action was only thwarted by the difficulty of laying hold of the dissident mediums. Alternatively, they could attempt to persuade the people that a 'political medium' was not a real one, that a real medium would never back the 'communist' guerrillas committed to the destruction of their 'native traditions' which the state upheld.

The best-documented example of this second choice is the persistent attack on the credibility of Chiwawa/Pondai. The files for the three chieftaincies of which Chiwawa/Pondai is the key ancestor contain assertion after assertion that Pondai is not a real medium. Almost every recorded genealogy contains a note next to the name of Chiwawa remarking that this *mhondoro* 'has no true medium at present'. Somehow the illusion had to be kept alive that 'real' mediums who genuinely spoke with the authentic voice of the ancestors gave their support to the state. And many members of the administrative staff and the local police seem to have begun to believe this themselves. In an extraordinary mixture of half-truth and wish fulfilment a consensus seems to have been arrived at that the older mediums were more in touch with the 'original' traditions of the people and hence must be opposed to the guerrillas. It was only the young hot-heads who put their traditions at such risks by opposing the people and the state.

As well as the soldiers sent to guard Mutota, another party was sent to guard the medium of Nehanda. By the time they reached her village in the far north of Dande she was no longer there. Together with three others mediums and an escort of ZANLA guerrillas, she had crossed the Zambezi River and was living in Mozambique, 'doing her command work, directing us in Zimbabwe', as guerrillas and mediums have told me. But her flight was interpreted by the district commisssioner as a kidnapping. On a typed list of the 'Spirit Mediums and spirits, *ngangas* etc. of Chief Matsiwo's area' in the files of the district commissioner, Sipolilo, next to the names of the mediums who accompanied Nehanda, is the following phrase written in ink: 'Subverted and being used by the ters'. But next to the name of Nehanda is written 'Abducted by ters with the help of 2 and 3' (the other two mediums). The two younger, little-known mediums may have been open to subversion but the district commissioner seems to have been convinced that senior mediums such as Mutota and Nehanda could not willingly have gone over to the guerrillas' side. The only true traditions are old traditions, the only real mediums are old mediums, the only trustworthy Shona are dead Shona, the ancestors, who – or so the district commissioner claimed to believe – inevitably support the state.

The death of Mutota/Kupara

The pressures put on the mediums by the district commissioners threatened not only their reputations but also their lives. In the north-east outside Dande, at least two mediums were shot as sell-outs by ZANLA guerrillas. One was the medium of Matare. The other, the medium of Perengeta, was unfortunate enough to be handed a fistful of money by a member of the security forces at a public meeting. Within Dande itself, no mediums lost their lives, though a few were severely beaten up by the army of the state. Mutota's position was altogether more complex and ambivalent.

It is of course impossible to account for individual choice and commitment by making use of symbolic oppositions. Nonetheless, it is not, I would think, entirely irrelevant that the fundamental structural opposition between Mutota and Chiwawa, which has emerged as a contradiction involving the rights and duties of these *mhondoro* and as a series of arguments and enmities between their mediums, found a further expression in their contrasting attitudes to the state at the time of the war.

All of Chiwawa/Pondai's professional life as a medium had been carried out in opposition to Mutota/Kupara who had rejected him and made numerous attempts to reduce his importance to the Korekore of the Valley. As he had never been tested or formally installed, Mutota/Kupara could argue that no account of his opinions should be taken. But for precisely the same reason, Chiwawa/Pondai was free from Mutota/Kupara's direct control. It seems probable that once Mutota/Kupara had formed his alliance with the state, the force of the opposition between these two mediums would have driven Chiwawa/Pondai into the arms of the guerrillas even had he not had sufficient reason for joining them on his own. And the force of this opposition works the other way too. Although Mutota/Kupara's position as the most senior *mhondoro* of numerous royal lineages seemed monumentally secure, in fact he was under very great pressure indeed. Over the colonial period (virtually the length of Kupara's professional career) the authority of the mediums had increased while that of the chiefs had dwindled away. This process had continued despite the state's attempts to give the chiefs their support. If the political order were to change and a new style of government take power, would the spirit mediums lose the authority they had achieved? If they did, Mutota/Kupara had more than any other medium to lose. More junior mediums welcomed the guerrillas because they undertook to recapture all the lost land. But if this promise was redeemed, would the new political masters treat Mutota/Kupara with the indulgence he had received from the old? Or would all their attentions be turned to the younger mediums like

Chiwawa/Pondai who had marched by their sides through the forests? With the district commissioner he knew where he stood and how much he could do to protect his followers. According to a district assistant's report, up to the last day of his life he continued to instruct his followers to obey the laws of the land: 'Listen to what the DC tells you. If anyone breaks the DCs laws there is no doubt that he will suffer.'

But as the war became more and more intense the old days of pleasant chats with the district commissioner and the exchange of gifts for information on traditions were over. Mutota/Kupara became, as the chiefs had before him, no more than a means of exerting the will of the state. Here is one of the last of the propaganda leaflets dropped from the air that mentioned his name:

A MESSAGE FROM THE GREAT MEDIUM OF MHONDORO MUTOTA TO ALL HIS PEOPLE
I know that my children Nehanda, Chidyamawuya and Chiwodza Mamero have been captured by the terrorists. And I see that Chiwawa has committed a great crime. The ancestral spirits do not want blood-shed in this country. I shall work with the Government. I shall not die helping terrorists, no! I know them. When the terrorists come to this area, they must be destroyed by the people working hand in hand with the soldiers.[25]

But when the soldiers came to his village, working hand in hand took on an altogether different meaning. The means by which Kupara had protected his reputation among his followers, the conscientious performance of his duties as medium, was made impossible. He could no longer observe the full set of ritual restrictions and his supplicants were prevented by the soldiers from consulting the *mhondoro* in privacy and peace.

Kupara's death has been interpreted by the people of Dande in a variety of ways. Some maintain that it was caused by the *mhondoro's* abhorrence of the smell of petrol brought into his village by the soldiers' vehicles. Others suggest that it may have been the smell of the onions the soldiers ate or of the cigarettes they smoked. But his son's account, quoted at the beginning of this chapter, points in another direction. He was 'wanted' by both sides. The performance of his duties was heavily restricted by the interrogation his visitors suffered at the hands of the security forces on the lookout for guerrillas who might come to consult him. The medium had been protected from the risk of 'abduction' but the identity of the *mhondoro* as an autonomous royal ancestor and owner of the land, free from contamination by the conquering whites, had been stripped away. It was impossible for Kupara to go on without losing every drop of the authority he had achieved with such pains over so many years. He was at least 70 years old and the precise cause of his death is unknown but it is hard not to think that it was hastened if not actually brought on by despair.

The triumph of Chiwawa/Pondai

In this chapter I have traced the development of the oppositions between the *mhondoro* Chiwawa and Mutota and between their mediums, oppositions I have categorised as structural, personal and historical. One last consequence of these oppositions remains to be described. The co-operation between Mutota/Kupara and the local district commissioner had an important effect on the way in which the war was conceptualised by the agents of the state. The nature of Chiwawa/Pondai's opposition to the state had an equally powerful effect on how the war was conceptualised by the ZANLA guerrillas in Dande. In a sense, long before he was arrested and sentenced, Chiwawa/Pondai had already worked out his revenge. For out of the opposition between the two mediums, between support for the resistance and support for the state, arose a radical transformation of the rituals carried out at his shrines.

If you think back to the description of the organisation of the shrines of the *mhondoro* in Chapter 4, you will remember that the key official of these shrines is the *mutapi*. The *mutapi* takes care of the day-to-day business of mediumship, especially of those matters which, when he is in a state of possession, the medium is unable to see to for himself. The *mutapi* is almost always also a village head and a senior member of an important lineage with a long and close connection with the province of 'his' *mhondoro*. Contrary to appearances, in local conception it is not the medium who is thought to open and maintain the channels of communication between the living and the dead, it is the *mutapi*. His job is to summon the *mhondoro* from where he is resting in the body of a lion, or roaming unseen in the depths of the forest, and to persuade him to return to the living, to resolve their disputes and to cure their ills. In sum, the *mutapi* intermediates between the two spheres of social life, the political sphere consisting of living women and men organised into households, villages, headmanships and chieftaincies, and the religious sphere, the sphere of the dead, organised around shrines, divided into spirit provinces and spirit realms and dominated by the mediums of the chiefs of the past.

Up till now I have used the term *mutapi* to designate the five lineages that perform these functions for Chiwawa at his shrines, two on the Escarpment and three in the Valley. But in fact, unlike all other *mhondoro*, Chiwawa does not have any *vatapi*. The individuals who perform these tasks for him say simply: 'We are Chiwawa's *vazukuru*' (grandchildren or descendants). In saying this they draw on the idea that everyone who lives within the *mhondoro's* spirit province is his *muzukuru* and, in the absence of a recognised *mutapi*, may perform such rituals as are necessary from time to time. Chiwawa's five lineages of *vazukuru/vatapi* have all the necessary credentials to fulfil their role and they are referred to as *vatapi* beyond the borders of Chiwawa's province. And yet they refuse this title. Why?

Answering this question leads to the heart of the changes that have taken place in Dande, changes which though immensely important are virtually invisible to the dim-sighted traveller until the journey from the Plateau down the Escarpment and deep into the peasants' conceptualisation of their own complex society has been made.

In fact, Chiwawa's innovation is very simple. The political sphere of chiefs and villages had been thoroughly absorbed into the colonial state. The chiefs had become civil servants with the powers of policemen. The headmen were tax collectors, and organisers of forced-labour gangs. Attempts had been made (less successfully in Dande than in other parts of the country) to restructure the villages so as to maximise the questionable advantages of the new agricultural policies. The old cycles of exchange between chiefs and their followers had fallen away. All in all, the political sphere was experienced as migrant labour, poverty and prisons, no part of it under the control of the people or the mediums of Dande. So Chiwawa/Pondai simply cut his ties with the political sphere and went his own way.

As Chiwawa/Pondai did not wish to speak through his *vatapi* to the de-ancestralised chiefs and all that their world contained, he spoke instead direct to the people. The officials who prepare his rituals were thought of simply as *vazukuru*, the descendants and followers of the *mhondoro*. And by severing his tie to the political sphere, Chiwawa/Pondai was able to triumph over it. To give just one practical example: Chiwawa/Pondai appointed one of his *vazukuru/vatapi* named Broom to the status of ward head (*sadunhu*). The present Chief Chitsungo insists that only he can promote men this way and that Broom is no more than a *sabhuku*, a village head. But those who live in Broom's village claim that he is a *sadunhu because Chiwawa said so*. It is no coincidence that Broom was one of the villagers most stalwart in support of the ZANLA guerrillas. (Figure 10.2 contrasts the new and old relationships between *mhondoro, mutapi*, chief, followers and the state.)

Thus when the ZANLA guerrillas made contact with the spirit mediums in Dande they entered a world in which the life of the ancestors had taken on a most pervasive and vibrant intensity. All aspirations, problems, conflicts, desires which in the past had been directed towards representatives of the political realm were now directed towards the *mhondoro* and their mediums. The ancestors were quite simply everywhere. They had trooped out of the forests, flooded the villages and thronged the air. 'The great spectacle of the past' had come into its own with a force that it had perhaps never achieved before.

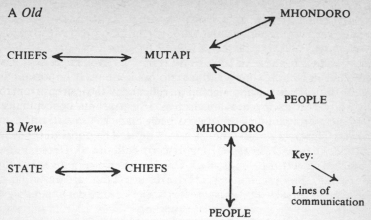

Figure 10.2   The changing lines of communication between ancestors and people

It is against this background that we must listen to the wave after wave of experiences and anecdotes reported by guerrillas and peasants of the miraculous, unprecedented happenings that occurred during the war. Wild animals protecting *mujibas*, snakes pointing the way to stores of food, spirits keeping people alive under water, trees talking, birds giving warnings and the like. For the world of the present had swung away and they were held for a time in the firm grasp of the ancestors, poised between the future and the past.

The same experiences are reported from all the other spirit provinces in Dande, and, as I suggested in the Introduction, from many other parts of Zimbabwe as well. How many other mediums dispensed with their *vatapi* and cut their ties with the present as Chiwawa did is not yet known. I anticipate that further research will produce further examples. In the meantime, we can speculate on why it should have been Chiwawa/Pondai out of all the other mediums in Dande who saw so clearly that the rituals he performed linked him to the world he abhorred.

Perhaps his long-standing opposition to a medium who had intimate ties with the local administration pointed the way. Perhaps it was the fact that the local district commissioner specifically rejected his authenticity and proclaimed him a charlatan, but then any medium who backed the guerrillas, who 'meddled in politics', was from this point of view *de facto* a fraud. What was unique to Chiwawa/Pondai was that he had never been tested, that he was to a large extent free of commitment to any other authority, medium or chief. He had had to rely entirely on the force of his own personality, his own will, his belief in his own powers to establish his substantial reputation.

The unencumbered, charismatic authority of Chiwawa leads on to the final aspect of this de-materialised, disembodied, thoroughly ancestralised world that I want to explore. In Chapter 9 I suggested that the *mhondoro* mediums had transferred legitimate political authority from the chiefs to the ZANLA guerrillas but this should not be taken to imply that they had established a stable political order. A war such as this one is inevitably experienced as an intermediary period, as a period between two established political orders. The guerrillas were fighting to introduce a political order of their own but, as they saw it, this would not come into being unless the ancestors desired that it should. Only if the rituals of the ancestors were performed could the coming of the new, pure world of the future be assured. This intermediary period of warfare had, in fact, definite millenarian overtones. They are certainly not dominant but if we listen with care it is impossible to deny that they are there.

To make an argument of this kind is to walk a tightrope. To say that there were millenarian aspects to the behaviour and the beliefs of the guerrillas is not to say that this is all that there was to them. One of the characteristics of millenarian movements is that the new worlds they anticipate have a tendency not to arrive. Though the present state of Zimbabwe is perhaps not entirely what all those who fought to create it desired or imagined, it does exist, it has come. The war was won and the new state was born out of armed conflict, out of successful military strategy, out of the courage, the persistence and the sacrifice of the guerrillas and the peasants in the countryside. Millenarian ritual activity could never have brought it into being on its own.

But the millenarian aspect of the struggle is the context within which many of its more unusual aspects fall into place. Listen, first of all, to the tone of this statement quoted earlier from a notebook written for me by an ex-*mujiba*:

> The prostitutes were killed because the comrades said: You are holding us back from winning our country. The comrades were saying: The country is ours, we blacks. People who are putting Ambi [skin lightening cream] on their faces were killed.[26]

Part of the meaning conveyed here is that unless prostitutes and others corrupted by white values were got rid of, the new world would not be able to come. This desire to use morally pure ritual actions to force the new world into being is, I believe, at the root of a great deal of the guerrillas' behaviour. Much of this behaviour successfully combines the millenarian with the utterly pragmatic. The killing of witches, those sources of absolute evil, implacably opposed to the *mhondoro*, is a necessary cleansing of this world to force the new one into existence but it is also an attempt to eradicate sell-outs who betray the guerrillas and bring down the all-too-real force of the army on their heads and on the heads of the peasants.

Secondly, this determination to clear out all the evil of the present world to prepare for the next helps to explain, I think, some of the brutality that characterised many of the contacts between guerrillas and their enemies. And, finally, this perspective adds something to our understanding of the meaning of the many political arguments that were put to the peasants.

I have already quoted one ex-guerrilla's account which reported that 'we explained national grievances, then colonialism, then neo-colonialism and capitalism. We explained that ours would be a socialist government and what that would mean to the masses.'[27] Much of the ZANU political programme, especially the policy of anti-racism, was well understood and accepted. But what of 'colonialism, neo-colonialism and capitalism'? I found no evidence that the inhabitants of Dande had more than the very vaguest idea of what these terms mean. Or, at least, of what these terms mean in a literate, urban political context. In Dande they acquired their own meaning as the names given to the bad world of the present that must be swept aside, while 'socialism' was the name of the good one that would arrive once this long and bitter but intermediate period of warfare was over.

It would be a mistake to imagine that the image of the world to come was based entirely on the 'great spectacle', on an imaginary vision of the past. True, the people were promised that they would regain their land in the name of the ancestors, but straightaway they would set about making use of all the modern technique of production and marketing that had, up till then, been denied them. The present world had been rejected because it worked to the peasants' severe disadvantage but, once this ancestral interregnum was over, the rewards would be better lives lived in comfortable surroundings, better food, better education for their children, better health care, participatory democracy, in short all the advantages that the modern world could bring. Nonetheless without the powers of the ancestors to transcend the material plane, to triumph over the political sphere, these rewards would always remain out of reach.

Chiwawa/Pondai's rejection of the political realm had one further manifestation that makes a fitting end to his history. A tale repeated to me many times in Dande told how, the morning after Chiwawa had been sentenced and imprisoned, his warders found him standing at his ease outside his cell. They jailed him again but as many times as they locked him up he would set himself free. It is useless to ask why in that case he did not run away and come home and get on with the war. The sour expressions that were turned on me when I was so foolish as to ask this question were well deserved. The meaning of this tale is revealed by a comparison with Mutota/Kupara who died, so the accounts of his death made clear, when the state intruded too deeply into his life. He had been killed by the forbidden smell of petrol from the vehicles of the police. Chiwawa/Pondai, on the other hand, cut his ties with the mundane world and triumphed over the police and the jailers of the state. Provided that their ritual prohibitions are observed, the power of the *mhondoro* is so vast it can never be overcome by any secular authority. No political power on earth could ever chain Chiwawa down.

NOTES

1 See genealogy of Chitsungo dated 12 December 1969, Per 5 Chitsungo in Ministry of Local Government Archives, Harare, Zimbabwe.

2 For a full exposition of the relationship between Mutota and the Korekore lineages of Dande and the northern Plateau see Garbett (1966a, 1969, 1977).

3 For trade routes in the north and north-east see Bhila (1982, p. 76). For the Chiweshe chieftaincy see Fynn N3/33/8 in the National Archives, Harare, Zimbabwe. For Dande Korekore generalogies see Per 5 Chitsungo and Kasekete. On the Tande view of Chiwawa: in a report of a meeting held on 11 December 1935 the 'Native Commissioner' notes that he was told by the Tande that in the past they had been 'much harassed by the Makorekore from the south, notably by the tribal *mhondoro* Chiwawa who had a fortress on a hill on the escarpment and detachments of warriors below in the three forts said to be made by the father of Chiwawa Kasekete'. But compare this with the report in Matthews (1966) where the leader of the conquest is said to have been Mutota. Perhaps the contrast between these accounts has significance for the oppositions between Chiwawa and Mutota I am exploring in this chapter.

4 Garbett (1977, p. 74).

5 I am grateful to Dr Garbett for this and other personal communications and for his generosity in allowing me to include them here. For Chiwawa's following in the 1960s, see Garbett (1963, p. 247).

6 Garbett (1977, p. 66).

7 Garbett (1963, p. 248); memo of meeting, 12 December 1967, in Per 5 Kasekete. Ministry of Local Govt. Harare. Zimbabwe.

8 The question of why it should have been Nyahuma who appointed the successors to this chieftaincy is discussed in Lan (1983, p. 242). Nyahuma had no especially close relationship with the Chitsungo chieftaincy as Figure 10. 1, above shows, though the chieftaincy was within part of his spirit province. All the names of the principal actors in this story, except for

those of the mediums, have been changed.
9   Letter of 18 March 1969, Per 5 Chitsungo.
10 Both letters dated 7 August 1970. See also letter dated 21 September 1970. All in Per 5 Chitsungo.
11 Ranger (1981, p. 9).
12 To some extent, being an 'ineffective old buffer' may be a technique of resistance. The previous Chief Chitsungo's incompetence was described in a number of reports. He insisted on handling all legal cases at his own court and never referred any to the court of the district commissioner; he refused to share money paid into his court with his councillors and, a sure sign of a man who knows his own mind, the district assistant complained that 'he forgets things discussed yesterday or even two hours ago'. See notes of July 1965 in Per 5 Chitsungo.
13 Ranger (1982b, p. 23).
14 There is no doubt that among some district commissioners at least the view of themselves as protectors of the traditions of the people was quite sincerely held. Some published articles or wrote long manuscripts on the subject. A number of these are valuable accounts of traditions as they were perceived and remembered at one moment in time, though the writers often imply that they have arrived on the scene to record these practices in the nick of time and just before they disappear down the plughole of history for ever. See especially Latham (1970, 1972) and White (1971). There are many earlier examples as well.
15 Abraham (1959). See also (1962, 1964, 1966). In Chapter 5 I suggested that Mutota was not in fact an ancestor at all, at least not an ancestor like the majority of the *mhondoro* of Dande but an anthropomorphic fertility principle. For a suggestion of how this fertility principle may have been converted into a *mhondoro* and of the effects this may have had on the religious organisation of Dande and the northern Plateau, see Lan (1983, p. 234).
16 The phrases in quotation marks are extracted from interviews with the two ex-district commissioners on which this account is based.
17 I found bundles of these leaflets abandoned in a government camp near the village of Mushumbi Pools in June 1980. A copy has been deposited in the National Archives, Harare.
18 Letter dated 29 November 1976, Per 5 Chitsungo.
19 For the fascinating case of Muchetera, the medium of the Zezuru *mhondoro* Chaminuka, whose career has similarities to those of Mutota/Kupara and the medium of Madzomba, see Ranger (1982a).
20 Letter dated 8 February 1972, Per 5 Chitsungo.
21 Accounts given to me in Dande of Chiwawa's success in keeping security forces out of his spirit provinces were confirmed by ex-district commissioners who had had responsibility for the area at the time. To conclude the story of the Chitsungo succession: Lazarus was appointed in March 1972 with a 'subsidy' of $1440 per annum. He was assassinated by ZANLA six years later at the height of the war in the Valley.
22 *Rhodesian Herald*, 19 April 1973; Parliamentary Debates, 29 March 1973; Volume 83, No. 15, Column 1072.

23 Frederikse (1984, p. 130).
24 A copy of this instruction has been deposited in the National Archives, Harare.
25 Frederikse (1984, p. 130).
26 Notebook 5.
27 For a fuller version of this quotation, see above, p. 127.

Plate 10   This photograph taken at the height of the war shows the mediums of Chipfene (left) and Chidyamauyu after they had joined the ZANLA forces in Mozambique

Plate 11   The medium of Chiodzamamera in his cotton field after his return to independent Zimbabwe

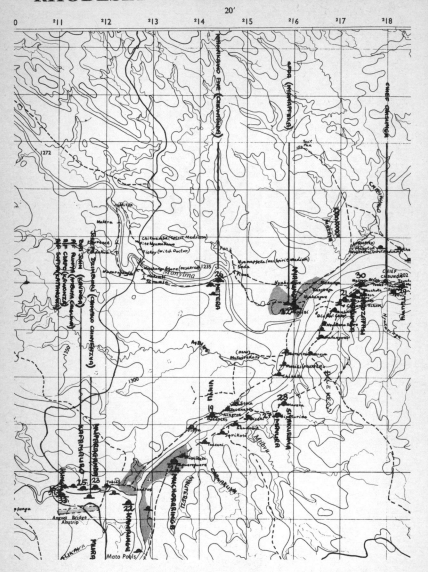

Plate 12   Fragment of a military map found in an ex-Rhodesian army camp.
The homes of spirit mediums have been inked in by security force officers.
These include Nyamapfeka, Chikwamba and Chimako.

Plate 13 George Kupara – the medium of Mutota, the most senior of all Korekore ancestors, for more than fifty years

Plate 14 Enos Pondai, the medium of Chiwawa, was jailed by the Rhodesian government for seven years for assisting ZANU guerrillas. He, alone of all mediums, had earlier challenged Kupara's authority in Dande. (See Chapter 10.)

Plate 15   The medium of Nehanda, hanged in 1895 (see Plate 1), bequeaths the authority of the ancestors to the first prime minister of Zimbabwe, Robert Mugabe. Many similar designs appeared on cloths printed to celebrate Independence in 1980

PART IV

To Zimbabwe and Beyond

Control of the idea of possession was one of the main objectives of the rulers of the Central African state systems, and the varying degrees to which they achieved it constitutes a large part of the history of Central African territorial cults.

Terence Ranger, 'Territorial Cults in the History of Central Africa', 1973, p. 596.

11
The Ancestors and the Party

Our alliance and solidarity within the Patriotic Front and our solidarity with the Front Line States, with OAU countries, with socialist countries, with other progressive countries and socialist and progressive organisations in non-socialist countries and with other liberation movements – such as SWAPO, PAC, ANC-SA, POLISARIO, FRETILIN, the PLO must continue . . . Zimbabwe must be free now. The people are anxiously waiting a new and independent state. To arms, all you brothers and sisters, to arms all you fathers and mothers: yes, everyone of you, comrades, workers and peasants, students and everyone, join on and fight on, bash the enemy for victory is in sight.[1]

Throughout the nineteenth and twentieth centuries, one problem had confounded the attempts of the Shona to mount resistance to colonialism. The individual chieftaincies of Mozambique, even groups of these chieftaincies, could not hope to compete with the strength of a Portuguese army of mercenaries. No more could the chiefs of Rhodesia survive individually the challenge of the well-equipped army of the British state. The problem, in a phrase, had been 'how to commit the masses to an effective enlargement of scale.' The spirit realms controlled by the mediums crossed the boundaries of chieftaincies and provided one solution to this problem. But spirit realms stretch no wider than a handful of chieftaincies and often they are related ones at that. The major contribution to resolving this problem was made by ZANU. With cells and branches throughout the country it achieved unprecedented unity across boundaries of lineage, of chieftaincy, of dialect, of clan. The role of the African nationalist parties is therefore the most important feature, and perhaps the only truly original one, that distinguishes the recent war from all the wars and rebellions of the past.[2]

In Part III I may have given the impression that the only way in which

ZANU and its guerrilla army ever established any legitimacy at all was by evoking the authority of the ancestors. As the extract from Robert Mugabe's 1978 New Year statement quoted above makes clear, this was not so. In presenting itself to the outside world, ZANU obviously needed to establish its legitimacy in terms quite different from those used by the guerrillas inside the country to establish theirs. The collaboration between guerrillas and peasant leaders was the experience of those who lived and fought within the borders of Zimbabwe rather than of the ZANU politicians who laid out party policy at some distance, both geographic and conceptual, from the peasants themselves. But how much did these politicians know of the collaboration that was taking place between the guerrillas and the mediums? And how far did they approve?

In the late 1960s and the very early 1970s, the ZANLA guerrillas received training by fighting alongside Frelimo in its struggle to liberate Mozambique. Frelimo was consistently opposed to collaboration with peasant religious leaders. It argued that religious leaders' claims were fraudulent and their practice irreconcilable with the principles of scientific socialism which Frelimo was attempting to instil amongst the Mozambiquan peasantry. It encouraged ZANU to take a similar line. But when ZANLA guerrillas reported that one consequence of their newly acquired skills as peasant mobilisers was contact with mediums who were firmly committed to resistance to the state, senior ZANU politicians operating out of Lusaka instructed them to recruit them. Indeed, they ordered that any elder who was sympathetic to the struggle should be recruited regardless of his status within the dominant political system. In addition to the mediums, militant chiefs such as Tangwena, Chiweshe and Makoni all became close associates of the guerrillas either inside or outside the country.[3]

The basis on which this decision was taken was what was known as the 'two-line policy', a strategy of combined long-term and short-term aims. The 'revolutionary transformation of the political and economic practice of the peasantry' was categorised as long term. The short-term goal was nationalist victory, to take control of the countryside so that the long-terms goals might in time be achieved. The two-line policy demanded 'flexibility' and 'pragmatism'. If the participation of spirit mediums could speed the nationalist victory, then this should be encouraged.[4]

Did the guerrilla commanders carry their policy of flexibility so far as to allow the spirit mediums to determine military strategy as many of their followers believe? The answer I have received from a number of ex-guerrilla commanders is, quite simply, no. Why then did the lower ranks of guerrillas and the peasants believe that they did?

The majority of the guerrillas were very young, often hardly more than adolescents, who had only recently left their fathers' villages. Especially in the later years, their period of training was very brief. Such political education as they enjoyed did not contradict the premises of their religious beliefs. The *mhondoro* are the warriors and the chiefs of the past. They are well known to be experts on war. From this point of view, it seemed obvious that if the mediums were involved with the struggle at all, their expertise would be drawn on, their instructions obeyed.

What of the magical protection that the guerrillas received from the mediums? The fact is that few if any of the guerrillas relied exclusively for their safety on magical precautions. Nor would the mediums have expected them to. Sound planning, courage and discipline were the recognised requirements of a successful military campaign. But just as few guerrillas were prepared to dispense with ancestral protection altogether.

This point is crucial. All the evidence suggests that guerrillas and peasants held two contrasting ideas in their heads at the same time and, by referring to both, arrived at effective courses of action. Ancestral protection and rigorous military discipline were both essential. The successes achieved confirmed this. Defeats were interpreted as due to tactical miscalculations and perhaps lapses of courage and at the same time ascribed to a failure to observe all the prohibitions the *mhondoro* demanded. The one train of thought does not preclude the other. The apparent contradiction between them is only apparent from one (and in the circumstances, an irrelevant) point of view.

ZANU/PF in the countryside

In mid-1979, as the war finally drew towards its end, ZANLA guerrillas travelled throughout the Valley and established a network of village committees. The purpose of these committees was to take over the administration of the countryside. In the first round of elections, many of the individuals who had served on the secret committees set up to support the guerrillas during the war were transferred from one style of committee to the next, but many other men and some women were elected as well. By the time the guerrillas finally withdrew altogether, the committees representing the interests of ZANU (now ZANU/PF) were firmly in control.[5]

The structure and to some extent the function of these committees varies from place to place throughout Zimbabwe. Within Dande they consist entirely of members of ZANU/PF (there is no other political party active in the area). Their structure has gone through a number of developments. At present, each committee represents one-hundred adults, male and female, who vote for a Chairman, a Secretary, a

Political Commissar and officers responsible for welfare, security, publicity of meetings, women's affairs, youth affairs and so on. Each officer has a deputy who is a full member of the committee. A separately elected branch committee has authority over five village committees and sends a delegate to a district committee which has direct contact with ZANU/PF headquarters.

At village level the committees are the means whereby the policies of ZANU/PF are communicated to the peasants and put into action. They are charged with allocating land to newcomers and overseeing all works necessary to the welfare of the village. For the first few years, they were also responsible for holding courts in which civil disputes could be heard and, if possible settled. If they were not resolved, they were referred to the branch committee and then to the district committee if necessary.[6]

If the village committees inherited the political authority once held by the guerrillas, what effect did this have on the spirit mediums? Has the arrival of participatory democracy finally left them behind?

Not at all. At the beginning of every village and branch committee meeting, all the men present remove their hats and shoes and perform the ritual clapping to the local *mhondoro* while his *mutapi* invokes his blessing on the business of the day. This ritual, which is repeated as a conclusion to the meeting, is a powerful reminder to the officers of the committees that their responsibility is not only to the people who have elected them but to the *mhondoro*, the owner of the land, as well. These officers were not, of course, appointed by the *mhondoro* as the chiefs were in the past. They are chosen by the people. But after elections have taken place, senior members of the committees visit their local spirit medium to inform the *mhondoro* and to ask for his approval and advice.

The belief that the ancestors support the committees has led to the Political Commissars acquiring a function in addition to those specified by the party, namely political education and the spreading and interpreting of current party policies. Within Dande, at least, the Political Commissar is also charged with protecting the area from witches. This should come as no surprise. The concept of 'witch' is, today as in the past, the negative of the concept '*mhondoro*'. Because the *mhondoro* have given their support to the committees, the committees defend the moral code they represent. If anyone breaks that code and is therefore categorised as a witch, it is the duty of the Political Commissar, as it was of the chiefs of the past, to take action against them.

In a few cases spirit mediums have been elected to serve on committees but this is rare. In most cases the traditional separation of the political and the religious, the rulers of the present and of the past, has been perpetuated. But there is nothing to stop mediums attending committee meetings and some do so regularly. In terms of local theory, the mediums are no more than men. What they say is no more worth the hearing than the words of anyone else. But the unique ambivalence of their personalities – part man, part ancestor – in fact lends great weight to any intervention they might make.

What if a spirit medium should object to a decision taken by a committee? Or speaking as the *mhondoro*, what if he should refuse to sanction the appointment of a committee official? As far as I know, this has not happened so far but it is likely that the same principles will apply in the present as in the past. The unshakeable assumption is that the *mhondoro* have great concern for the welfare of the people. Where the action of a medium in opposing an elected official appears to be motivated by self-interest, suspicions about the authenticity of his possession will arise. Where the *mhondoro*'s opinions, as conveyed by the medium, are perceived as altruistic, as beneficial to the people as a whole, they will be heard with respect and, usually, acted upon.

Of the chairmen of the branch committees it is said, *ndimambo zvino*, he is now the chief. This does not mean that he is like a chief, or that he is acting as or for the chief. The word *mambo* is applied to anyone who acts with the authority of the ancestors. The old chiefs no longer have this authority. As branch chairmen do, they are the *mambo* of today. However he is unlike past *mambos* in one respect at least. Once installed, chiefs ruled for life. The branch chairman, like all other officers, is elected for just three years. After this he must stand down, though he may if he chooses put up for election again. Moreover, if at any time during his period in office he loses the support of the electorate he may be voted down and replaced. The question this raises is whether the political committees will find themselves capable of recreating the old links between the earth and the sky, the world of the living and of the dead. Will branch chairmen at their deaths become *mhondoro*, establish branch-size spirit provinces and control the fertility of the fields that, in life, their ancestors the guerrillas won back from the whites?

It will, I am sure, be a good fifty years before the answer is known. For the moment the *mhondoro* that exist are newly charged with energy from their great success in the war and they can, if they wish to, supply all the fertility required.

With the exception of the achievement of Independence itself, the establishment of these committees is the most important outcome of the liberation struggle. They bring to a conclusion the series of transformations of political authority that began when the chiefs were incorporated into the emergent white state. First the mediums added political authority to the religious authority they already held. Then the old duality re-emerged during the intermediate period of the war with the guerrillas as the political half of the partnership. At the end of the

211

war, the guerrillas handed over their authority to committees elected by the villagers. By giving their support to these committees, the mediums have achieved remarkable continuity. The authority of the *mhondoro*, alongside that of the party, continues to legitimate the political process.

A major effect of the setting up of the committees was to challenge three long-established inequalities in Dande social life. The first is that between commoner and royal. Today all adult men are equally entitled to a leading role in political life. The chiefs retain some prestige as the descendants of the *mhondoro* but they are entitled to no automatic political or economic privilege on that account. Like any other villager they may stand for election to the Party Committees. Within Dande, although a number of ex-headmen have been returned to positions of authority, only one chief has been voted into power. The rest have no formal authority within the new political order at all.[7]

Within Chiwawa's spirit provinces, the distinction between chiefs and ordinary people has suffered an additional blow. Chiwawa/Pondai was released from jail in 1979 under the terms of an amnesty after serving seven years of his twenty-five-year sentence. During one of his first possession rituals following his return to Dande, he declared that if a person finds a pangolin in the bush they no longer need to present it either to the chief or to the *mhondoro*. They are free to eat it themselves. Everyone who lives in his spirit provinces is a descendant of the *mhondoro* and equally entitled to the wild fruits of the earth.

The second inequality that the structure of the committees has challenged is that between women and men. The third is that between elders and the young.

When the guerrillas came into the countryside the section of the population to whom they offered the most direct challenge were the male elders. The vast majority of the guerrillas were unmarried and therefore not of adult status. And many of them were female. By transforming themselves into warriors, the archetypal male role, and by wandering far from their fathers' homes with neither husbands nor chaperones, the women achieved a dramatic break with the past and they were fully conscious that they had done so.

Today the majority of the women who had acquired practical experience of living and fighting alongside men as their moral and intellectual equals are either in the army or the towns and are not available to share this experience with the women who stayed behind. Although women are eligible for election to village committees, in practice very few are chosen and even fewer are elected to senior positions. The women who are elected are almost invariably the wives of unusually wealthy or prestigious husbands. Though there are those who wish to consolidate and extend the progress achieved during the war, in the face of determined male opposition they all too easily fall victim to

212

the pre-war male conceptualisation of women as no more than the providers of biological fertility and domesticity to the men.

By and large, male elders have manipulated the committees to maintain their dominant position. The inequalities between the genders and between the generations are not experienced by them as a problem and in the absence of the political will which the guerrillas provided, they are happy to allow wartime practice to lapse in this time of peace.

But the ease with which this dominant group has reasserted itself cannot be explained simply by the withdrawal of the militants. If the guerrillas had wished to institute full-scale democracy, to place women and unmarried men at the centre of a new political arena from which the men's-house and the tumble-down authority of the chiefs had been cleared, why did they fail?

At least part of the answer is that the challenge which the guerrillas offered to the entrenched interests of the male elders was muffled by the cloak of ancestral legitimacy. The elders accepted their displacement by their juniors because the ancestors approved of the authority they had achieved. The effect of this was that the guerrillas were able to get their way without undertaking a programme of education that might have ensured that these advances be maintained and perhaps even extended when the war was over and they had left the countryside.

The authority of the ancestors is conjured up by contrasting their perfect and permanent life-in-death with the biological processes of human birth and decay. These processes are conceived of as harmful and pollutant. By means of ritual they are symbolically attributed to women. The glory of the ancestors requires that women be thought of as expendable and worthless. By this denigration, the containment of women within the private, domestic sphere is made to seem inevitable while male domination of the key institutions of the society goes unchallenged.

That the spirit mediums, the principle exponents of this ideology, were chosen by the guerrillas to instruct them in a moral code of protective behaviour had the effect that the symbolism that supports the profession of the medium was carried into the professional life of the combatant. Menstruation was regarded as a source of acute danger to the guerrillas, both male and female. Despite the accession of women to senior military positions, the notion that feminity is made up of equal parts of weakness and danger survived intact into the post-war world.

Despite this, many of the mediums themselves encourage the participation of women in local politics. In general the mediums' support for progressive development has been consistently strong. They are enthusiastic about the new schools built in Dande over the last four years and make no objection to the opening of dispensaries and clinics. Although there is a range of diseases which they believe should be treated (or should be treated first) by them, there are many others for which they accept the greater competence of Western medicine.

Moreover, in more than one case I know of, mediums have begun to make use of some Western medicines themselves. Many mediums today ride in cars and buses and go into shops. One medium even runs a shop of his own.

To interpret these changes as a liberalisation of past attitudes is to miss their real importance. In the past, this set of ritual prohibitions made a symbolic protest against the exploitation of blacks by the white-dominated capitalist markets but they did not oppose the markets, nor indeed the whites themselves. When the ending of the war was followed by ZANU's electoral victory, the need for these prohibitions fell away. To all questions about why what was forbidden is now permitted, the mediums reply that their *mhondoro* were consulted and they approve. The war is over. The hostility between black and white is at an end. It is all one Zimbabwe now. The mediums feel that under their control, the beneficial aspects of white society should now be absorbed.[8]

The only prohibitions that are still universally enforced among mediums are those which stress the essential nature of the *mhondoro* by opposition to the processes of life and death. Possession still occurs only when the moon is visible. The *chisi* days of *chiropa* and *rusere* remain days of rest from all non-domestic labour.

As the ancestors have affiliations to individual lineages, it might have been expected that their mediums would oppose the collaboration of members of different lineages in co-operative production. Two co-operative schemes have been set up in Dande since Independence, both with assistance from OXFAM. In both, communal fields are cultivated by women and men who have volunteered to participate and who retain fields of their own. The proceeds from one co-operative have been used to make a down payment on a tractor to which co-operative members have privileged access. In the other case, the proceeds were used to part-finance the purchase of a grinding mill for the use of which co-operative members pay a lower fee than other villagers.

The chairman of the tractor-owning group is the medium of Chiodzamamera who, with Chipfene and Chidyamauyu, returned to Zimbabwe in 1979. When not in use this tractor is parked outside the medium's home. Compare this to the vehicles said to have caused the death of Mutota/Kupara. Once again it is clear that the only Western goods fatal to *mhondoro* mediums are those used to the disadvantage of the medium's followers. Chiodzamamera has, on his own initiative, set up yet a third co-operative, this one of farmers who wish to experiment with a newly available serum which protects cattle against tsetse fly but who cannot afford to purchase it on their own.

All in all, the experience of the years since Independence shows that, now as in the past, the mediums do not simply keep pace with and reflect changes in the economic and political spheres. In some cases at least. they actually lead the way.

NOTES

1 Mugabe (1983, p. 18).
2 The phrase is from Ranger (1968, p. 446).
3 For Tangwena see Holleman (1969). For Makoni see Ranger (1982b). This account is based on interviews with Cde Josiah Tungamirai. Cde Henry Hamadziripi. Cde George Rutinhiri. Cde Mayor Urimbo all in Harare in December 1980 and January 1984.

   A question that would repay further research is whether the mediums and other traditional healers with whom Frelimo had contact in Mozambique were able to supply a source of symbolic resistance similar to that of the Shona *mhondoro* mediums with their 'great spectacle of the past'. From the small amount of information available it seems that the Frelimo attitude derived from their experience of traditional healers whose contribution was no more than the provision of protective medicines which quickly proved ineffective against bullets. Perhaps the Frelimo approach would have been different had their first contacts been with the Shona *mhondoro* in Tete. Manica and Sofala provinces.

4 The phrases in quotation marks are extracted from interviews with ex-guerrilla commanders.

   As far as I have been able to trace there was only one period when the desirability of the ancestral legitimacy that the guerrillas had acquired was seriously questioned. This was during the eighteen months that followed the assassination of ZANU president Herbert Chitepo in March 1975. Most of the ZANU leadership were imprisoned in Lusaka and the struggle was advanced by a group of younger politicians and military leaders who were drawn from both ZANU and ZAPU to form the Zimbabwean Peoples' Army (ZIPA).

   The rapid rise and demise of ZIPA has been dealt with in detail elsewhere (Martin and Johnson, 1981; Astrow, 1984). The only feature of its history that concerns us here is that at this time an attempt was made to put into practice some of the Marxist-Leninist ideas that this group of politicians had acquired in the political schools in ZANLA camps in Mozambique. A move was made to shift the focus of the mobilisation campaign from the peasants to the urban proletariat and to promote a version of 'scientific socialism' that admitted no compromise with peasant religious thought or practice. From this point of view, the struggle required no other legitimacy than a determination to put these socialist principles into action. When ZIPA fell, this rejection of ancestral authority fell with it and the 'two-line policy' was re-established.

5 ZANU/PF is the name adopted by ZANU at the time of the elections in 1980 to distinguish it from a new party formed by ex-members of ZANU that had taken over its name during the period that the original ZANU had been part of the Patriotic Front. The Patriotic Front was the title used to refer to ZANU and ZAPU together during their period of military and political co-operation. When this coalition broke apart, the title was retained by ZAPU for use during the election campaign.

6 Criminal cases were referred to the police and then to the magistrates' and other state courts.

7 At a meeting held soon after Independence, the elders of Dande agreed that it would be better to do away with the chiefs altogether. They remain only because it is the policy of the present government to recognise them and to continue to pay them a salary for 'cultural and historical' reasons.

8 The process by which the prohibitions were abandoned was explained to me as follows: The mediums' co-operation with the guerrillas necessitated their riding in military vehicles, eating food out of tins, coming into contact with whites and so on. As they were forced to ignore these restrictions in the war and 'have got used to doing so', and as the *mhondoro* approve, they continue to ignore them in the peace.

12
The Ancestors
and the State

Newscaster: *Good morning. This is the Zimbabwe Broadcasting Corporation. Here is the news. Zimbabwe will become a new state with effect from midnight tonight . . . Among the ceremonies will be a royal salute, the lowering of the Union Jack, and the raising of the Zimbabwe flag. It will be followed by the blessing of the new flag and the swearing in of the President elect, Mr. Banana, and the Prime Minister-elect Mr. Mugabe . . . It's five past seven. On we go with music – the music of Zimbabwe! Listen now to the voices of our comrades with 'Mbuya Nehanda'. (Song, by the ZANU – PF Ideological Choir)*

Grandmother Nehanda,
You prophesied,
Nehanda's bones resurrected,
ZANU's spear caught their fire
Which was transformed into ZANU's gun,
The gun which liberated our land.

The exploiters of Zimbabwe
Were cannibals drinking the masses' blood,
Sucking and sapping their energy.
The gun stopped all this.
Grandmother Nehanda,
You prophesied.

Extract from transcripts of a broadcast by the Zimbabwean Broadcasting Corporation on 17 April 1980.[1]

During the election campaign and at the Independence ceremonies that followed, the contribution made by the ancestors to the successful outcome of the war was acknowledged and celebrated. The ancestor who received the most attention and the greatest praise was Ambuya

Nehanda, the *mhondoro* whose mediums had participated both in the first liberation struggle, the rebellion of 1896, and in the second. The enemy, the Rhodesian state, 'the exploiters of Zimbabwe', described in the song quoted above as a gang of witches 'drinking the masses' blood', had been defeated with the aid of the *mhondoro* who was thought of as the earliest, the most important and the most senior of them all.

Countless songs were performed about her. Recordings of these songs sold in their thousands. Her image, incorporated into a design printed on materials and made up into headscarves and dresses was everywhere to be seen, brought back to life by the bobbing and ducking of thousands of women in the jubilant and dancing crowds. On a specially printed banner that was hung wherever the new nation state was welcomed, Nehanda's head and shoulders hovered above those of Robert Mugabe, the warrior of the past guiding, supporting and recommending this triumphant warrior of the present. Within six months, schools and, with particular aptness, a maternity hospital had been named in her honour. There was no doubt that Ambuya Nehanda, the grandmother of all the ancestors, had taken the whole of Zimbabwe under her care. (See Plate 15, between pp. 204–5.)

With Nehanda established as the *mhondoro* who protects the whole of the new nation state, it is almost as if Zimbabwe had come to be regarded as a single spirit province. To some extent, this is how the relationship between ancestors and territory was conceptualised by the guerrillas in Dande. Although the borders of Zimbabwe were drawn up in the late nineteenth century, the idea that they correspond to some ancient polity over which the ancestors ruled long ago was powerfully felt during the war. All the restrictions that were imposed by the *mhondoro* mediums on the guerrillas were observed only within the borders of Rhodesia as it then was. As soon as they crossed into Mozambique, the guerrillas were free to have sex, to shoot wild animals and to eat any food they pleased. The reason is at once obvious and profound. They were autochtons only within the borders of their own country. Only there did they need to imitate the habits and preferences of the ancestors to ensure that they would receive their protection. Before they crossed from Mozambique back into Zimbabwe they would wash themselves in a river and, purified, place themselves once more under the protection of their national *mhondoro*. Today in Dande it is said that Nehanda has two spirit provinces. One is her traditional territory known as Tsokoto near the northern border on the banks of the Msengezi River. The other is the whole country of Zimbabwe.

All nationalisms make use of metaphors of the land, of soil and earth, of territory and boundary, of monuments and graves, of the heroes of the past who are the ancestors of the nation. The symbolism of the *mhondoro* gains its extraordinary effectiveness as an expression of the struggle for Zimbabwe from its ability to combine the economic and political aspects of this struggle in a single unforgettable image: the chiefs of the past, independent and prosperous, benign and generous to their followers, in sole possession and control of their bountiful, fertile lands. It is an image that has proved attractive to ministers of state and senior members of ZANU/PF. The ancestors, the original and legitimate owners of the country, are nowadays charged with protecting the nation against its new potential 'conquerors', for example the South African state or the more abstract but no less real forces of neo-colonialism and so on. (See Plate 5, between pp. 118–19.)

Let me give you one example. Here is an extract from a speech made by Robert Mugabe in reaction to a threat by the British government to withdraw a part of its promised aid:

> The Prime Minister, Mr. Mugabe, swearing by the name of the legendary anti-British spirit medium Ambuya Nehanda, vowed that his government would confiscate white-owned land for peasant resettlement if Mrs. Thatcher suspends promised British compensation . . . 'If they do that we will say 'Well and good, you British gave us back the land because you never paid for it in the first place. The land belongs to us. It is ours in inheritance from our forefathers', the Prime Minister said.[2]

Statements of this kind do not of course represent the full extent of the state's rhetorical repertoire but they are among its most potent elements.

We are more than familiar with Shona politicians claiming legitimacy for their rule over the land in the name of the ancestors, but over the last few years, an important change in the articulation of ancestral authority had taken place.

In 1981 an Act of Parliament known as the Traditional Medical Practitioners Act passed into law. The purpose of this Act was to establish a Traditional Medical Practitioners Council and to give legal standing to ZINATHA (the Zimbabwe National Traditional Healers Association) which had been in existence for some years though in competition with a number of other traditional healers' associations which have since been disbanded. The function of the Council according to the Act will be 'to supervise and control the practice of traditional medical practitioners and to foster research into, and develop the knowledge of, such practice.'

The Council is required to set up a register of all traditional medical practitioners. Once they are registered, those whose healing techniques do not include possession may add the initials TMP (Traditional Medical Practitioner) after their name. Those who are proficient at possession may use the letters SM (Spirit Medium). The explicit function of this body is to organise and centralise the practice of TMPs and SMs so that they can provide a service to the community parallel to the Western-style medicine made available in clinics and hospitals throughout the country.

But the Act goes further. It allows for TMPs or SMs who do not measure up to the standards of the Council to be expelled. The council may 'order the suspension of the registered person for a specified period from practising as a traditional medical practitioner or performing any act specially pertaining to the practice of TMPs.' In addition, if individuals make use of these titles when they have not been registered, they are liable to a fine of $1000 or imprisonment for two years.[3] It is only necessary to point out that the Council consists of twelve members of whom five are appointed by the Minister of Health and that six members constitute a quorum of this Council for it to be clear that, to all intents and purposes, the government has provided itself with an agency fully capable of declaring who is and who is not a legitimate and authentic spirit medium.

Of course one, and perhaps the predominant, effect of this legislation will be that mediums whose curing techniques are either ineffective or harmful will not be allowed to put the safety of the public at risk. But curing has long been only one of the duties of the *mhondoro* mediums. Another is the choosing and installing of the political leadership.

At a public meeting in Dande in 1982 a senior *mhondoro* medium, speaking in trance, described his dismay at the slow rate of progress achieved by the government in fulfilling their promise of economic aid to the Dande region. He reminded his listeners of the contribution that he and other mediums had made to the struggle. His warning was perfectly clear. It was, he said, the *mhondoro* who had enabled the present government to come to power. If they failed the people and therefore failed the ancestors, the *mhondoro* would transfer their authority elsewhere.

The *mhondoro* mediums provided the resistance with the set of symbols with which its moral authority was expressed. They lent it their skills, their knowledge, and the weight of their prestige. It was inevitable that after the successful conclusion of the war they should feel that the power to control the destiny of the new nation was in their hands.

A number of other Dande mediums have complained of the neglect they have suffered since Independence and of the failure of the government to reward them for the help which they gave. One circumstance that has contributed to this feeling of neglect is the recent removal of authority from the party village committees which operate, in Dande at least, under the jurisdiction of the ancestors. The committees have been subordinated to two new administrative bodies. First, the authority to hear and resolve disputes has been transferred to the so-called Primary Level Courts. Operated by a judge and two assessors who are elected from an area corresponding roughly to the old wards of the chiefs, these courts fall under the Ministry of Justice. Secondly, most of the other powers which were inherited by the committees from the guerrillas have been inherited in turn by the District Councils established under the Ministry of Local Government. These Councils, also based more or less on the old ward system, require only one individual to represent a constituency of some thousands of people, and deal with all the major issues such as education, transport, economic development and so on.

The ZANU/PF committees have therefore been left with almost no functions at all except to inform the villagers of new party policies, to hear minor disputes and to look after village matters such as sanitation and the allocation of new sites for homes. The overall effect has been to remove power from ZANU/PF with its direct experience of the liberation struggle in the countryside and from the hands of the villagers themselves and surrender it to the institutions of government which are based in the capital and staffed largely by career politicians and civil servants.

At present, the likelihood that the mediums will actually transfer their allegiance, and that of the ancestors, away from ZANU/PF and the government is slight, though the possibility that if they did so the chiefs might be the beneficiaries is perhaps one of the reasons that the chiefs' old relationship of subservience and dependence on the state has been perpetuated from the previous government. But the threat that they might is significant because it is a threat to that special sort of legitimacy which only the ancestors can provide and which, in addition to the legitimacy it has obtained by its overwhelmingly popular democratic election, the government elected in 1980 claims for itself.

In effect the Traditional Medical Practitioners Act entrenches in law precisely that control over the mediums that political authorities of the past, whether chiefs or district commissioners, attempted to enforce in order to discredit mediums who opposed them. The state emphasises its own 'descent' from the ancestors thus minimising the importance of that other technique by which the *mhondoro* are represented on earth, possession (see Figure 9.1, above). To take a very long historical view indeed, the present state of play is reminiscent of Dos Santos' account of the 'king' Quiteve in 1609. It was to Quiteve rather than to the mediums that his followers turned to for rain and though the 'king' periodically consulted his ancestors, the role of the medium was relatively undeveloped, the ancestor choosing a medium at random from amongst those attending the royal ceremonies.[4]

One final point about the relationship between the ancestors and the state. It comes at the end not because I consider it insignificant but so that everything that has gone before can be reconsidered in its light.

It is the unique quality of the Shona spirit mediums that they are able to present a complex 'performance' of the past combined with a vision of the future in a way that enhances the peoples' belief in the value of their much maligned history and thereby strengthens their belief in their ability to create a better future. Among the particular skills of the mediums that were called upon during the war was their ability to accumulate followings that crossed chiefly boundaries. These they put at the disposal of the nationalist leaders. And the most senior of the *mhondoro* mediums, those of Nehanda and, to a lesser extent, Mutota were able to command loyalties that stretched far beyond local priorities, that extend almost to the nation as a whole.

Almost but not quite, for the ancestors that have occupied our attention for so many pages are the ancestors of only one of the ethnic groups of Zimbabwe. The Shona make up the majority of the population but the efforts of the Ndebele, the Shangaan, the Sotho, the Venda and the other ethnic minorities were also highly significant to the achievement of Independence. So far, however, only the religious and political institutions of the Shona have contributed to the symbolism of the new state.

If Zimbabwe is the spirit province of the great Shona ancestor Nehanda, then it follows that there are two distinct Zimbabwes. There is the nation/spirit province, owned by the ancestors of the Shona people in which the Shona have the perpetual, inextinguishable right of autochthons to live and govern forever. And there is the territory that was Rhodesia, the borders of which were drawn by politicians in Britain and Portugal with no regard for the peoples who lived within them, with a history less than a hundred years long. Within this second Zimbabwe live the Shona but also the Ndebele, the Shangaan, the whites, and the other marginal ethnic groups as well.

From the point of view of Dande, the two Zimbabwes are one. From many other parts of the country this is not so. Will the Ndebele and the other small populations accept that the Shona ancestors can provide them with their fertility or will they insist on maintaining their own integrity, insist, that is, that their own ancestors, their own political traditions should also form part of the symbolism of the new state?

Since Independence, numbers of ex-guerrillas loyal to ZAPU have taken up arms against the new state. By this action they declare their belief that the state does not adequately represent the interests of the Ndebele people. Of the two Zimbabwes, one, the Zimbabwe of Nehanda and the other Shona *mhondoro*, Zimbabwe the spirit province, has survived numerous transformations in the past and will no doubt survive many more. But it seems clear that the peaceful survival of the other Zimbabwe, the modern nation state, requires more than the benefits that any one set of ancestors can provide.

NOTES

1 Frederikse (1984, p. 326).
2 The Guardian, 10 October 1983, See also election speeches quoted in Ranger (1985, p. 213).
3 Traditional Medical Practitioners Act of 1981. See Part I, para 3, 4, 12; Part II, para 27; Part V, para 31. Though the Act does not make it obligatory that all mediums should register, the intention is plain that all TMPs and SMs should do so. The Act also gives the Council the power to declare registered in an honorary capacity anyone whom it decides should be included.
4 This historical sequence invites further research, perhaps along the following lines:

In early accounts of the Shona, chiefs are frequently described as 'divine' (e.g. Bullock, 1928). On the basis of Portuguese documents Randles (1981, p. 62) describes them in this way and Mudenge (1972, p. 96), says the same of the Rozvi *mambos*, the eighteenth- and nineteenth-century successors to the Mutapas. What 'divinity' usually means in this context is rain-making power. And yet, as we have seen, in recent times chiefs have had no divine powers at all and few or no ritual responsibilities. I speculate that at a time of conquest and state formation, when areas of land are being absorbed within a centralised polity, the claim by the ruler to rights in the newly conquered land would be expressed by a claim to be able to control the rain in that area and thus to divine 'rain-maker' status. As the centre weakens, so rain-making powers are taken back by individual political units. This interpretation fits very well the transformations of the Musikavanhu cult described by Rennie (1979). In this case, the original ancestor, said to be a fugitive Rozvi *mambo* was able to bring rain by himself because of certain charms he possessed. In time the chiefs lost these charms and rain-making power was taken over by mediums possessed by the spirits of the original *mambos*.

The life-bringing power of the state was symbolised by fire as well as water. 'The Monomotapa once every year sent emissaries throughout his empire, carrying with them fire from him; on the approach of these emissaries, everybody had to extinguish their fires and then re-light them from the royal flame. If a village refused to carry out this ceremony of submission, the army was sent to bring it back to its allegiance' (Randles 1981, p. 60). In Barwe, an eastern province of the Mutapa state, this fire was lit and handed on by the medium of the senior *mhondoro* of the royal lineage (Isaacman 1973, p. 396).

223

Conclusion

This study of guerrilla warfare has provided an unusual perspective on one of the classic themes of modern anthropology: political change at the level of the village. Nonetheless, the greater part of this book has been taken up with describing what has stayed the same. I have argued that the cluster of abstract ideas, symbolic associations and ritual performances that make up the political ideology of Dande has survived the upheavals of colonisation and of war virtually unaltered. Like a cork afloat on the sea, it has risen above and overcome each wave of history as, one by one, they have rushed up and broken on the shore.

But the survival of this ideology contains a paradox. I have laid a good deal of stress on the assimilation of the ZANLA guerrillas into established peasant categories. By following certain ritual prohibitions they gained acceptance as autochthons, the warriors of the past returned in new guise, as quasi-descendants of the *mhondoro*. But it was never possible that the guerrillas would be totally assimilated into this category. They were and they remain something new. The paradox is that the only reason that the guerrillas were allowed to occupy these ancient categories is that they were *not* the warriors of the past. Battle axes and spears are all very well to wave in the air in order to identify newcomers with old causes, but if the guerrillas had *only* waved battle axes and spears and left their machine guns at home, if they had tried to revive the old techniques of resistance which had failed time and again rather than introducing new ones, their reception by the peasants would have been altogether different. It would seem that, in a changing world, ideology and ritual must constantly seek out new raw material to feed upon, to ingest and absorb in order to grow to meet the challenges change brings, and in order to remain essentially unchanged.

The guerrillas brought with them a set of categories which they intended to cast over the heads of the peasants like so many lassos. The peasants were the '*povo*', the 'masses' who were to be organised, mobilised, educated and 'conscientised'. But as they entered Dande they stepped into the categories which history, like an old bearded hunter seeding the forest with traps, had laid out in wait for them. Throughout the years of the war, ever-more peasants were organised, mobilised and educated sometimes by gentle means, sometimes not. But it was necessary first for the guerrillas to win the approval of the ancestors, to be seen as their tools, almost, one might say, as the passive mediums of their will. And thus the old set of categories survived not as a blunted relic but at the very cutting edge of this latest attempt to make the old world new.

It is sometimes assumed that protracted guerrilla warfare inevitably leads to the development of revolutionary consciousness among guerrillas and peasants alike. One problem with this assumption is that it is hard to know what the term 'revolutionary' means in terms as abstract as these. And as to being 'inevitable', the conceptual gains achieved by the process of making a war all too often fade almost entirely away, like mist after rain, as a new elite replaces the last in the still-warm seats of power and the peasants return to their villages and fields and a life hardly changed accept that the promises the leaders once made now give way to demands that they work even harder. But putting this possibility aside, is there a sense in which the term 'revolutionary' can be usefully applied to the history we have journeyed through here?

If to be revolutionary means to make a complete break with the past then it cannot, but nor can it elsewhere. A total break must always be perceived as chaos. Without guidance from the past, how can we know what has changed, what has stayed the same? But if there can be revolution with continuity, then I think that the term is fully appropriate for describing the replacement of the chiefs by the village committees as the source of ancestral authority and law.

The political ideology of Dande derives from a conceptualisation of the relationship between lineage and land as a product of the passing of time. The lineage that has lived within a territory the longest is considered its owner and, as its owner, it or its ancestors can ensure its fertility. Because they and they alone can do this, anyone else who makes his home on their land is subject to their authority. When the leaders of these 'original' or royal lineages, the chiefs, were thought to have betrayed their own ancestors, these ancestors, through their mediums, transferred their authority first to the guerrillas and then to the village committees. This process was revolutionary precisely because the ancestors supported it. The ancestors will always seek some representative among the living. If they had not endorsed the guerrillas and the committees, most likely they would have continued to endorse the chiefs or found some other means of giving order to the countryside alien to the experience of the war. They endorsed the system of participatory democracy that the committees put into practice and thus a radically new and fully legitimate political era began. As ever, we can only see the depths of the changes that have occurred if it is first clear how much has stayed the same.

And it is not only the authority of the ancestors that has survived. Even more impressive is the survival of their mediums, not only through a decade of guerrilla warfare but over the entire length of the century that saw colonialism in and saw it out. Indeed, the mediums did a great deal better than merely survive. The detail of their ritual practice has remained consistent in a most remarkable way.

To trace back to Dos Santos' account of 1609 or even to Pacheco's of 1861 would require a book in itself. Nonetheless one or two points are worth making.

I have quoted a number of times from the descriptions of the rituals of the mediums scattered throughout Pacheco's journal. Alongside these are detailed accounts of rituals performed by the chiefs both in Dande and in the neighbouring district of Chidima. These royal rituals are totally unlike anything one might observe today or that one might read of in Kingsley Garbett's account of Dande twenty years ago. They have a richness, a complexity and a pervasiveness that are today entirely absent. The descriptions of the *mhondoro* mediums, by contrast, might have been written yesterday.[1]

When Pacheco wrote, Dande was a semi-independent province of the decaying Mwene Mutapa state. Over the last 120 years that state has collapsed and disappeared, Dande has been split in two by the boundary with Mozambique, the chiefs have been incorporated into an authoritarian, highly centralised colonial state, a nationalist campaign has grown to maturity and ten years of bitter civil war have culminated in the inauguration of a new democratic state with a new system of administration in the countryside. The same period began with a surplus-producing, trading economy with complex cycles of tribute and support linking chiefs to followers. Under colonial pressure this economy became reliant on a very high level of migrant labour combined with semi-subsistence production, and the period has ended with the introduction, though on a small scale, of collective cultivation. Through all this the mediums have continued to get possessed, to roar like lions, to be tested and to bring the rain in precisely the same way. How can this extraordinary consistency be explained?

Through their rituals the mediums have represented to the peasants a vision of the past as it was lived before the settlers arrived. Whether or not this past is in any sense 'real', whether for example what the mediums wear is the same as one might see on photographs of the chiefs of the past if such existed, is quite beside the point. Throughout the colonial period, many of the economic and political changes that took place were characterised as undesirable. Amongst the least desirable of these was the subordination of the chiefs to the settler state. The rituals that surrounded them fell into disrepair. To maintain them would have been to endorse these agents of the state. But the spirit mediums retained their independence and their rituals cleared a space within which the peasants could express their resistance to the present and experience once again, if only for an instant at a time, the good life as they imagined it had been lived in the past. As long as the mediums continued to allow the long-dead chiefs to address their followers, so long were the peasants able to retain their sense of the value of their past and of their present despite the waves of humiliation and contempt to which they were subjected day after day. So long could they cherish and increase their hopes that in time they would regain their land and re-establish their political autonomy once again.

Unlike most of the neighbouring peoples who practise male or female initiation, the Shona have no other major ritual in their cultural repertoire. When the chiefly rituals fell into decay, only the rituals of possession remained as the moment in the peasants' lives when they felt themselves to be most profoundly themselves no matter what pressures they were up against in the outside world.

Until the structure of ancestral authority finally cracks up and gives way, any attempt to establish political legitimacy will only succeed if it obtains the endorsement of the ancestors. For the ultimate test of the legitimacy of any political system is its ability to provide fertility, to ensure that the crops grow, that the people prosper and are content. Since the achievement of Independence the state of Zimbabwe has acquired legitimacy from the endorsement it has received from Nehanda and other senior *mhondoro*. The cycle that began with the decay of the royal rituals has come full circle and the focus of ritual attention has returned to the political leadership, the descendants of the ancestors or at least those who rule in their name.

Today this large-scale, highly centralised polity has subjected the mediums to more rigorous legislation than they had ever experienced in the past. But legislation, even at its sharpest end, can do no more than fetter their bodies, and their bodies – the vessels of the ancestors – are the least important part of them. The concern of the ancestors for their descendants will never cease. For the moment, the mediums have been edged to the side of the stage but the day may come when they return to the centre again.

NOTES

1 Pacheco's comments on a possession ritual he observed are given on page 45 above. Here is his account of the functions of the mediums:

He sends sunshine and rain when it pleases him. He foretells the future of the Natives, he forecasts the disasters that will fall upon them, he gives judgement on all the matters submitted to him . . . he is submitted to the most scrutinising tests which consist of naming all the Mùanamotapùas from Mutato to the present ruler and of describing the most important events that took place in each reign as well as the specification name by name of all the leading men who owned insignia which they keep for this sole purpose . . . After this he starts roaring like a lion and then . . . he goes to the place where the spell is broken and the lion stays there and the Unvuza (medium) goes back to the village. But he does not stop being active. He is present at all the disputes, studies them and judges them to pass sentence if he thinks he will benefit from that. (Pacheco, 1883, p. 44).

Here are three examples of royal rituals:

As soon as an emperor dies . . . all the princes of his house leave the districts where they rule and gather at the Zimbabwe (capital) of the deceased. The opposing chief, hearing the news, gathers all his forces and the princes of his family and, crossing the Zambezi, marches on the Zimbabwe of the deceased where there is a fierce fight which is repeated over and over until he defeats them. (Pacheco, 1883, p. 26).

They have an unavoidable custom: if two chiefs meet they must fight until one dies. (Pacheco, 1883, p. 48).

On the death of a chief all the population of the district, dressed in the most indecent way imaginable, come to gather to mourn at the village the great loss they have suffered and at the same time behave in the most unruly manner, killing, wounding and robbing anyone passing through the territory where the death occurred until a new chief is proclaimed. (Pacheco, 1883, p. 44).

Appendix:
Methodology
and Sources

There were two main reasons for the choice of Dande as a research site. First, Dande lies within one of the first of the operational zones declared by ZANLA, the military wing of ZANU. Fighting occurred there between the beginning of the war in 1972 and the cease-fire in 1979. In planning this research it seemed likely that the interaction between guerrillas and local people in which I was interested would have taken place there with some intensity. The second reason was that research had been carried out in Dande by the historian Donald Abraham and the anthropologist Kingsley Garbett in the late 1950s and early 1960s. The advantages of having detailed accounts of the social organisation and oral tradition of the period twenty years before my study began were very great, providing me with a baseline against which the changes that occurred during and because of the war could be measured.

I arrived in Dande in October 1980, having made a brief exploratory visit in June the same year. This was seven months after Independence, ten months after the cease-fire. During the last years of the war, the majority of the population had been forced into concentration camps, the so-called 'protected villages', in order to limit the amount of assistance they could give the guerrillas. By October 1980, the dispersal of the peasants from these camps was in its last stages. Many returned to the burnt-out sites of their home villages but others chose to remain near the areas where the camps had been sited. This demographic disruption made the systematic collection of data on kinship and economics especially difficult. On the other hand, the fact that people from a large number of local religious traditions had taken up residence side by side in the new communities provided me with a broader range of religious and political experience and knowledge than is usually found in so small a space.

Approximately two-thirds of my time in Dande (October 1980 to

May 1982) was spent in my base village at the foot of the Escarpment. During the remaining months I visited twelve other villages in Dande as well as four on the Plateau. These villages crossed seven chieftaincies and five hierarchies of mediums. Visits extended from a few days to a few weeks. In all cases I visited each village at least twice, often three or four times. As well as day-to-day contact with friends, neighbours and my adopted kin. I held a large number of more formal interviews with mediums, their assistants (*vatapi*), their patients and visitors to their shrines; with members of village and branch committees and with district councillors; with ex-guerrillas, with ex-members of the security forces and with ex-district assistants. All these interviews were conducted in ChiKorekore, the local dialect of Shona. Copies of recordings of these interviews as well as transcripts in Shona and English have been deposited in the National Archives, Harare.

In addition, I held a number of interviews in Harare with ZANU politicians who had been guerrilla leaders in Dande in the early 1970s and also with ex-district commissioners who had held authority for Dande and the neighbouring districts under the Rhodesian Front government. These interviews were in English and were not recorded. A few follow-up interviews with ex-guerrillas were held in Harare in January 1984.

As to the historical record: after the ZANU/PF victory in the 1979 elections, large quantities of government records and documents of the war including records of state trials were systematically destroyed by government officers who feared that they would be used to incriminate servants of the old regime. I arrived in Sipolilo District early enough to find that some of the files had not yet been purged and a fragmentary record of the war against the mediums in this district thus escaped the shredding machines. I was given access to the district commissioner's files on all the chieftaincies in the district (classification Per 5 in the archives of the Ministry of Local Government) as well as a compendium of information on mediums abstracted from all districts in the country.

As to the mediums themselves: obtaining information from long-dead people presents some special problems. The knowledge that mediums acquire in the course of their professional careers is usually made available to others in one type of social situation only, that in which a clearly defined problem requires solution. Whether the problem is sickness, irreconcilable rivalry for the position of chief or the failure of the rain, the statements made by the *mhondoro* spirit through the medium will be directed towards the resolution of the problem. Questions are rarely put for the sake of intellectual speculation or disinterested research. The state of possession only acquires its full meaning and reality in terms of the relationship between a medium and his or her client or patient who believes in the authenticity of the

231

medium's possession and desires the help of the *mhondoro*.

The many questions I put to the various *mhondoro* I was permitted to visit were quite out of the ordinary. I was interested in the knowledge the *mhondoro*/mediums had about the ancestors and their descendants in order to write an account of them, and I was interested in the techniques used by mediums to acquire this knowledge and to pass it on. I was interested in the state of possession itself.

All the mediums I spoke to knew that I would interview other mediums as well and that I was, in a sense, testing the limits of their knowledge and the integrity of their practice. Although this did not preclude the development of a certain intimacy with several of the mediums, it did mean that the relationship between the mediums and myself differed far more from that between them and their clients than if the subjects of my study had been, for example, teachers or conventional politicians. It seems likely that the information I recorded from the mediums was of a different sort from that which might have been recorded during possessions at which I was not present and at which my sort of questions were not asked.

Moreover, it was necessary to establish the degree to which the answers given to questions (mine and others) by the spirits were conventionalised, the degree to which the answers would be different depending on which *mhondoro*/medium was questioned and on the circumstances in which the questioning took place. The partial solution I found to this attempt to estimate the individual creativity of the mediums was the simple expedient of asking all *mhondoro*/mediums the same set of questions irrespective of which tradition of *mhondoro* they belonged to, as well as to put the same questions to numbers of other people whether or not they were reputed to have particular knowledge of the past or the ways of the mediums, women as well as men, children as well as adults. In addition, I attended possession sequences at which 'real' problems were put to the *mhondoro*. But this was not always easy to do.

For reasons which I discuss in Chapter 9, *mhondoro*/mediums generally refuse to allow whites to be present when they become possessed. All fifteen mediums whom I interviewed were willing to discuss the aspects of their lives and work in which I was interested. But in all cases certain questions brought the response that this was information unknown to the medium and only the *mhondoro* itself would be able to answer. For most of my twenty months in Dande I carried a letter from the ZANU/PF National Political Commissar requesting all mediums to help me with my research. Nonetheless, in some cases, I was refused permission to question the spirits directly or to be present when they took possession of their mediums. In the majority of cases, however, permission was given and interviews with the *mhondoro* were held.

Bibliography

Abraham, D. P. (1959), 'The Monomotapa dynasty', *NADA,* no. 36, pp. 58–84.

Abraham, D. P. (1962), 'The early political history of the kingdom of Mwene Mutapa 850–1589', in *Historians in Tropical Africa: Proceedings of the Leverhulme Inter-Collegiate History Conference, September 1960* (Salisbury: University College of Rhodesia and Nyasaland), pp. 61–90.

Abraham, D. P. (1964), 'Ethno-history of the empire of Mutapa. Problems and methods', in J. Vansina, R. Mauny and L. V. Thomas (eds), *The Historian in Tropical Africa: Studies Presented and Discussed at the Fourth International African Seminar at the University of Dakar–Senegal, 1961* (London: Oxford University Press), pp. 104–26.

Abraham, D. P. (1966), 'The roles of "Chaminuka" and the *mhondoro*-cults in Shona political history', in E. Stokes and R. Brown (eds), *The Zambezian Past* (Manchester: Manchester University Press), pp. 28–46.

Alpers, E. A. (1968), 'The Mutapa and Malawi political systems to the time of the Ngoni invasions', in T. O. Ranger (ed.), *Aspects of Central African History* (London: Heinemann), pp. 1–28.

Arrighi, G. (1973), 'Labour supplies in historical perspective: a study of the proletarianization of the African peasantry in Rhodesia', in G. Arrighi and J. S. Saul, *Essays on the Political Economy of Africa* (New York: Monthly Review Press), pp. 180–234.

Astrow, A. (1984), *Zimbabwe: A Revolution that Lost its Way?* (London: Zed Books).

Axelson, E. (1967), *Portugal and the Scramble for Africa 1875–1891* (Johannesburg: Witwatersrand University Press).

Balandier, G. (1970), *Political Anthropology* (Harmondsworth: Penguin).

Beach, D. N. (1977), 'The Shona economy: branches of production', in R. H. Palmer and N. Parsons (eds), *The Roots of Rural Poverty in South Central Africa* (London: Heinemann), pp. 37–65.

Beach, D. N. (1979), '"Chimurenga": the Shona rising of 1896–97', *Journal of African History*, vol. 20, no. 3, pp. 395–420.

Beach, D. N. (1980), *The Shona and Zimbabwe, 900–1850* (Gweru: Mambo Press).

Beach, D. N. (1983), 'The Rozvi in search of their past', *History in Africa*, vol. 10, pp. 12–34.

Beach, D. N. and De Noronha, H. (1980), *The Shona and the Portuguese 1575–1980* (Department of History, University of Zimbabwe, typescript).

Beattie, J. (1969), 'Spirit mediumship in Bunyoro', in J. Beattie and J. Middleton (eds), *Spirit Mediumship and Society in Africa* (London: Routledge & Kegan Paul), pp. 159–70.

Bhebe, N. M. B. (1979), 'The Ndebele and Mwari before 1893: a religious conquest of the conquerors by the vanquished', in J. M. Schoffeleers (ed.), *Guardians of the Land* (Gweru: Mambo Press), pp. 287–95.

Bhila, H. H. K. (1974), 'Munhumutapa: the history and mis-spelling of a Shona term', *Rhodesian History*, vol. 5, pp. 79–80.

Bhila, H. H. K. (1982), *Trade and Politics in a Shona Kingdom. The Manyika and Their Portuguese and African Neighbours, 1575–1902* (London: Longman).

Bloch, M. and Parry, J. (eds) (1982), *Death and the Regeneration of Life* (Cambridge: Cambridge University Press).

Bourdillon, M. F. C. (1970), 'Peoples of Darwin: an ethnographic survey of the Darwin District', *NADA*, vol. 10, no 2, pp. 103–14.

Bourdillon, M. F. C. (1971), 'Some aspects of the religion of the eastern Korekore' (unpublished DPhil thesis, University of Oxford).

Bourdillon, M. F. C. (1979), 'The cults of Dzivaguru and Karuva amongst the N. E. Shona peoples', in J. M. Schoffeleers (ed.), *Guardians of the Land* (Gweru: Mambo Press), pp. 235–55.

Bourdillon, M. F. C. (1982), *The Shona Peoples* (Gweru: Mambo Press, 2nd edn).

Bullock, C. (1928), *The Mashona* (Cape Town: Juta).

Campbell, A. C. (1957), 'Chimombe', *NADA*, no. 34, pp. 31–7.

Chavunduka, G. (1978), *Traditional Healers and the Shona Patient* (Gweru: Mambo Press).

Chavunduka, G. (1982), *Witches, Witchcraft and the Law in Zimbabwe* (Harare: Zinatha Occasional Papers, no. 1).

Chigwedere, A. (1980), *From Mutapa to Rhodes* (Harare: Longman).

Chitepo, H. (1974), 'Soko Risina Musoro', in S. M. Mutswairo, *Zimbabwe* (Washington, DC: Three Continents Press).

Colson, E. (1969), 'Spirit possession among the Tonga of Zambia', in

J. Beattie and J. Middleton (eds), *Spirit Mediumship and Society in Africa* (London: Routledge & Kegan Paul), pp. 69–103.

Colson, E. (1971), *The Social Consequences of Resettlement* (Manchester: Manchester University Press, Kariba Studies, IV).

Colson, E. (1977), 'A continuing dialogue: prophets and local shrines among the Tonga of Zambia', in R. Werbner (ed.), *Regional Cults* (London: Academic Press, ASA Monograph, no. 16), pp. 119–39.

Daneel, M. L. (1970), *The God of the Matopo Hills* (The Hague: Mouton).

Daneel, M. L. (1971), *Old and New in Southern Shona Independent Churches,* Vol. 1, *Background and Rise of the Major Movements* (The Hague: Mouton).

Daneel, M. L. (1974), *Old and New in Southern Shona Independent Churches*, Vol. 2, *Church Growth–Causative Factors and Recruiting Techniques* (The Hague: Mouton).

Davidson, B., Slovo, J. and Wilkinson, A. R. (1976), *Southern Africa. The New Politics of Revolution* (Harmondsworth: Penguin).

Dillon-Malone, C. (1978), *The Korsten Basketmakers* (Manchester: Manchester University Press).

Edwards, W. (1928), 'Sacred places', *NADA*, vol. 6, pp. 23–4.

Fanon, F. (1967), *The Wretched of the Earth* (Harmondsworth: Penguin).

Fortes, M. (1959), 'Descent, filiation and affinity: a rejoinder to Dr Leach. Part II', *Man*, vol. 59, pp. 206–12.

Frederikse, J. (1984), *None But Ourselves. Masses vs Media in the Making of Zimbabwe* (London: Heinemann).

Fry, P. (1975), *Spirits of Protest: Spirit Mediums and the Articulation of Consensus among the Zezuru of Southern Rhodesia* (Cambridge: Cambridge University Press).

Garbett, K. (1963a), 'The political system of a Central African tribe with particular reference to the role of spirit mediums' (unpublished PhD thesis, University of Manchester).

Garbett, K. (1963b), 'The Land Husbandry Act of Southern Rhodesia', in D. Biebuyck (ed.), *African Agrarian Systems* (London: Oxford University Press), pp. 185–202.

Garbett, K. (1966a), 'Religious aspects of political succession among the Valley Korekore (N. Shona)', in E. Stokes and R. Brown (eds), *The Zambezian Past* (Manchester: Manchester University Press), pp. 137–70.

Garbett, K. (1966b), 'The Rhodesian chief's dilemma: government officer or tribal leader', *Race*, vol. 8, no. 2, pp. 113–28.

Garbett, K. (1967), 'Prestige, status and power in a modern Valley Korekore chiefdom', *Africa*, vol. 37, no. 3, pp. 307–26.

Garbett, K. (1969), 'Spirit mediums as mediators in Valley Korekore society', in J. Beattie and J. Middleton (eds), *Spirit Mediumship and*

Society in Africa (London: Routledge & Kegan Paul), pp. 104–27.

Garbett, K. (1977), 'Disparate regional cults and a unitary field in Zimbabwe', in R. Werbner (ed.), *Regional Cults* (London: Academic Press, ASA Monograph, no. 16), pp. 55–92.

Gelfand, M. (1959), *Shona Ritual* (Cape Town: Juta).

Gelfand, M. (1962), *Shona Religion* (Cape Town: Juta).

Gelfand, M. (1977), *The Spiritual Beliefs of the Shona* (Gweru: Mambo Press).

Gwassa, C. G. J. (1972), 'African methods of warfare during the Maji Maji War, 1905–1907', in B. A. Ogot (ed.), *War and Society in Africa* (London: Frank Cass), pp. 123–48.

Hannan, M. (1974), *Standard Shona Dictionary* (Salisbury: Rhodesian Literary Bureau, 2nd edn).

Hodgson, J. (1982), *The God of the Xhosa* (Cape Town: Oxford University Press).

Hodza, A. C. and Fortune, G. (1979), *Shona Praise Poetry* (London: Oxford University Press).

Holleman, J. F. (1952), *Shona Customary Law* (London: Oxford University Press).

Holleman, J. F. (1953), *Accommodating the Spirit Amongst Some North-Eastern Shona Tribes* (London: Oxford University Press, Rhodes-Livingstone Paper, no. 22).

Holleman, J. F. (1969), *Chief, Council and Commissioner: Some Problems of Government in Rhodesia* (Assen: Afrika-Studiecentrum).

Isaacman, A. F. (1973), 'Madzi-Manga, Mhondoro and the use of oral Chikunda of south central Africa', *Journal of African History,* vol. 13, no. 3, pp. 443–61.

Isaacman, A. F. (1973), 'Madzi-Manga, Mhondoro and the use of oral traditions – a chapter in Barue religious and political history', *Journal of African History,* vol. 14, no. 3, pp. 395–409.

Isaacman, A. F. (1976), *The Tradition of Resistance in Mozambique: Anti-Colonial Activity in the Zambezi Valley 1850–1921* (London: Heinemann).

Isaacman, A. and Isaacman, B. (1977), 'Resistance and collaboration in Southern and Central Africa, *c.* 1850–1920', *International Journal of African Historical Studies,* vol. 10, no. 1, pp 31–62.

Kaschula, B. P. (1965a), 'Delineation Report for Sipolilo District: Dande Tribal Trust Land' (report presented to State Department, Government of Rhodesia).

Kaschula, B. P. (1965b), 'Notes on some of the Mhondoros (spirit mediums) in the Sipolilo District of Rhodesia' (appended to report above).

Kuper, A. (1982), *Wives for Cattle: Bridewealth and Marriage in Southern Africa* (London: Routledge & Kegan Paul).

Lan, D. (1983), 'Making history: spirit mediums and guerrilla war in the Dande area of Zimbabwe' (unpublished PhD thesis, University of London).

Lancaster, C. S. (1974), 'Ethnic identity, history and "tribe" in the Middle Zambezi valley', *American Ethnologist*, vol. 1, pp. 707–30.

Lancaster, C. S. (1981), *The Goba of the Zambezi* (Norman: Oklahoma University Press).

Latham, C. J. K. (1970), 'Dzimbadzemabgwe', *NADA*, vol. 10, no. 2, pp. 24–30.

Latham, C. J. K. (1972), 'Munhumutapa: oral traditions', *NADA*, vol. 10, no. 4, pp. 77–82.

Latham, C. J. K. (1975), 'Some notes on the tribes in the Mount Darwin, Rushinga and Centenary Districts', *NADA*, vol, 11, no. 2, pp. 168–80.

Levi-Strauss, C. (1968), *Structural Anthropology* (London: Allen Lane).

Levi-Strauss, C. (1969), *Totemism* (Harmondsworth: Penguin).

Livingstone, D. (1956), *The Zambezi Expedition of David Livingstone 1858–1863* (London: Chatto & Windus, 2 vols, Central African Archives, Oppenheimer Series, no. 9).

Long, N. (1968), *Social Changes and the Individual. A Study of the Social and Religious Responses to Innovation in a Zambian Rural Community* (Manchester: Manchester University Press).

MacGaffey, W. (1970), 'The religious commissions of the Bakongo', *Man*, vol. 5, no. 1 (ns), pp. 27–38.

Malaba, L. (1980), 'Supply, control and organisation of African labour in Rhodesia', *Review of African Political Economy*, no. 18, pp. 7–28.

Martin, D. and Johnson, P. (1981), *The Struggle for Zimbabwe: The Chimurenga War* (London: Faber).

Matthews, J. B. (1966), 'An account of the history of the Vatande', *NADA*, vol. 9, no. 3, pp. 31–2.

Maxey, K. (1975), *The Fight for Zimbabwe* (London: Rex Collings).

Mitchell, D. (1982), *Who's Who 1981–1982: Nationalist Leaders in Zimbabwe* (Harare: Diana Mitchell).

Mitchell, J. C. (1961), 'Chidzere's tree: a note on a Shona land-shrine and its significance', *NADA*, no. 38, pp. 28–35.

Mudenge, S. I. (1972), 'The Rozvi empire and the *feira* of Zumbo' (unpublished PhD thesis, University of London).

Mudenge, S. I. (1976), 'The Dominicans at Zumbo', *Mohlomi, Journal of Southern African Historical Studies*, vol. 1, pp 32–63.

Mudenge, S. I. (forthcoming), *The History of Munhumutapa* (Harare: Zimbabwe Publishing House).

Mugabe, R. G. (1983), *Our War of Liberation* (Gweru: Mambo Press).

Mugabe, R. G., Nkomo, J., and Zvogbo, E. (1978), *Zimbabwe: The Final Advance* (Oakland: LSM Press).

Mutswairo, S. M. (1974), *Zimbabwe* (Washington, DC: Three Continents Press).

Newitt, M. D. D. (1973), *Portuguese Settlement on the Zambezi: Exploration, Land Tenure and Colonial Rule in East Africa* (London: Longman).

Pacheco, A. M. (1883), 'Uma Viagem de Tet ao Zumbo' in Beach and De Naronha (1980).

Palmer, R. H. (1977), *Land and Racial Domination in Rhodesia* (London: Heinemann).

Palmer, R. H. and Parsons, N. (eds) (1977), *The Roots of Rural Poverty in Central and Southern Africa* (London: Heinemann).

Pongweni, A. J. C. (1983), *What's in a Name? A Study of Shona Nomenclature* (Gweru: Mambo Press).

Radcliffe-Brown, A. R. (1950), 'Introduction' to A. R. Radcliffe-Brown and D. Forde (eds), *African Systems of Kinship and Marriage* (London: Oxford University Press).

Randles, W. G. L. (1981), *The Empire of Monomotapa* (Gweru: Mambo Press).

Ranger, T. O. (1963a), 'The last days of the empire of Mwene Mutapa', in *The History of the Central African Peoples* (17th Conference of the Rhodes-Livingstone Institute, Lusaka).

Ranger, T. O. (1963b), 'Revolt in Portuguese East Africa: the Makombe rising of 1917', in K. Kirkwood (ed.), *St Antony's Papers No. 15 (African Affairs No. 2)* (London: Chatto & Windus), pp. 54–80.

Ranger, T. O. (1967), *Revolt in Southern Rhodesia 1896–7* (London: Heineman).

Ranger, T. O. (1968), 'Connexions between primary resistance movements and modern mass nationalism in East and Central Africa, Part I', *Journal of African History*, vol. 9, no. 4, pp. 437–53.

Ranger, T. O. (1973), 'Territorial cults in the history of Central Africa', *Journal of African History*, vol. 14, no. 4, pp. 581–97.

Ranger, T. O. (1979), *Revolt in Southern Rhodesia 1896–7* (London: Heinemann, 1st paperback edn).

Ranger, T. O. (1981), 'Poverty and prophetism: religious movements in the Makoni District 1929–1940', University of Zimbabwe History Department, Henderson Seminar Paper, no. 51.

Ranger, T. O. (1982a), 'The death of Chaminuka: spirit mediums, nationalism and the guerilla war in Zimbabwe', *African Affairs*, vol. 81, no. 324, pp. 349–69.

Ranger, T. O. (1982b), 'Tradition and travesty: chiefs and the administration in the Makoni District, Zimbabwe 1960–1980', *Africa*, vol. 52, no. 3, pp. 20–41.

Ranger, T. O. (1985), *Peasant Consciousness and Guerrilla War in Zimbabwe* (London: James Currey).

Rennie, J. K. (1979), 'Transformations of the Musikavanhu territorial cult in Rhodesia', in J. M. Schoffeleers (cd.), *Guardians of the Land* (Gweru: Mambo Press), pp. 257–85.

Richards, A. I. (1940), 'The political system of the Bemba tribe – North-Eastern Rhodesia' in M. Fortes and E. E. Evans-Pritchard (eds), *African Political Systems* (London: Oxford University Press), pp. 83–120.

Roberts, R. S. (1974), 'The making of a Rhodesian myth', *Rhodesian History*, vol. 5, pp. 89–92.

Sithole, N. (1977), *Roots of Revolution: Scenes from Zimbabwe's Struggle* (London: Oxford University Press).

Stead, W. H. (1946), 'The clan organization and kinship system of some Shona tribes', *African Studies*, vol. 5, no. 1, pp. 1–20.

Strathern, A. (1973), 'Kinship, descent and locality: some New Guinea examples', in J. Goody (ed.), *The Character of Kinship* (Cambridge: Cambridge University Press), pp. 21–33.

Theal, G. McG. (1898–1903), *Records of South Eastern Africa* (Cape Town: Government Printers, 9 vols).

Thornton, R. (1963), *The Zambezi Papers of Richard Thornton* (London: Chatto & Windus, 2 vols).

Van Onselen, C. (1976), *Chibaro. African Mine Labour in Southern Rhodesia 1900–1933* (London: Pluto Press).

Weinrich, A. K. H. (1971), *Chiefs and Councils in Rhodesia* (London: Oxford University Press).

Weinrich, A. K. H. (1977), *The Tonga People of the Southern Shore of Lake Kariba* (Gweru: Mambo Press).

White, J. D. (1971), 'Some notes on the history and customs of the Urungwe District', *NADA*, vol. 10, no. 3, pp. 33–72.

Windrich, E. (1975), *The Rhodesian Problem: A Documentary Record, 1923–1973* (London: Routledge & Kegan Paul).

Index

Abraham, D.P. 17, 101, 108n6, 187, 230
affines 34, 37, 85–6
African Affairs Amendment Act 186
Ambuya Nehanda (senior royal ancestor) xvi, 6–7, 8n5, 147–8, 217–18; characteristics 4, 72; at Independence 217–18, 219; in myths 75–6, 81–91; as a rain spirit 72; in Shona literature 6–7
  19th century medium (Charwe) 6, 72
  later mediums 72
  recent medium (Kunzaruwa): death 5; in the war 3–6, 194
animal symbolism 36, 39, 157–8, 159
ancestral spirits 31–9; protect guerrillas xv, xvii, 4, 157–66; *see also mhondoro, midzimu*
Apostolic church, *see* churches
assistant to mediums (*mutapi*) 48, 59–68; authority 61–8; duties 59–60, 65, 115; as headman 62; knowledge 60; in myth 79; as *munyai* 63–5; and territory 60, 62
authority: of chiefs 19–22, 32–4, 61–8, 137–53, 166–74, 185; of elders 212–13; of guerrillas 149–53, 164–74; of mediums 65–8, 139–53; of men over women 25–7, 212–13; of *mhondoro* 21, 34–5, 54, 59, 61–8, 97, 139–53, 210; of mediums' assistants 61–8; of native commissioners 137, 138,

145–7, 173, 184–94; of village committees 210, 220–1
autochthons 14, 19, 24, 74, 82–91, 98–107, 171

Beach, D.N. 77, 101, 108n6, 154n3
beer 27, 32, 46, 92
Bhila, H.H.K. 101–2
blood 82, 91–8, 151–2, 160
Bourdillon, M.F.C. 22
bride price 21
bride service 21, 28n11
Bullock, C. 141

cattle: absence in Dande 13; and ancestors 103
Chaminuka (Zezuru royal ancestor) 6, 8n6
Chapoto (Chikunda chief) 17
Chidyamauyu (Korekore royal ancestor) 5, 214
chiefs: burial 69, 93; after death 32–4; authority 19–22, 32–4, 61–8, 137–53, 166–74, 185, 210, 212; of Dande 137; and guerrillas 166–74; legitimacy 59, 61–4, 139–53, 185–94; and mediums 56–68, 136–46, 166–74, 221; as owners of land 19–20, 34, 67, 69, 98; in the past 56, 227–8, 229n1; payments to 21, 137; post-war status 212; and Rozvi state 15; succession 26, 56–9, as tax-collectors 18, 137; under

240